Progress, War, and Reaction:
1900–1933

The Structure of American History

DAVIS R. B. ROSS, ALDEN T. VAUGHAN,
AND JOHN B. DUFF, EDITORS

VOLUME I
Colonial America: 1607–1763

VOLUME II
Forging the Nation: 1763–1828

VOLUME III
The Nation in Crisis: 1828–1865

VOLUME IV
The Emergence of Modern America: 1865–1900

VOLUME V
Progress, War, and Reaction: 1900–1933

VOLUME VI
Recent America: 1933 to the Present

Progress, War, and Reaction: 1900–1933

edited by Davis R. B. Ross
COLUMBIA UNIVERSITY

Alden T. Vaughan
COLUMBIA UNIVERSITY

John B. Duff
SETON HALL UNIVERSITY

THOMAS Y. CROWELL COMPANY
NEW YORK · ESTABLISHED 1834

COPYRIGHT © 1970 BY
THOMAS Y. CROWELL COMPANY, INC.
ALL RIGHTS RESERVED

Except for use in a review, the reproduction or utilization of this work in any form or by any electronic, mechanical, or other means, now known or hereinafter invented, including photocopying and recording, and in any information storage and retrieval system is forbidden without the written permission of the publisher.

L. C. Card 78-101951

Series design by Barbara Kohn Isaac

Manufactured in the United States of America

Preface

The Structure of American History is designed to introduce undergraduate students of United States history and interested general readers to the variety and richness of our historical literature. The six volumes in the series offer selections from the writings of major historians whose books have stood the test of time or whose work, though recent, has met with unusual acclaim. Some of the selections deal with political history, some with diplomatic, some with economic, and others with social; all however offer thoughtful and provocative interpretations of the American past.

The volumes, with seven substantial selections in each, cover the following chronological periods:

    I. Colonial America: 1607–1763
   II. Forging the Nation: 1763–1828
  III. The Nation in Crisis: 1828–1865
  IV. The Emergence of Modern America: 1865–1900
   V. Progress, War, and Reaction: 1900–1933
  VI. Recent America: 1933 to the Present

Each volume opens with a general introduction to the period as a whole, in which we have suggested major themes that give coherence to the era and have outlined briefly the direction of past and recent scholarship. An editors' introduction precedes each selection; in these we have not sought to tell the reader what he is about to encounter but rather to identify the selection's author, establish its historical setting, and provide its historiographical context. Finally, a short bibliographical essay follows each selection, in which the reader is introduced to a wide range of related literature.

Several criteria guided us in our choice of readings: the distinction of the author, the significance of his interpretation, the high literary quality of his style. Because we conceived of the series as a supplement to, rather than a substitute for, the reading usually assigned in college-level survey courses, we have tried to avoid material that merely expands in detail the coverage offered in the traditional textbooks; we have sought, instead, selections from works that shed new light and raise new questions, or at the very least provide a kind of reading experience not customarily encountered in traditional assignments. For, at bottom, *The Structure of American History* stems from the editors' conviction that the great works of historical writing should not be reserved for the graduate student or the professional scholar but should be made available to those readers who can perhaps best benefit from an early encounter with Francis Parkman, Samuel Eliot Morison, Allan Nevins, Oscar Handlin, and their peers. We want college students to know from the outset that the stuff of history is neither the textbook nor the latest article in a scholarly journal. What has often inspired us, as teachers and writers of history, and what we hope will inspire students and lay readers, is history written by the great practitioners of the art: men who have written with vigor and grace the results of their own meticulous research and meditation.

In order to make our selections as extensive as possible, we have, with reluctance, omitted all footnotes. We urge readers to remember that the authority of each historian rests largely on the documentation he offers in support of his statements, and that readers who wish to investigate the evidence on which a historian has based his argument should refer to the original published version—cited on the first page of each selection. Readers are also reminded that many of the books recommended in the bibliographical notes appended to each selection are obtainable in paperback editions. We have refrained from indicating which volumes are currently in paper for the list of paperbacks grows too rapidly. We refer those interested to R. R. Bowker Company, *Paperbound Books in Print*, available at the counter of most bookstores.

D.R.B.R.
A.T.V.
J.B.D.

Contents

Introduction	1
The Spanish-American War JULIUS W. PRATT	4
The Status Revolution and Progressive Leaders RICHARD HOFSTADTER	39
Roosevelt versus Taft—1912 MARK SULLIVAN	67
Entry into World War I ARTHUR S. LINK	108
The Supreme Infanticide THOMAS A. BAILEY	149
Manners and Morals in the 1920's FREDERICK LEWIS ALLEN	180
The Great Crash: Cause and Consequence JOHN KENNETH GALBRAITH	217

Introduction

Two concepts dominate the history of the United States during the first third of the twentieth century. One is the emergence of the nation as a world power, with the attendant difficulties and challenges of new departures in foreign policy. The second concept concerns the development of the reform impulse from the progressive movement to the New Deal.

Three of the selections in this volume deal with diplomatic history. The first of them is concerned with how the United States got into war with Spain in 1898. The results of the Spanish-American War were certainly imperialistic, whether in a direct sense as with acquisition of the Philippine Islands, or indirectly through the creation of a virtual protectorate over Cuba, or tangentially through such policies as the Roosevelt Corollary or Dollar Diplomacy designed to meet new responsibilities and opportunities in the Caribbean. But although imperialism, and in particular economic imperialism, has been associated with the outcome of the war, it is not widely accepted as a motivation for entering into the war, for the reasons given in the selection from Julius Pratt's *Expansionists of 1898*.

As will be seen in the excerpt from Arthur Link's biography of Woodrow Wilson, much more controversy surrounds intervention in 1917. Opponents of American belligerency abounded during the neutrality period, were not completely silenced either by the war or the Allied victory, and probably represented a majority opinion in the 1920's. By then only a few people, it appeared, still believed that unrestricted submarine warfare forced the United States to declare war on Germany. Many wondered why and how the country had gotten involved in European affairs at all. The prevailing opinion was one of disillusionment with large policies and overseas adventures as evidenced by the Senate's failure to endorse the Versailles Treaty and the League of Nations.

The Senate shifted with changes in public attitude toward the League. In the spring of 1919, American acceptance of membership in the proposed international peace-keeping body seemed beyond question. By the fall, the isolationist impulse, carefully nurtured by certain politicians and periodicals, had begun to reassert itself. Approval of the treaty was then possible only with reservations aimed at retaining the right of Congress to decide the country's role in the League. The editors' selection from Thomas A. Bailey's study of the defeat of the treaty attempts to pinpoint the responsibilities and the reasons for this failure in American statesmanship.

The national consensus that turned against the League also included a pronounced illiberal reaction against the Progressivism of the previous two decades. Although it has been contended that the progressive cause was not entirely moribund during the 1920's, it surely did not excite the public interest as it had during the Roosevelt-Wilson years. For fifteen years the nation had witnessed a ferment of reform: economic reform striking at the monopolistic tendency of the large corporations, social reform aimed at protecting the rights of women and children and to a lesser extent of the workingman, political reform directed against the corrupt politicians and their allies in business and organized crime. One of the selections examines the leadership of the progressive movement, if such a term can be applied to what was really not an organized effort, and offers some intriguing insights into the motivation of those who wanted to make America over. Progressivism reached its apogee in the presidential campaign of 1912 as the major candidates contended not over the desirability of the ends sought by reformers but over means to obtain those ends. From the writings of the most prominent political reporter and analyst of the times, we have tried to recapture the flavor of the inner politics of the Republican Party in that dramatic year.

These two extracts of political history are counterbalanced by the selections chosen for the 1920's. They reflect the mood of the prosperity decade, of a population caught up in the excitement of flush times, ballyhoo, and sensationalism, but heading for a financial debacle that would begin the longest period of economic depression in our history. The first examines the morals of the jazz age, long an item of fascination for journalists and motion-picture makers as well as historians, while the other is a lively, irreverent, but intelligible guide through the tangled background of the stock market crash of 1929.

The Spanish-American War

Julius W. Pratt

At the end of the Spanish-American War, the United States Ambassador to Great Britain, John Hay, wrote to his friend Theodore Roosevelt, "It has been a splendid little war, begun with the highest motives, carried on with magnificent intelligence and spirit, favored by that fortune which loves the brave." Splendid is a strange word for describing mortal combat. Perhaps we may charitably conclude that Hay meant if we must have wars, let us have short ones, and the war with Spain lasted only ten weeks. We can hardly agree, however, that the war was carried on with magnificent intelligence, as the Congressional investigations quickly revealed. To be sure, fortune certainly did favor the Americans: as Bismarck cynically observed, there appeared to be a special providence for drunkards, fools, and the United States of America. But what of the high motives? Certainly contemporary American opinion saw the war as a humanitarian crusade to liberate the Cuban people. The United States, as the exemplar of freedom for the whole world, had a moral obligation to further the cause of liberty by eliminating the last vestiges of Old World aristocracy from the Western Hemisphere.

Source: Julius W. Pratt, *Expansionists of 1898* (Baltimore: Johns Hopkins Press, 1936), pp. 230–278. Reprinted by permission of the Johns Hopkins Press.

Also mixed in with a crusade of pronouncements about expelling the cruel Spaniards was much talk of bringing to the island a morally superior civilization; and in all of this there was a great deal of downright racism. A popular preacher, the Reverend Josiah Strong, foresaw the Anglo-Saxon race as destined "to dispossess mainly weaker races . . . assimilate others and mold the remainder," while the historian John W. Burgess glorified the ability of the Teutonic peoples to supervise civilization. The poet Rudyard Kipling, the high priest of English imperialism, exhorted the American people to

> Take up the White Man's burden—
> Send forth the best ye breed—
> Go bind your sons to exile
> To serve your captives' need;

Within a few years, the Americans had indeed taken up "the White Man's burden" to the extent of possessing Puerto Rico, the Hawaiian Islands, Guam, and the Philippine Islands. The war ostensibly begun to free the people of a Caribbean island had ended with the United States in possession of a Pacific empire. How had it happened? Some writers sought an answer by determining who had made money out of the war, and a Marxist interpretation soon evolved. In a classic study, an English economist, J. A. Hobson, found the roots of imperialism lying in the desire of financiers and industrialists to secure markets and opportunities for investment. He did not deny that real and powerful motives of pride and prestige together with the idea of a civilizing mission figured as causes of imperial expansion. The dominant motive, however, remained economic, "a drive towards enlarged export trade" created by the "excess of capitalist production over the demands of the home market." The Spanish-American War, he charged, "put several millions of dollars into the pockets of Mr. Pierpont Morgan and his friends." Drawing heavily on Hobson's work, Nikolai Lenin called imperialism the last stage of capitalism.

The Spanish-American War

In the following selection Julius W. Pratt (b. 1888), through a careful study of business periodicals, attempts to gauge the extent to which economic factors brought on the war. He concludes that while American businessmen demanded the retention of the fruits of the war, in particular the Philippine Islands, they had, in the months before the declaration of war, been perhaps the strongest force against war, fearing it as a threat to the general business revival that had begun with William McKinley's election. Pratt, who had previously published a study of expansionism during the War of 1812, believed that advocates of a large policy for the United States in foreign affairs, men like Theodore Roosevelt, Henry Cabot Lodge, and Alfred Thayer Mahan, proclaiming a new Manifest Destiny, overrode the reluctance of the business community and convinced the country of the necessity of acquiring territory in the Caribbean and the Pacific. But Pratt's thesis has not proved entirely satisfactory. Later scholars feel he erred in confining his research to trade journals and not digging into the correspondence of business executives, which reveals a deep concern over the excess capacity of the American economy. Moreover, it now appears that many of the conservative business journals opposed to intervention had begun to change their position by March 1898. The tide of events beginning with the publication of the De Lome letter in early February, followed by the mysterious sinking of the battleship *Maine* in Havana Harbor, and culminating with a significant speech by the conservative and formerly strongly anti-war Senator Redfield Proctor of Vermont on March 17 carried important segments of the business community toward war. Walter La Feber, one of the strongest dissenters from Pratt's thesis, contends that by the end of March business opinion had moved to a position of preferring the shock of war to continued uncertainty over the Cuban situation.

Several studies have emphasized the significance of the circulation battle between William Randolph Hearst's *New York Journal* and Joseph Pulitzer's *New York*

World. Through gross distortions of the situation in Cuba, through crude sensationalism and rampant emotionalism, the yellow press played a significant, albeit indefensible, role in creating a popular demand for intervention. But it has been often asked why the public responded so strongly to the newspaper exaggerations. Richard Hofstadter suggests that the nation was experiencing a deep psychic crisis in the 1890's of which yellow journalism was a symptom. After identifying the sectional and political elements most enthusiastic for the war and most susceptible to war propaganda as the Populist section of the country, those areas most frustrated by the economic and political history of the decade, he concluded that the war with Spain provided the backcountry with a convenient outlet for their frustrations. William McKinley, a politician with his ear close to the ground, proved unable or unwilling to resist the popular clamor. His lack of courage has earned him the almost universal censure of historians, for if any consensus has emerged out of the historiography of the crisis of 1898, it is that the war with Spain was needless.

The joint resolutions of Congress embodying the ultimatum to Spain had, in the amendment offered by Senator Teller, disclaimed any intention of exercising "sovereignty, jurisdiction or control" over Cuba and had declared it to be the purpose of the United States, after pacifying the island, to leave its government and control to the Cuban people. To some, at least, of the expansionist group, this act of renunciation seemed unfortunate; yet they considered it no very serious obstacle to their plans. Whitelaw Reid, of the New York *Tribune*, in an interview published in the Paris *Matin*, announced that the United States had assumed responsibility for the maintenance of good government in Cuba, and that if the insurgents should prove incapable of conducting such a government, American responsibility would continue. But the

Teller Amendment referred to Cuba alone; it said nothing of Spain's other possessions, and it is apparent that no serious expansionist felt bound to apply the spirit of the amendment elsewhere than in Cuba.

Beveridge's speech, delivered a few days after the declaration of war, was quoted in the last chapter. Heartily in accord with him were such other young enthusiasts as Theodore Roosevelt and Henry Cabot Lodge—men thoroughly imbued with the concept of the "new manifest destiny." Three days after the battle of Manila Bay, Lodge wrote to Henry White: "We hold the other side of the Pacific, and the value to this country is almost beyond recognition." On no account, he said, must we "let the islands go . . . they must be ours under the treaty of peace." Shortly thereafter, in response to an appeal from Roosevelt not to "make peace until we get Porto Rico, while Cuba is made independent and the Philippines at any rate taken from the Spaniards," Lodge assured his Rough Rider correspondent that a substantial military force would be sent to the Philippines, that Puerto Rico would surely not be forgotten, and that

> Unless I am utterly and profoundly mistaken the Administration is now fully committed to the large policy that we both desire.

A few days later he made it clear that Hawaii, too, was embraced in the "large policy." Whitelaw Reid, also, undertook to inform the European public that the United States had no thought of relinquishing either the Philippines or Puerto Rico.

In other words, the young imperialists who had espoused the "large policy" of Lodge and Roosevelt knew precisely what use to make of the war with Spain. Their aims were partly patriotic or political: they would build up American sea power and claim for the United States its proper place among the nations of the world. But such a program was inseparable from economics. Sea power, as expounded by Mahan, was largely a matter of the control of world trade, and world trade, especially the trade of the Pacific, had figured largely in the various expansionist pronouncements. . . . Territorial expansion, in the minds of men like Lodge and Beveridge, found its justification largely in the control which it would give over markets and trade routes. It is pertinent, therefore, to enquire whether the war with Spain and the accompanying acquisition of insular possessions were, in reality, the results of economic pressure; whether, that is, business interests in the United States shared the aspirations of such intellectuals as Mahan, Lodge, Roosevelt, and Beveridge.

So reliable a scholar as Professor H. U. Faulkner has asserted that "the great cause for the war" with Spain is to be found in the fact that by 1898 the United States was "sufficiently advanced for financial imperialism," implying that the war was fought for markets and fields for investment. This interpretation was directly contradicted by the late James Ford Rhodes, who declared quite as categorically that "the financial and business interests of the country were opposed to the war." We may well enquire, therefore, what was, in reality, the attitude of American business both to the war (or to the intervention in Cuba, which brought on the war) and to the question of territorial expansion.

We may begin with a generalization, the evidence for which will be presented as the chapter proceeds. American business, in general, had strongly opposed action that would lead to war with Spain. American business had been either opposed or indifferent to the expansionist philosophy which had arisen since 1890. But almost at the moment when the war began, a large section of American business had, for reasons that will become apparent, been converted to the belief that a program of territorial expansion would serve its purposes. Hence business, in the end, welcomed the "large policy" and exerted its share of pressure for the retention of the Spanish islands and such related policies as the annexation of Hawaii and the construction of an isthmian canal.

One public man to whom the welfare of American business was of so much concern that he may almost be considered its spokesman in the Senate was McKinley's friend, Mark Hanna. No one was more unwilling than he to see the United States drift into war with Spain. To Hanna, in the words of his biographer, "the outbreak of war seemed to imperil the whole policy of domestic economic amelioration which he placed before every other object of political action." Hanna's attitude appears to have been identical with that of leading business men. This conclusion is based not only upon the few published biographies of such men, but also upon the study of a large number of financial and trade periodicals, of the proceedings of chambers of commerce and boards of trade, and of material in the *Miscellaneous Files* of the Department of State, containing numerous letters and petitions from business men and organizations.

That business sentiment, especially in the East, was strongly anti-war at the close of 1897 and in the opening months of 1898 is hardly open to doubt. Wall Street stocks turned downward whenever the day's news seemed to presage war and climbed again with information favorable to peace. Bulls and bears on the market were those who anticipated, respectively, a peaceable and a warlike solution of the Cuban question. The "jingo," in Congress or the press, was an object of intense dislike to the editors of business and financial journals, who sought to counteract his influence by anti-war editorials in their columns. Boards of trade and chambers of commerce added their pleas for the maintenance of peace to those of the business newspapers and magazines. So marked, indeed, was the anti-war solidarity of the financial interests and their spokesmen that the jingoes fell to charging Wall Street with want of patriotism. Wall Street, declared the Sacramento *Evening Bee* (March 11, 1898), was "the colossal and aggregate Benedict Arnold of the Union, and the syndicated Judas Iscariot of humanity." Senator Thurston, of Nebraska, charged that opposition to war was found only among the "moneychangers," bringing from the editor of *The American Banker* the reply that "there is not an intelligent, self-respecting and civilized American citizen anywhere who would not prefer to have the existing crisis culminate in peaceful negotiations." This anti-war attitude on the part of several leading financial journals continued up to the very beginning of hostilities. The New York *Journal of Commerce and Commercial Bulletin* declared on February 28 that the only possible excuses for war would be (1) a finding by the naval board investigating the "Maine" disaster that the ship had been destroyed by an official act of the Spanish Government; or (2) a refusal by Spain to make reparation if the board should hold that she had failed to exercise due diligence in safeguarding the vessel. Either of these events it held to be almost inconceivable. The *Commercial and Financial Chronicle* expressed the belief on March 12 that the opposition of the financial interests would yet prevent war; and on April 2 the same journal branded as "monstrous" the proposition to settle the Cuban and "Maine" questions by war while the slightest chance remained for a peaceful solution. On April 16, after the House of Representatives had passed the Cuban resolutions, the Boston *Journal of Commerce* declared: "Sober second thought had but little to do with the deliberations. . . . The members were carried off their feet by the war fever that had been so persistently worked up since the Maine explosion. . . ."

The reasons for this attitude on the part of business are not far to seek. Since the panic of 1893 American business had been in the doldrums. Tendencies toward industrial revival had been checked, first by the Venezuela war scare in December, 1895, and again by the free silver menace in 1896. But in 1897 began a real revival, and before the end of the year signs of prosperity appeared on all sides. The New York *Commercial* conducted a survey of business conditions in a wide variety of trades and industries, from which it concluded that, "after three years of waiting and of false starts, the groundswell of demand has at last begun to rise with a steadiness which leaves little doubt that an era of prosperity has appeared." January, 1898, said the same article, is "a supreme moment in the period of transition from depression to comparative prosperity." This note of optimism one meets at every turn, even in such a careful and conservative sheet as the *Commercial and Financial Chronicle*. As early as July, 1897, this paper remarked: "We appear to be on the eve of a revival in business"; and in December, after remarking upon the healthy condition of the railroads and the iron industry, it concluded: "In brief, no one can study the industrial conditions of today in America without a feeling of elation. . . ." The *Wall Street Journal* found only two "blue spots" in the entire country: Boston, which suffered from the depressed demand for cotton goods, and New York, where senseless rate cutting by certain railroads caused uneasiness. "Throughout the west, southwest and on the Pacific coast business has never been better, nor the people more hopeful."

A potent cause for optimism was found in the striking expansion of the American export trade. A volume of exports far in excess of those of any recent year, a favorable balance of trade of $286,000,000, and an especially notable increase in exports of manufactures of iron, steel, and copper convinced practically every business expert that the United States was on the point of capturing the markets of the world. "There is no question," said one journal, "that the world, generally, is looking more and more to the United States as the source of its supply for very many of the staple commodities of life." Especially elated were spokesmen of the iron and steel industry. Cheaper materials and improved methods were enabling the American producer to undersell his British competitor in Europe and in the British possessions, and Andrew Carnegie was talking of a great shipbuilding yard near New York to take advantage of these low costs. The *Iron Age,* in an editorial on "The Future of Business," foretold the abolition of the business cycle by means of a better planned economy, consolidation of railroads and industries, reduction of margins of profit, higher wages, and lower prices to consumers. To this fair prospect of a great business revival the threat of war was like a spectre at the feast. A foreign complication, thought the *Commercial and Financial Chronicle* in October, 1897, would quickly mar "the trade prosperity which all are enjoying." Six months later (April 2, 1898), after a discussion of the effect of war rumors on the stock exchange, it declared: ". . . Every influence has been, and even now is, tending strongly towards a term of decided prosperity, and that the Cuban disturbance, and it alone, has arrested the movement and checked enterprise." The *Banker and Tradesman* saw in the Cuban complication the threat of a "material setback to the prosperous conditions which had just set in after five years of panic and depression." The same journal summarized a calculation made by the Boston *Transcript* showing that in February, 1898, the wave of prosperity had carried the average price of twenty-five leading stocks within 5½ points of the high for the preceding ten years and 30 points above the low of 1896, and that the Cuban trouble had, in a little over two months, caused a loss of over ten points, or more than one-third of the recent gain. "War would impede the march of prosperity and put the country back many years," said the *New Jersey Trade Review*. The *Railway Age* was of the opinion that the country was coming out of a depression and needed peace to complete its recovery. "From a commercial and mercenary standpoint," it remarked, "it seems peculiarly bitter that this war should have come when the country had already suffered so much and so needed rest and peace."

The idea that war could bring any substantial benefits to business was generally scouted. It would endanger our currency stability, interrupt our trade, and threaten our coasts and our commerce, thought the *Commercial and Financial Chronicle*. It would "incalculably increase the loss to business interests," said the *Banker's Magazine*; while the *United States*

Investor held that war was "never beneficial from a material standpoint, that is, in the long run." The *Railroad Gazette* predicted that war would result in "interruption of business enterprise of every kind, stopping new projects and diminution of the output of existing businesses and contraction of trade everywhere." Railroads would lose more than they would gain. Even arms manufacturers were not all agreed that war would be desirable. Journals speaking for the iron and steel industry also argued that war would injure business. It "would injure the iron and steel makers ten times as much as they would be benefited by the prevailing spurt in the manufacture of small arms, projectiles and steel plates for war ships," in the opinion of one of these. The *American Wool and Cotton Reporter* of New York and the *Northwestern Miller* of Minneapolis agreed that war was never materially beneficial in the long run, while trade journals in Atlanta, Chattanooga, and Portland, Oregon, saw as fruits of the approaching conflict only destruction, debt, and depressed industry.

Many conservative interests feared war for the specific reason that it might derange the currency and even revive the free-silver agitation, which had seemed happily dead. The subsidence of that agitation and the prospect of currency reform were among the hopeful factors at the close of 1897. It was not uncommonly charged that the jingoes were animated in part by the expectation that war would lead to inflation in paper or silver. The New York *Journal of Commerce,* in an editorial on "The Breeding Grounds of Jingoism," had called attention to the fact that the jingoes were generally silverites, including in their number "the financiers who desire to force bankruptcy on the country as a means of breaking down the gold standard," and had quoted with approval an editorial from another paper charging that Senator Morgan's championship of the Cuban insurgents was part of "his wild scheming in the interest of the silver standard." The *Commercial and Financial Chronicle* endorsed this view, declaring that many of the Cuban agitators "are only interested in the establishment of a free-silver standard, a plan which they think war would advance." Similar views were expressed by the *American Banker* of New York, the *United States Investor* of Boston, and the *Rand-McNally Bankers' Monthly* of Chicago. The last-named quoted from a speech of Secretary of the Treasury Gage, delivered in Chicago in February, 1898, in which he had declared that "it would be scarcely possible for this nation to engage in war in its present condition . . . without a suspension of specie payments and a resort to further issues of Government notes." A war of any duration, in the opinion of the *United States Investor,* would certainly derange the currency and reduce business to a gambling basis.

Something of a freak among New York financial journals was the *Financial Record,* which, in November, 1897, denounced "the cowardice of our Administration in refusing the phenomenally brave Cubans the commonest rights of belligerency" as "a disgrace to the United States," and argued that war with Spain, far from depressing securities or injuring business, "would vastly increase the net earning power of every security sold on our market today." The mystery of this jingo attitude is explained when we discover that this journal had been a warm advocate of the free coinage of silver.

Business opinion in the West, especially in the Mississippi Valley, appears to have been less opposed to war and less apprehensive of its results than that of the Atlantic coast. The Kansas City Board of Trade, at the beginning of 1897, had urged recognition of Cuban independence. The Cincinnati Chamber of Commerce, at a meeting on March 29, 1898, adopted "amidst much enthusiasm" resolutions condemning Spain for cruelties to the Cubans and the destruction of the "Maine" and calling for a "firm and vigorous policy which will have for its purpose—peacefully if we can, but with force if we must—the redress of past wrongs, and the complete and unqualified independence of Cuba." The Chicago *Economist* denied that war would seriously hurt business or endanger the gold standard and asserted that the liberation of Cuba, by peace or war, would mean another star of glory for the United States and would produce "results of the highest value to mankind." The *Rand-McNally Bankers' Monthly,* of the same city, while opposing war, called attention to the fact that while the war scare had demoralized the stock market, "general business activity apparently received an impetus." Similarly the *Age of Steel* (St. Louis), while much preferring peace, "when not secured at the price of national honor," comforted its readers with the thought that although foreign trade might suffer, home trade and industries would be stimulated by war. A St. Louis bank president, Mr. Lackland, believed that war would "cause a boom in many lines of business in this country . . . and give employment to a large number of persons who are now out of work." The Chattanooga *Tradesman* stated on March 1, 1898, that a "small prospect" of war had already stimulated the iron trade in certain lines and had benefited the railroads by hurrying forward shipments of grain and other commodities in anticipation of war prices. The *Mining and Scientific Press,* of San Francisco, while holding that, in general, war "lets loose havoc and waste, and entails destructive expense," conceded that "to nearly everything related to the mining industry the war will be a stimulus."

Even in New York, business men saw some rays of light piercing the war clouds. Stock market operators, according to the *Wall Street Journal,* just after the "Maine" explosion, "did not look for any great break in the market, because actual war with Spain would be a very small affair compared with the Venezuela complication with Great Britain." Their expectation was for a drop in stocks at the beginning of hostilities, followed by a resumption of the recent advance. In fact, the first shock might well be followed by a boom. "The nation looks for peace," declared *Dun's Review,* March 5, "but knows that its sources of prosperity are quite beyond the reach of any attack that is possible." *Bradstreet's* contrasted the jumpiness of Wall Street over war news with "the calm way in which general business interests have regarded the current foreign complications," and *Dun's Review* of March 12 stated that no industry or branch of business showed any restriction, while some had been rapidly gaining, that railroads were increasing their profits while speculators sold their stocks, and that there was a growing demand for the products of all the great industries.

Despite such expressions as these, there seems little reason to question the belief that an overwhelming preponderance of the vocal business interests of the country strongly desired peace. By the middle of March, however, many organs of business opinion were admitting that a war with Spain might bring no serious disaster, and there was a growing conviction that such a war was inevitable. In the Senate on March 17, Senator Redfield Proctor, of Vermont, described, from his own observation, the terrible suffering of the Cuban "reconcentrados." Proctor was supposedly no sensationalist, and his speech carried great weight. The *Wall Street Journal* described its effect among the denizens of the Street. "Senator Proctor's speech," it said, "converted a great many people in Wall Street, who have heretofore taken the ground that the United States had no business to interfere in a revolution on Spanish soil. These men had been among the most prominent in deploring the whole Cuban matter, but there was no question about the accuracy of Senator Proctor's statements and as many of them expressed it, they made the blood boil." The *American Banker,* hitherto a firm opponent of intervention, remarked on March 23 that Proctor's speech showed an intolerable state of things, in view of which it could not understand "how any one with a grain of human sympathy within him can dispute the propriety of a policy of intervention, so only that this outraged people might be set free!" It still hoped, however, for a peaceful solution, declaring that the United States ought to urge the Cubans to accept the Spanish offer of autonomy. That this growing conviction that something must be done about Cuba was by no means equivalent to a desire for war, was clearly revealed a few days later. Rumors circulated to the effect that Spain was willing to sell Cuba and that J. P. Morgan's return from a trip abroad was connected with plans to finance the purchase. "There is much satisfaction expressed in Wall Street," said the *Wall Street Journal,* "at the prospects of having Cuba free, because it is believed that this will take one of the most disturbing factors out of the situation. . . . Even if $200,000,000 is the indemnity demanded it is a sum which the United States could well afford to pay to get rid of the trouble." Even $250,000,000, it was thought, would be insignificant in comparison with the probable cost of a war.

It remains to examine the attitude of certain American business men and corporations having an immediate stake in Cuba, or otherwise liable to be directly affected by American intervention. Much American capital, as is well known, was invested in the Cuban sugar industry. Upon this industry the civil war fell with peculiarly devastating effect, not only cutting off profits on capital so invested, but also crippling a valuable carrying trade between Cuba and the United States. Naturally enough, some firms suffering under these conditions desired to see the United States intervene to end the war, though such intervention might lead to war between the United States and Spain. In May, 1897, a memorial on the subject bearing over three hundred signatures was presented to John Sherman, Secretary of State. The signers described themselves as "citizens of the United States, doing business as bankers, merchants, manufacturers, steamship owners and agents in the cities of Boston, New York, Philadelphia, Baltimore, Savannah, Charleston, Jacksonville, New Orleans, and other places, and also other citizens of the United States, who have been for many years engaged in the export and import trade with the Island of Cuba." They called attention to the serious losses to which their businesses had been subjected by the hostilities in Cuba and expressed the hope that, in order to prevent further loss, to reestablish American commerce, and also to secure "the blessings of peace for one and a half millions of residents of the Island of Cuba now enduring unspeakable distress and suffering," the United States Government might take steps to bring about an honorable reconciliation between the parties to the conflict.

Another memorial, signed by many of the same subscribers, was presented to President McKinley on February 9, 1898, by a committee of New York business men. It asserted that the Cuban war, which had now continued for three entire years, had caused an average loss of $100,000,000 a year, or a total loss of $300,000,000 in the import and export trade between Cuba and the United States, to which were to be added "heavy sums irretrievably lost by the destruction of American properties, or properties supported by American capital in the Island itself, such as sugar factories, railways, tobacco plantations, mines and other industrial enterprises; the loss of the United States in trade and capital by means of this war being probably far greater and more serious than that of all the other parties concerned, not excepting Spain herself."

The sugar crop of 1897–1898, continued the memorial, appeared for the most part lost like its two predecessors, and unless peace could be established before May or June of the current year, the crop of 1898–1899, with all the business dependent upon it, would likewise be lost, since the rainy season of summer and fall would be required "to prepare for next winter's crop, by repairing damaged fields, machinery, lines of railways, &c." In view of the importance to the United States of the Cuban trade and of American participation "in the ownership or management of Cuban sugar factories, railways and other enterprises," the petitioners hoped that the President would deem the situation "of sufficient importance as to warrant prompt and efficient measures by our Government, with the sole object of restoring peace . . . and with it restoring to us a most valuable commercial field."

How much weight such pressure from special interests had

with the administration there is no way of knowing. But it is to be noted that the pressure from parties directly interested was not all on one side. Mr. E. F. Atkins, an American citizen who divided his time between Boston and his sugar plantation of Soledad near Cienfuegos, Cuba, which he had developed at a cost of $1,400,000, had been able, through protection received from the Spanish Government and through a corps of guards organized and paid by himself, to continue operations throughout the period of the insurrection. He was frequently in Washington, where he had influential friends, during both the Cleveland and McKinley administrations and worked consistently against the adoption of any measures likely to provoke war.

Unlike some of the sugar plantations, American-owned iron mines in Cuba continued to do active business despite the insurrection. Three American iron and manganese enterprises in a single province of Santiago claimed to have an investment of some $6,000,000 of purely American capital, a large proportion of which was in property which could easily be destroyed. "We are fully advised as to our status in case of war," wrote the representative of one company to the Assistant Secretary of State, "and that this property might be subject to confiscation or destruction by the Spanish Government." War between Spain and the United States, wrote the president of another company, "will very likely mean the destruction of our valuable plant and in any event untold loss to our Company and its American stockholders." An American cork company with large interests in Spain; a New York merchant with trade in the Mediterranean and Black Sea; a Mobile firm which had chartered a Spanish ship to carry a cargo of timber—these are samples of American business interests which saw in war the threat of direct damage to themselves. They are hardly offset by the high hopes of an enterprising gentleman of Norfolk, "representing a party of capitalists who are enthusiastic supporters of the Government," who applied to the State Department for a letter of marque "to enable us to lawfully capture Spanish merchant vessels and torpedo boats," adding: "We have secured option on a fine steam vessel, and on receipt of proper documents will put to sea forth with."

It seems safe to conclude, from the evidence available, that the only important business interests (other than the business of sensational journalism) which clamored for intervention in Cuba were those directly or indirectly concerned in the Cuban sugar industry; that opposed to intervention were the influence of other parties (including at least one prominent sugar planter) whose business would suffer direct injury from war and also the overwhelming preponderance of general business opinion. After the middle of March, 1898, some conservative editors came to think intervention inevitable on humanitarian grounds, but many of the most influential business journals opposed it to the end.

We can now turn to the question whether American business was imperialistic; whether, in other words, business opinion favored schemes for acquiring foreign territory to supply it with markets, fields for capital investment, or commercial and naval stations in distant parts of the world. American business men were not unaware of the struggle for colonies then raging among European nations. Did they feel that the United States ought to participate in that struggle?

We have seen above that the rising tide of prosperity was intimately connected with the increase in American exports, particularly of manufactured articles. That the future welfare of American industry was dependent upon the command of foreign markets was an opinion so common as to appear almost universal. The New York *Journal of Commerce* pointed out, early in 1897, that the nation's industrial plant had been developed far beyond the needs of domestic consumption. In the wire nail industry there was said to be machinery to make four times as many nails as the American markets could consume. Rail mills, locomotive shops, and glass factories were in a similar situation. "Nature has thus destined this country for the industrial supremacy of the world," said the same paper later in the year. When the National Association of Manufacturers met in New York for its annual convention in January, 1898, "the discussion of ways and means for extending this country's trade, and more particularly its export business, was, in fact, almost the single theme of the speakers," according to *Bradstreet's,* which added the comment: "Nothing is more significant of the changed attitude toward this country's foreign trade, manifested by the American manufacturer today as compared with a few years ago, than the almost single devotion which he pays to the subject of possible export-trade extension."

But if business men believed, prior to the opening of the war with Spain, that foreign markets were to be secured through the acquisition of colonies, they were strangely silent about it. To the program of colonial expansion which for almost a decade had been urged by such men as Mahan, Albert Shaw, Lodge, Roosevelt, and Morgan, business had remained, to all appearances, either indifferent or antagonistic. To the business man, such a program was merely one form of dangerous jingoism. A large section of business opinion had, indeed, favored plans for the building of a Nicaraguan canal with governmental assistance, and some spokesmen for business had favored annexation of the Hawaiian Islands. But beyond these relatively modest projects few business men, apparently, wished to go. Two of the most important commercial journals, the New York *Journal of Commerce* and the *Commercial and Financial Chronicle,* had stoutly opposed both the canal scheme and Hawaiian annexation. The former satirized the arguments of the proponents of both schemes. "We must certainly build the canal to defend the islands, and it is quite clear that we must acquire the islands . . . in order to defend the canal." The canal was not only unnecessary, but unless fortified at each end and patrolled by two fleets, it would be a positive misfortune. Such protection—"the price of jingoism"—might "easily cost us $25,000,000 a year, besides the lump sum that will be required for the original investment, and there is absolutely no excuse whatever in our commercial or our political interests for a single step in this long procession of expenses and of complications with foreign powers." As for Hawaii and Cuba, neither was fit for self-government as a state,—and the American constitution provided no machinery for governing dependencies. The Hawaiian Islands would have no military value unless the United States were to build a great navy and take an aggressive attitude in the Pacific. The *Commercial and Financial Chronicle* saw in colonies only useless outposts which must be protected at great expense, and the St. Louis *Age of Steel* warned lest the expansion of the export trade might "lead to territorial greed, as in the case of older nations, the price of which in armaments and militarism offsets the gain made by the spindle and the forge."

Colonies were not only certain to bear a fruit of danger and expense; they were valueless from the commercial point of view. Did not the colonies of Great Britain afford us one of the most valuable of our export markets? Did we not trade as advantageously with Guiana, a British colony, as with independent Venezuela? "Most of our ideas of the commercial value of conquests, the commercial uses of navies and the commercial advantages of political control," said the New York *Journal of Commerce,* dated back to times when colonial policies were designed to monopolize colonial trade for the mother country. The *Commercial and Financial Chronicle* believed that the current European enthusiasm for colonies was based on false premises; for although trade often followed the flag, "the trade is not always with the home markets of the colonizer. England and the United States are quite as apt to slip in with their wares under the very Custom-House pennant of the French or German dependency." Outright opposition, such as this, to the idea of colonial expansion is not common in the business periodicals examined; much more common is complete silence on the subject. Positive and negative evidence together seem to warrant the conclusion that American business in general, at the opening of 1898, was either indifferent to imperialism, or definitely opposed. Confidence in the continued expansion of the export trade was based upon faith in the working of natural forces in a world given over largely to a system of free trade. American industry had reached a point where it could meet the world on more than even terms in both the price and the quality of its products. Given a fair chance, these products would make their own way. Government could aid them, not by acquiring colonial markets but by removing or lowering the barriers that restricted imports of raw materials and exchange commodities. To one who has in mind the subsequent tariff history of the United States, it is surprising to discover the amount of free-trade sentiment which found expression in these months of 1897–1898. The preoccupation of Congress with the raising of duties in the Dingley Act was disturbing to those interested in the export trade. "It is pitiful," said the *Journal of Commerce,* "to see the national legislature bending its whole force to readjusting the trammels of a system which can only obstruct, and closing its eyes to the manifest, though unconscious, struggling of industry for a freedom that will enable it to compete successfully in any market of the world." The futility of expecting to increase exports while at the same time barring out imports was stressed by more than one writer for business journals, and a change toward free trade in American policy was freely predicted. "We are gradually losing our fear of the bugaboo of cheap foreign labor," said the *Iron Age,* "and are slowly realizing that we hold the key of the position, since there are no indications that European manufacturers will ever displace us in the van of progress." The *American Machinist* declared that the recent growth in the export trade showed that in many lines the tariff was a dead letter, that goods which could be sold under the nose of the foreign producer no longer needed protection in the home market, and that the machinery interests would in all probability bring pressure to bear on Congress "toward action which will equalize these matters." The Chattanooga *Tradesman* was convinced that the great development in the export of manufactures was certain to have upon tariff policy an effect "both broad and radical," and the president of the Baltimore Chamber of Commerce, speaking on the same theme to that body in December, 1897, predicted that "the day is not so far distant when free trade, in some measure, at least, will become part of our political faith."

In a free-trade world, colonies would be of no importance. But if countries to which American producers looked for their markets should adopt restrictive policies, then a change in the American attitude might easily occur. Two events in the late fall of 1897 gave warning that the world at large might not continue hospitable to American products. The first was an address by Count Goluchowski, Austro-Hungarian Foreign Minister, to the Austro-Hungarian Delegations, in which he complained of the "destructive competition with transoceanic countries" and warned that the peoples of Europe "must fight shoulder to shoulder against the common danger, and must arm themselves for the struggle with all the means at their disposal." The twentieth century, he declared, would be a "period marked by a struggle for existence in the politico-commercial sphere," and "the European nations must close their ranks in order successfully to defend their existence."

In the United States, the Austrian's pronouncement was generally interpreted as aimed principally at this country. It caused widespread comment but little serious alarm. Many papers doubted the possibility of any European cooperation to exclude American products, pointing out that a stoppage of trade would injure Europe more than the United States, since we provided Europe with necessities in return for commodities most of which were either luxuries or articles that we could produce ourselves. Even if Europe should exclude our products, thought the New York *Commercial*, we should find an outlet in those other markets now cherished by Europe.

This opinion was shared by the Philadelphia *Ledger,* which believed that, though concerted action in Europe might cripple our markets there, our trade with South America and the Far East could not "be directly disturbed through any European alliance." But the New York *Journal of Commerce,* in a thoughtful editorial, took a more serious view of the speech. In their determined quest for markets, it said, the industrial nations of Europe were following two courses: acquisition of colonies and the enactment of discriminatory tariffs. Hitherto each country had worked alone, but now there were signs of the rise of alliances or combinations in tariff policy. Since Austria-Hungary had a trade of but $10,000,000 a year with the United States, the idea put forward by Count Goluchowski must have been initiated elsewhere, and the paper suggested that a probable source was Russia, which had reason to seek to restrict the markets for American staples in both Europe and Asia.

The suspicion voiced by the *Journal of Commerce* that behind the Austrian's speech might lie concealed a threat to the American market in the Far East seemed partially confirmed within a few days, with the coming of news of European aggressions in China. Under the color of retaliation for the death of two German missionaries, a German force, on November 14, expelled the Chinese garrison at Tsingtau, at the mouth of Kiaochow Bay, seized the forts and occupied the port. Eight days later the German Government presented its formal demands, which included a naval station on Kiaochow Bay and the grant of the sole right to build railways and open coal mines in Shantung. By early in January, 1898, China had yielded all, and a convention to that effect was signed March 6. Meanwhile, within a week after the occupation of Tsingtau, Russian warships arrived at Port Arthur, and by May, 1898, China had agreed to the lease to Russia for twenty-five years of Port Arthur, Dalny, and other territory in the Liaotung peninsula. Compensating advantages were demanded and received by Great Britain and France, and by July 1, 1898, the partition of China had to all appearances begun.

Here were deeds more ominous than any words could be. They touched American business sentiment in a particularly sensitive spot, for though American trade with China was, in 1897, less than two per cent of its total foreign trade, exports to China in that year were almost double those of 1896, and there was a widespread belief that China was to provide an exceedingly important market for the surplus products of the United States. While some papers made light of the danger to American business presented by the Chinese crisis, and others professed to see positive advantages to the United States in the development of China under European direction, the less optimistic saw a probability that American trade would find itself discriminated against or excluded altogether by the partitioning powers. Mr. Charles Denby, former Minister to China, in a note published in the *American Banker,* warned that with the seizure of territory, American commercial treaties with China "fall to the ground, and spheres of influence hostile to American commerce spring into existence." Similar alarm was voiced by numerous papers in all parts of the country, by none more vehemently than the New York *Journal of Commerce.* This paper, whose attitude hitherto might be characterized as pacifist, anti-imperialist, and devoted to the development of commerce in a free-trade world, saw the foundation of its faith crumbling as a result of the threatened partition of China. Declaring that free access to the markets of China, with her 400,000,000 people, would largely solve the problem of the disposal of our surplus manufactures, the *Journal* came out not only for a stern insistence upon complete equality of rights in China, but unreservedly also for an isthmian canal, the acquisition of Hawaii, and a material increase in the navy—three measures which it had hitherto strenuously opposed. Nothing could be more significant than the manner in which this paper was converted in a few weeks, justifying its change on each point by the needs of the hour in the Far East.

Finding the Department of State, under Secretary Sherman, quite unimpressed by the seriousness of the Chinese situation, the *Journal of Commerce* itself initiated a movement to arouse the Executive to a defense of American interests. At the paper's suggestion, a Committee on American Interests in China was organized in New York to work for concerted action by chambers of commerce in important cities. As a direct result of this propaganda, a committee of the Chamber of Commerce of the State of New York laid before that body on February 3, 1898, a report on "American Treaty Rights in China" and a memorial to the President of the United States. The report summarized the history of the acquisition of commercial rights through treaties with the Chinese Government and argued that those rights were seriously endangered by the recent aggressions of European powers. American products, it pointed out, were already virtually excluded from French Cochin China—an omen of what was to be expected elsewhere if France and other powers made good their positions on Chinese soil. "The Administration at Washington," the report continued, "seems to be supine about the present menace to those important interests of our citizens in China. . . . Under these circumstances it would seem that unless those concerned in our export trade take steps to agitate the matter and to have their interests safeguarded, nobody else will do it." The memorial to the President, which was promptly adopted by the Chamber, pictured the growing importance of American trade with China and the new dangers threatening it and respectfully urged that steps be taken "for the prompt and energetic defense of the existing treaty rights of our citizens in China, and for the preservation and protection of their important commercial interests in that Empire."

Within a few weeks similar action was taken by the Chambers of Commerce or Boards of Trade of Philadelphia, San Francisco, Baltimore, Boston, and Seattle. Not content with this action, a group of merchants interested in the Eastern trade held a meeting on March 3, at 59 Wall Street, New York, to form a permanent organization for the protection of that trade. A few days later, with the cooperation of the New York Chamber of Commerce, they took steps to organize the American China and Japan Association, to foster and safeguard the interests of citizens of the United States and others concerned in the trade with those empires and to secure and disseminate information relating thereto. The organization was not perfected until June 16. By that time the battle of Manila Bay had broadened the American outlook in the Orient, and the organization followed suit, changing its title to the American Asiatic Association and including in its field of interest American trade not only in China and Japan, but also in "the Philippine Islands, and elsewhere in Asia and Oceania." Promptly upon its organization, the Association put itself into communication with the Department of State, offering its services for consultation or cooperation.

In the light of this widespread and intense interest in the preservation of the Chinese market, we can perhaps understand why American business, which had been, to all appearances, anti-war and anti-imperialist, was filled with sudden enthusiasm at the news of Dewey's victory at Manila Bay. Not only did the news dissipate all fears of a long and costly war and send stock prices rapidly upward; still more important, it seemed to place in American hands, all unexpectedly, the key to the trade of the Orient. The attack on the Spanish fleet at Manila had been anticipated for months and well advertised by the American press. Some papers had speculated upon the value of the islands as an American colony and had foreseen that a victory there might greatly alter our relation to the imbroglio in China. But for most, this thought did not occur until arrival of the news that the Spanish fleet was destroyed and Dewey safely in possession of Manila Bay. Then, at last, business men joined the jingoes in their acclaim of imperial conquests. Senator Lodge's exclamation—"We hold the other side of the Pacific, and the value to this country is almost beyond recognition"—was matched by many a formerly conservative business journal. It was not the intrinsic value of the Philippines or their trade that most impressed American writers, though this angle of the subject was not overlooked. Rather, their importance appeared to lie in their position as a gateway to the markets of Eastern Asia.

It has been shown that the aggressions of the European powers in China had converted the New York *Journal of Commerce* to the belief that the United States must dig an isthmian canal, acquire Hawaii, and enlarge its navy. The same paper now took the lead in insisting that the newly won vantage point in the Philippines be retained and utilized to uphold American rights in China. However disconcerting might be our possession of Manila to European plans in the Far East, we must deal with it as a "factor in the protection of our interests in that part of the world." Hitherto we had "allowed Great Britain to fight our battle for an open market in China: with our flag floating within 500 miles of Hong Kong we shall be able to give that policy something more than merely moral support in the future." There was thus "introduced a most formidable element of resistance to all that France and Russia at least seem to be working for in Asia." To return the islands to Spain or to dispose of them to England or any other power, said the same paper a few days later, "would be an act of inconceivable folly in the face of our imperative future necessities for a basis of naval and military force on the Western shores of the Pacific."

Endorsement of these views came rapidly from all sides. "Some broad-minded men," said the *Wall Street Journal*, May 5, "believe that the United States should retain enough interest in the Philippines to be sure of a coaling station and a naval base in Asiatic waters, under belief that the breaking up of China will make it necessary for this country to be in a position to protect, not only the existing trade with the far east, but the enormously greater trade likely to be developed in the next 25 years." The *American Banker,* of May 11, while absolving the United States from entering the war for any selfish purpose, declared that it could not relinquish the territories which it had been forced to seize, with the result that its diplomacy would no longer be a negative quantity in European counsels, "particularly not as respects the inevitable partition of the Chinese Empire. That a war with Spain," it added, "should have transpired at precisely this time, when Europe is tending to divide a considerable section of the inhabited earth, is a coincidence which has a providential air." The *Banker and Tradesman* likewise discerned the hand of Providence in bestowing the Philippines upon the United States at a time when Russia, France, and Germany were threatening American trade in China, and asked whether we could rightly throw away "a possession which would be of such great advantage to us in maintaining and defending our interests in this part of the globe." It asserted later that the answer to the question of the open door in China "was given, as European nations very well know, when Dewey entered Manila Bay and won his glorious victory." Similar views appeared in the *Age of Steel,* the *Iron Age,* the *United States Investor,* and the *Financial Record. Bradstreet's* thought the possession of Manila would greatly accelerate the growth of American trade in Asia and predicted that that city "might in time even rival Hong Kong as a distributive trade center." The New York *Commercial,* using figures supplied by the Bureau of Statistics in Washington, pointed out that countries closely adjacent to the Philippines contained 850,000,000 people and purchased over one billion dollars worth of goods a year, mostly articles which might be grown or manufactured in the United States. "With the Philippines as a three-quarter way house, forming a superb trading station, the bulk of this trade should come to this country." The New York Chamber of Commerce, in a report on "American Interests in China," argued that, in face of the prospect that European spheres of influence in China might become permanent territorial acquisitions, the only course by which the United States could protect her interests appeared to be active participation in politics on the "dangerous ground of the Far East"—a participation which might be "hastened and materialized through our possible occupation of the Philippine Islands."

The insistence that the Philippines be retained, for the sake of their own trade and as a gateway to Asiatic markets, was confined to no one section of the country. In the South, business men saw in possession of the islands assurance of the continued growth of the marketing of American cotton goods in China. The Pacific Coast, very naturally, displayed a lively interest. In Dewey's victory, the *Mining and Scientific Press* saw an earnest that the coast cities would be transformed from the back door to the front door of civilization. "The guns that destroyed the Spanish fleet in Manila Bay thundered a warning to the nations of our approaching commercial supremacy in the Orient." The *Commercial Bulletin of Southern California* believed acquisition of the Philippines would greatly hasten the growth of trans-Pacific trade and asserted it was with this expectation that "Pacific Coast people so generally favor territorial expansion." The *Daily Commercial News and Shipping List,* of San Francisco, thought the coast people would make determined efforts for the retention of the Philippines. The Chamber of Commerce of Seattle and the Chamber of Commerce, Merchants' Association, and Manufacturers' and Producers' Association of San Francisco petitioned the President to retain not only the Philippines, but the Caroline and Ladrone Islands, "and all other lands which are now, or may hereafter be acquired in the present war with Spain," in the interests of humanity and the Oriental trade of the United States. Even James J. Hill, who had been a strong opponent of the war, stated to a newspaper reporter that if it rested with him, he would retain the Philippines. "If you go back in the commercial history of the world," he was reported as saying, "you will find that the people who controlled the trade of the Orient have been the people who held the purse strings of nations."

It must not be inferred that business opinion was unanimous in favor of retaining the Philippines. There was an undercurrent of opposition or indifference. The New York *Journal of Commerce,* just before the signing of the peace protocol, deplored the fact that timid people were shrinking from imperialism and that "the business men of the country are maintaining a deathlike silence." The *Commercial and Financial Chronicle* was cautious, pointing out that Spain's distant possessions had proved her most vulnerable point—a fact from which the United States might learn a lesson—and hoping that the United States might yet find a way to avoid such a dangerous responsibility. The Baltimore *Journal of Commerce* was, in July, strongly opposed to annexation, and two months later held that no one yet knew whether "our position as wetnurse to Cuba, proprietors of Porto Rico and pantata to the Philippines is likely to bring us profit or loss." The *Iron Age,* which early in the summer had been strongly for expansion was by September harboring qualms as to the real value of colonies to the business man. Everett Frazar, president of the American Asiatic Association, was personally a warm supporter of annexation, but the Association held upon its table for months without action a resolution on the subject. The San Francisco *Call,* representing the California and Hawaiian sugar interests of the Spreckels family, was strongly opposed to annexation, arguing not only that Anglo-Saxons had no aptitude for tropical colonization, but also frankly warning Californian sugar-beet growers of the danger of competition from Philippine cane-sugar.

There is no way of measuring accurately the strength of business opinion for and against the retention of the Philippines. Judging opinion as best we can from the available expressions of it, it seems safe to conclude that after the battle of Manila Bay American business became definitely imperialistic—that is, if a wish to retain the Philippines is an evidence of an imperialistic attitude. It seems certain, too, from the prominence given to the Chinese situation in nearly every discussion of the value of the islands, that the conversion of business opinion was accomplished by the combination of a European threat against the freedom of the American market in China, present and prospective, with the dramatic coup of the American fleet in a fine harbor so near the Chinese coast. In one paper, the New York *Journal of Commerce,* there appears with beautiful clarity the shift of position induced by the action of the European Powers in China. In November, 1897, against all schemes of colonial or naval expansion; in December, for a canal, Hawaii annexation, and a big navy; in May and thereafter, for retention of the entire Philippine archipelago and aggressive assertion of American rights in China—the *Journal* reveals a process of thought which perhaps occurred less clearly and consciously in the minds of many business men.

Having concluded that the Philippines were wholesome and digestible, business was disposed to treat itself to more of the same diet. The venture in the Philippines strengthened immeasurably the demand for the annexation of Hawaii. "The battle of Manila Bay," said the *Journal of Commerce,* May 31, "makes it imperative that we should establish permanent arrangements which will make the [Hawaiian] islands a halfway house on the road to the Philippines." But there were other Pacific islands that beckoned. "Bridge the Pacific!" cried the Philadelphia *Press.* "With the Philippines go the Carolines, a Spanish possession, Samoa and the Hawaiian Islands complete the chain." The war in the Pacific, the prospect of new possessions there, and the voyage of the "Oregon" also gave new force to the demand for an isthmian canal. In the Caribbean, business interests not only insisted that the United States needed Puerto Rico for its strategic and commercial value, but suggested that it might prove impossible to adhere to the Teller Amendment, which had pledged the United

States not to annex Cuba. The New York *Journal of Commerce,* voicing skepticism as to the capacity of the Cubans for orderly government, declared: "The Teller amendment ... must be interpreted in a sense somewhat different from that which its author intended it to bear." The American flag must float over Cuba until law and order were assured. American covetousness in the Caribbean was not limited to the Spanish islands. The New York *Commercial,* which in March had commended Lodge's proposal for the purchase of the Danish Islands, now saw signs that the British West Indies might be interested in coming under the American flag and urged that the Bahamas, Jamaica, and Bermuda be not lost sight of during the war. The *Journal of Commerce,* endorsing the same idea, remarked: "Our people are now in an expansive mood and there is a deep and strong American sentiment that would rejoice to see the British flag, as well as the Spanish flag, out of the West Indies."

Merchants and manufacturers now saw in the acquisition of colonies a partial solution of the disposal of surplus American products. European countries, prejudiced against our goods, said the New York *Commercial* (evidently recalling Count Goluchowski's speech), had acquired colonial markets while we had none; but the acquisition of the Spanish islands would supply the lack; their development by American capital would stimulate the demand for the products of our fields and factories. We should regulate their customs in a manner to favor our own industries and shipping and discourage those of other countries. This proposed procedure was condemned by the *Journal of Commerce,* the *Commercial and Financial Chronicle,* and other journals and organizations, which insisted that after urging the "open door" in China we must adhere to the same principle in our new possessions. But whether the door was to be open or closed to the rest of the world, an active and lucrative trade with the new possessions was widely anticipated. "One way of opening a market is to conquer it ... ," said the *Railway World* in August. "Already our enterprising merchants are beginning to organize to take possession of the markets which our army and navy have opened to them." The Chicago *Inter-Ocean,* in a series of interviews with merchants and manufacturers in several cities, found them "very generally waking up to the opportunities which the war has brought at a moment when the immense increase of our manufacturing capacity has rendered foreign outlets absolutely necessary to us." The Bureau of Statistics reported large numbers of inquiries from all parts of the country, but chiefly from the great producing and business centers, as to the imports of Cuba and Puerto Rico. Not only the trade prospects but also the opportunities for American capital and skill to develop the resources of the islands excited enthusiasm. A national bank for Hawaii was organized immediately after passage of the annexation resolution. Similar plans were afoot for Puerto Rico and Cuba, and enterprising Americans were studying financial conditions in the Philippines. "Railroad building may be expected to boom in all the islands which may fall under the influence of the United States," said *Rand-McNally Bankers' Monthly.* Cane sugar and tobacco growing would receive an impetus. "The forests may also be made to yield handsome returns, . . . and in fact every industry, so long under the blighting rule of Spain, will be exploited and made to show the advantages accruing from better government and wider enterprise."

American business had yielded reluctantly to the necessity of a war with Spain, forced upon the United States by popular reaction to the distressing situation in Cuba. It had not foreseen, or if it foresaw had feared, the colonial responsibilities to which such a war might lead. But when Dewey's dramatic victory on the first of May offered a Far Eastern base from which the threatened markets in China might be defended, it had gladly accepted the result, and long before the conclusion of peace with Spain, it was building high hopes upon the supposed opportunities for trade and exploitation in a string of dependencies stretching from the Philippines to Puerto Rico.

For Further Reading

Two short and sprightly histories of the Spanish-American War are Walter Millis, *The Martial Spirit* (1931), and Frank Freidel, *The Splendid Little War* (1958). Although Theodore Roosevelt's *The Rough Riders* (1899) should not be overlooked, there is much valuable material in Margaret Leech, *In the Days of McKinley*, and H. Wayne Morgan, *America's Road to Empire* (1965). Arthur Weinberg, *Manifest Destiny* (1935), discusses the phenomenon of expansion throughout American history. Pratt's monograph on the movement in 1898 may be supplemented with Foster Rhea Dulles' *The Imperial Years* (1956) and a still valuable older work, French E. Chadwich's *The Relations of the United States and Spain: The Spanish-American War* (2 vols., 1911). For contemporary opinions on the nation's need to expand, see Josiah Strong, *Our Country: Its Possible Future and Its Present Crisis* (1885), and Alfred T. Mahan, *The Influence of Sea Power on History: 1660–1783* (1890).

J. A. Hobson, *Imperialism: A Study* (1902), the original statement on the economic causation of the war, should be supplemented by Walter La Feber, *The New Empire: An Interpretation of American Expansionism, 1860–1898* (1963). For the role of the newspaper, see Joseph E. Wisan, *The Cuban Crisis as Reflected in the New York Press, 1895–1898* (1934), Marcus M. Wilkerson, *Public Opinion and the Spanish-American War* (1932), and two biographies by William A. Swanberg, *Citizen Hearst* (1961) and *Pulitzer* (1967). Orestes Ferrara, *The Last Spanish War: Revelations in Diplomacy* (1937), views the war from a Spanish perspective. The thesis that the war presented a safe discharge for domestic resentments is presented in Richard Hofstadter, "Manifest Destiny and the Philippines" in Daniel Aaron, ed., *America in Crisis* (1952). Hofstadter located this psychosis chiefly in the rural areas of Populist strength, but a subsequent study by Ernest R. May, *Imperial Democracy: The Emergence of America as a Great Power* (1961), found more evidence of hysteria in cities and towns. For the related issue of the acquisition of the Hawaiian Islands, consult Sylvester K. Stevens, *American Expansion in Hawaii* (1945), William Adam Russ, Jr., *The Hawaiian Republic, 1894-1898* (1961), and William L. Langer, *The Diplomacy of Imperialism, 1890-1902* (1935).

The Status Revolution and Progressive Leaders

Richard Hofstadter

*I*n 1906, in a characteristic burst of exasperation, President Theodore Roosevelt added a new word to the American political lexicon when he called those writers engaged in exposing public and private corruption "muckrakers." The reforming journalists reminded him of the man with the muckrake in John Bunyan's *Pilgrim's Progress* "who was offered the celestial crown for his muckrake, but would neither look up nor regard the crown he was offered but continued to rake the filth on the floor." Roosevelt was unfair, to say the least. The success of the muckrakers in educating the public to the need for reform made it possible for men like Roosevelt himself to gain support for political programs and social proposals of such consequence that the years between 1900 and 1917 are commonly described as the progressive era.

Progressivism pervaded all links of government. On the local level, spurred on by Lincoln Steffens' blistering

Source: Richard Hofstadter, *The Age of Reform: From Bryan to F.D.R.* (New York: Alfred A. Knopf, Inc., 1955), pp. 134–161. Copyright © 1955 by Richard Hofstadter. Reprinted by permission of the author and publisher.

indictment of municipal corruption in *The Shame of the Cities*, reformers took control of cities as diverse as Boston and Toledo, San Francisco and Jersey City. Samuel M. "Golden Rule" Jones of Toledo gained national attention by introducing free kindergartens, night schools, and public playgrounds. Despite the opposition of both the Democratic and Republican parties, he won reelection four times. In Cleveland and Milwaukee, Tom Johnson and Emil Seidel won for their cities reputations as the best governed in America. Throughout the country, city governments became more efficient through the introduction of the commission and city manager plans. On the state level, progressive governors such as Woodrow Wilson in New Jersey, Hiram Johnson in California, Albert Cummins in Iowa, and Robert M. LaFollette in Wisconsin secured legislation reducing the power of the railroads and the great corporations, revising tax codes and improving the conditions of industrial employment. The presidential administrations of Roosevelt, Wilson, and to a lesser degree of William Howard Taft moved to regulate the trusts, secure consumer benefits, and conserve natural resources. The state legislatures and the national congresses of these years responded to popular agitation by introducing such political innovations as direct primaries, short ballots, and constitutional amendments providing for a graduated income tax, the direct election of United States senators, and eventually woman's suffrage. The people were also given the opportunity to participate more directly in politics through such devices as the initiative, referendum, and recall. Along with these official public efforts went private efforts to cure society's ills. Settlement houses reflected humanitarian concern for the unfortunate of the city slums, organized charity replaced haphazard giving, and throughout the country churchmen who had once stoutly defended the doctrine of laissez-faire now endorsed the Social Gospel preached by Walter Rauschenbusch and became leaders in the purpose of making over, as Rauschenbusch expressed it, "an antiquated and immoral economic system."

What forces produced this remarkable ferment? As noted earlier, the muckrakers helped by informing the public of the seamy side of American life. But the literature of protest can be traced back to as early as 1880 when Henry George published *Progress and Poverty,* which had, to be sure, caused a considerable discussion and some little activity, but had produced no compelling demand for reform. Richard Hofstadter (b. 1916), rejects the interpretation that Progressivism issued from Populism, for this does not explain why Populism failed in the depression decade of the 1890's and Progressivism succeeded in the more prosperous decade that followed. Why should so many people of conservative bent, who had strongly opposed Bryan in 1896, embrace almost his entire program ten years later? Hofstadter finds the answer to this paradox in the leadership of the new movement. It was the urban middle class throughout the nation, not the agrarian reformers of the South and the Middle West, who provided the support for a wide range of reforms. In the following selection, he contends that the urban gentry went into politics as the result of a status revolution that had deprived them of the deference that had once been theirs. Although the status revolution thesis first appeared in a study of California progressives by George Mowry, Hofstadter's elaboration of it gained wider attention and helped establish his current reputation as the profession's leading intellectual historian. His works are also distinguished by effective employment of the techniques of the behavioral and social scientists and by an unfailing tendency to generate controversy.

The status revolution interpretation, for example, has been vigorously challenged. Several students of urban America deny his charge that "together with the native conservative and the political indifferent, the immigrants formed a potent mass that limited the range and achievements of Progressivism." This statement ignores the reform contributions of a large ethnic group like the Jews, or the support which individual leaders like Al Smith,

Robert F. Wagner, or David I. Walsh gave to many progressive measures. It is quite true that many of the progressive reforms left the immigrant peoples cold. They resented the reformers' efforts to destroy the political machines because the Tammany-type organizations had been solicitous of the newcomers, providing them with jobs, getting them out of trouble with the police, or sending a basket of food in times of desperate need. Why support the direct primary when it probably meant a diminishing of the boss's influence? Why endorse municipal efficiency when it meant fewer jobs? One progressive leader complained, "The immigrant lacks the faculty of abstraction. He thinks not of the welfare of the community but only of himself." The trouble with this reasoning, as Oscar Handlin has pointed out, was that precious little thought was given to their welfare. They had to consider their own interests for no one else would. But when it came to social and economic reforms, the bread and butter issues, the progressive leaders could expect and did receive the support of the urban masses. Even political reforms, generally regarded with suspicion, would be endorsed if the particular situation warranted it. J. Joseph Huthmacher has shown how the urban working class in Massachusetts supported the initiative and referendum in order to bypass the rural-dominated state legislature. Future historians of Progressivism will have to ponder the implications of such evidence before locating the causes of the movement in the quest of the middle class for status and deference.

Curiously, the Progressive revolt—even when we have made allowance for the brief panic of 1907 and the downward turn in business in 1913—took place almost entirely during a period of sustained and general prosperity. The middle class, most of which had been content to accept the conservative leadership of Hanna and McKinley during the period of crisis in the mid-nineties, rallied to the support of Progressive leaders in both parties during the period of well-being that followed. This fact is a challenge to the historian. Why did the middle classes undergo this remarkable awakening at all, and why during this period of general prosperity in which most of them seem to have shared? What was the place of economic discontents in the Progressive movement? To what extent did reform originate in other considerations?

Of course Progressivism had the adherence of a heterogeneous public whose various segments responded to various needs. But I am concerned here with a large and strategic section of Progressive leadership, upon whose contributions the movement was politically and intellectually as well as financially dependent, and whose members did much to formulate its ideals. It is my thesis that men of this sort, who might be designated broadly as the Mugwump type, were Progressives not because of economic deprivations but primarily because they were victims of an upheaval in status that took place in the United States during the closing decades of the nineteenth and the early years of the twentieth century. Progressivism, in short, was to a very considerable extent led by men who suffered from the events of their time not through a shrinkage in their means but through the changed pattern in the distribution of deference and power.

Up to about 1870 the United States was a nation with a rather broad diffusion of wealth, status, and power, in which the man of moderate means, especially in the many small communities, could command much deference and exert much influence. The small merchant or manufacturer, the distinguished lawyer, editor, or preacher, was a person of local eminence in an age in which local eminence mattered a great deal. In the absence of very many nationwide sources of power and prestige, the pillars of the local communities were men of great importance in their own right. What Henry Adams remembered about his own bailiwick was, on the whole, true of the country at large: "Down to 1850, and even later, New

England society was still directed by the professions. Lawyers, physicians, professors, merchants were classes, and acted not as individuals, but as though they were clergymen and each profession were a church."

In the post-Civil War period all this was changed. The rapid development of the big cities, the building of a great industrial plant, the construction of the railroads, the emergence of the corporation as the dominant form of enterprise, transformed the old society and revolutionized the distribution of power and prestige. During the 1840's there were not twenty millionaires in the entire country; by 1910 there were probably more than twenty millionaires sitting in the United States Senate. By the late 1880's this process had gone far enough to become the subject of frequent, anxious comment in the press. In 1891 the *Forum* published a much-discussed article on "The Coming Billionaire," by Thomas G. Shearman, who estimated that there were 120 men in the United States each of whom was worth over ten million dollars. In 1892 the *New York Tribune,* inspired by growing popular criticism of the wealthy, published a list of 4,047 reputed millionaires, and in the following year a statistician of the Census Bureau published a study of the concentration of wealth in which he estimated that 9 per cent of the families of the nation owned 71 per cent of the wealth.

The newly rich, the grandiosely or corruptly rich, the masters of great corporations, were bypassing the men of the Mugwump type—the old gentry, the merchants of long standing, the small manufacturers, the established professional men, the civic leaders of an earlier era. In a score of cities and hundreds of towns, particularly in the East but also in the nation at large, the old-family, college-educated class that had deep ancestral roots in local communities and often owned family businesses, that had traditions of political leadership, belonged to the patriotic societies and the best clubs, staffed the governing boards of philanthropic and cultural institutions, and led the movements for civic betterment, were being overshadowed and edged aside in the making of basic political and economic decisions. In their personal careers, as in their community activities, they found themselves checked, hampered, and overridden by the agents of the new corporations, the corrupters of legislatures, the buyers of franchises, the allies of the political bosses. In this uneven struggle they found themselves limited by their own scruples, their regard for reputation, their social standing itself. To be sure, the America they knew did not lack opportunities, but it did seem to lack opportunities of the highest sort for men of the highest standards. In a strictly economic sense these men were not growing poorer as a class, but their wealth and power were being dwarfed by comparison with the new eminences of wealth and power. They were less important, and they knew it.

Against the tide of new wealth the less affluent and aristocratic local gentry had almost no protection at all. The richer and better-established among them found it still possible, of course, to trade on their inherited money and position, and their presence as window-dressing was an asset for any kind of enterprise, in business or elsewhere, to which they would lend their sponsorship. Often indeed the new men sought to marry into their circles, or to buy from them social position much as they bought from the bosses legislation and franchises. But at best the gentry could only make a static defense of themselves, holding their own in absolute terms while relatively losing ground year by year. Even this much they could do only in the localities over which they had long presided and in which they were well known. And when everyone could see that the arena of prestige, like the market for commodities, had been widened to embrace the entire nation, eminence in mere localities ceased to be as important and satisfying as once it had been. To face the insolence of the local boss or traction magnate in a town where one's family had long been prominent was galling enough; it was still harder to bear at a time when every fortune, every career, every reputation, seemed smaller and less significant because it was measured against the Vanderbilts, Harrimans, Goulds, Carnegies, Rockefellers, and Morgans.

The first reaction of the Mugwump type to the conditions of the status revolution was quite different from that later to be displayed by their successors among the Progressives. All through the seventies, eighties, and nineties men from the upper ranks of business and professional life had expressed their distaste for machine politics, corruption, and the cruder forms of business intervention in political affairs. Such men were commonly Republicans, but independent enough to bolt if they felt their principles betrayed. They made their first organized appearance in the ill-fated Liberal Republican movement of 1872, but their most important moment came in 1884, when their bolt from the Republican Party after the nomination of James G. Blaine was widely believed to have helped tip the scales to Cleveland in a close election.

While men of the Mugwump type flourished during those decades most conspicuously about Boston, a center of seasoned wealth and seasoned conscience, where some of the most noteworthy names in Massachusetts were among them, they were also prominent in a metropolis like New York and could be found in some strength in such Midwestern cities as Indianapolis and Chicago. None the less, one senses among them the prominence of the cultural ideals and traditions of New England, and beyond these of old England. Protestant and Anglo-Saxon for the most part, they were very frequently of New England ancestry; and even when they were not, they tended to look to New England's history for literary, cultural, and political models and for examples of moral idealism. Their conception of statecraft was set by the high example of the Founding Fathers, or by the great debating statesmen of the silver age, Webster, Sumner, Everett, Clay, and Calhoun. Their ideal leader was a well-to-do, well-educated, high-minded citizen, rich enough to be free from motives of what they often called "crass materialism," whose family roots were deep not only in American history but in his local community. Such a person, they thought, would be just the sort to put the national interest, as well as the interests of civic improvement, above personal motives or political opportunism. And such a person was just the sort, as Henry Adams never grew tired of complaining, for whom American political life was least likely to find a place. To be sure, men of the Mugwump type could and did find places in big industry, in the great corporations, and they were sought out to add respectability to many forms of enterprise. But they tended to have positions in which the initiative was not their own, or in which they could not feel themselves acting in harmony with their highest ideals. They no longer called the tune, no longer commanded their old deference. They were expropriated, not so much economically as morally.

They imagined themselves to have been ousted almost entirely by new men of the crudest sort. While in truth the great business leaders of the Gilded Age were typically men who started from comfortable or privileged beginnings in life, the Mugwump mind was most concerned with the newness and the rawness of the corporate magnates, and Mugwumps and reformers alike found satisfaction in a bitter caricature of the great businessman. One need only turn to the social novels of the "realists" who wrote about businessmen at the turn of the century—William Dean Howells, H. H. Boyesen, Henry Blake Fuller, and Robert Herrick, among others—to see the portrait of the captain of industry that dominated the Mugwump imagination. The industrialists were held to be uneducated and uncultivated, irresponsible, rootless and corrupt, devoid of refinement or of any sense of noblesse. "If our civilization is destroyed, as Macaulay predicted," wrote Henry Demarest Lloyd in an assessment of the robber barons, "it will not be by his barbarians from below. Our barbarians come from above. Our great money-makers have sprung in one generation into seats of power kings do not know. *The forces and the wealth are new, and have been the opportunity of new men. Without restraints of culture, experience, the* pride, or even the inherited caution of class or rank, these men, intoxicated, think they are the wave instead of the float, and that they have created the business which has created them. To them science is but a never-ending repertoire of investments stored up by nature for the syndicates, government but a fountain of franchises, the nations but customers in squads, and a million the unit of a new arithmetic of wealth written for them. They claim a power without control, exercised through forms which make it secret, anonymous, and perpetual. The possibilities of its gratification have been widening before them without interruption since they began, and even at a thousand millions they will feel no satiation and will see no place to stop."

Unlike Lloyd, however, the typical Mugwump was a conservative in his economic and political views. He disdained, to be sure, the most unscrupulous of the new men of wealth, as he did the opportunistic, boodling, tariff-mongering politicians who served them. But the most serious abuses of the unfolding economic order of the Gilded Age he either resolutely ignored or accepted complacently as an inevitable result of the struggle for existence or the improvidence and laziness of the masses. As a rule, he was dogmatically committed to the prevailing theoretical economics of *laissez faire*. His economic program did not go much beyond tariff reform and sound money—both principles more easily acceptable to a group whose wealth was based more upon mercantile activities and the professions than upon manufacturing and new enterprises —and his political program rested upon the foundations of honest and efficient government and civil-service reform. He was a "liberal" in the classic sense. Tariff reform, he thought, would be the sovereign remedy for the huge business combinations that were arising. His pre-eminent journalist and philosopher was E. L. Godkin, the honorable old free-trading editor of the *Nation* and the New York *Evening Post*. His favorite statesman was Grover Cleveland, who described the tariff as the "mother of trusts." He imagined that most of the economic ills that were remediable at all could be remedied by free trade, just as he believed that the essence of government lay in honest dealing by honest and competent men. Lord Bryce spoke of the Mugwump movement as being "made more important by the intelligence and social position of the men who composed it than by its voting power." It was in fact intellect and social position, among other things, that insulated the Mugwump from the sources of voting power. If he was critical of the predatory capitalist and their political allies, he was even more contemptuously opposed to the "radical" agrarian movements and the "demagogues" who led them, to the city workers when, led by "walking delegates," they rebelled against their employers, and to the urban immigrants and the "unscrupulous bosses" who introduced them to the mysteries of American civic life. He was an impeccable constitutionalist, but the fortunes of American politics had made him an equally firm aristocrat. He had his doubts, now that the returns were in, about the beneficence of universal suffrage. The last thing he would have dreamed of was to appeal to the masses against the plutocracy, and to appeal to them against the local bosses was usually fruitless. The Mugwump was shut off from the people as much by his social reserve and his amateurism as by his candidly conservative views. In so far as he sought popular support, he sought it on aristocratic terms.

One of the changes that made Progressivism possible around the turn of the century was the end of this insulation of the Mugwump type from mass support. For reasons that it is in good part the task of these pages to explore, the old barriers melted away. How the Mugwump found a following is a complex story, but it must be said at once that this was impossible until the Mugwump type itself had been somewhat transformed. The sons and successors of the Mugwumps had to challenge their fathers' ideas, modify their doctrinaire commitments to *laissez faire*, replace their aristocratic preferences with a startling revival of enthusiasm for popular government, and develop greater flexibility in dealing with the demands of the discontented before they could launch the movement that came to dominate the political life of the Progressive era. But if the philosophy and the spirit were new, the social type and the social grievance were much the same. The Mugwump had broadened his base. One need not be surprised, for instance, to find among the Progressive leaders in both major parties a large number of well-to-do men whose personal situation is reminiscent of the Mugwumps of an earlier generation. As Professor George Mowry has remarked, "few reform movements in American history have had the support of more wealthy men." Such men as George W. Perkins and Frank Munsey, who may perhaps be accused of joining the Progressive movement primarily to blunt its edge, can be left out of account, and such wealthy reformers as Charles R. Crane, Rudolph Spreckles, E. A. Filene, the Pinchots, and William Kent may be dismissed as exceptional. Still, in examining the lives and backgrounds of the reformers of the era, one is impressed by the number of those who had considerably more than moderate means, and particularly by those who had inherited their money. As yet no study has been made of reform leaders in both major parties, but the systematic information available on leaders of the Progressive Party of 1912 is suggestive. Alfred D. Chandler, Jr., surveying the backgrounds and careers of 260 Progressive Party leaders throughout the country, has noted how overwhelmingly urban and middle-class they were. Almost entirely native-born Protestants, they had an extraordinarily high representation of professional men and college graduates. The rest were businessmen, proprietors of fairly large enterprises. None was a farmer, only one was a labor-union leader, and the white-collar classes and salaried managers of large industrial or transportation enterprises were completely unrepresented. Not surprisingly, the chief previous political experience of most of them was in local politics. But on the whole, as Chandler observes, they "had had little experience with any kind of institutional discipline. In this sense, though they lived in the city, they were in no way typical men of the city. With very rare exceptions, all these men had been and continued to be their own bosses. As lawyers, businessmen, and professional men, they worked for themselves and had done so for most of their lives. As individualists, unacquainted with institutional discipline or control, the Progressive leaders represented, in spite of their thoroughly urban backgrounds, the ideas of the older, more rural America." From the only other comparable study, George Mowry's survey of the California Progressives, substantially the same conclusions emerge. The average California Progressive was "in the jargon of his day, 'well fixed.' He was more often than not a Mason, and almost invariably a member of his town's chamber of commerce. . . . He apparently had been, at least until 1900, a conservative Republican, satisfied with McKinley and his Republican predecessors."

While some of the wealthier reformers were self-made men, like John P. Altgeld, Hazen Pingree, the Mayor of Detroit and Governor of Michigan, and Samuel ("Golden Rule") Jones, the crusading Mayor of Toledo, more were men of the second and third generation of wealth or (notably Tom Johnson and Joseph Fels) men who had been declassed for a time and had recouped their fortunes. Progressive ideology, at any rate, distinguished consistently between "responsible" and "irresponsible" wealth—a distinction that seems intimately related to the antagonism of those who had had money long enough to make temperate and judicious use of it for those who were rioting with newfound means.

A gifted contemporary of the Progressives, Walter Weyl, observed in his penetrating and now all but forgotten book *The New Democracy* that this distinction between types of wealth could often be seen in American cities: "As wealth accumulates, moreover, a cleavage of sentiment widens between men who are getting rich and the men who *are* rich.

The old Cincinnati distinction between the 'stick-'ems' (the actual pork-packers) and the rich 'stuck-'ems' is today reflected in the difference between the retired millionaires of New York and the millionaires, in process or hope, of Cleveland, Portland, Los Angeles, or Denver. The gilt-edged millionaire bondholder of a standard railroad has only a partial sympathy with timber thieves, though his own fortune may have originated a few generations ago in railroad-wrecking or the slave and Jamaica rum trade; while the cultured descendants of cotton manufacturers resent the advent into their society of the man who had made his 'pile' in the recent buying or selling of franchises. Once wealth is sanctified by hoary age . . . it tends to turn quite naturally against new and evil ways of wealth getting, the expedients of prospective social climbers. The old wealth is not a loyal ally in the battle for the plutocracy; it inclines, if not to democratic, at least to mildly reformatory, programs . . . the battle between the plutocracy and the democracy, which furiously wages in the cities where wealth is being actually fought for, becomes somewhat gentler in those cities where bodies of accumulated wealth exercise a moderating influence. Inheritance works in the same direction. Once wealth is separated from its original accumulator, it slackens its advocacy of its method of accumulation."

Weyl realized, moreover, that so far as a great part of the dissenting public was concerned, the central grievance against the American plutocracy was not that it despoiled them economically but that it overshadowed them, that in the still competitive arena of prestige derived from conspicuous consumption and the style of life, the new plutocracy had set standards of such extravagance and such notoriety that everyone else felt humbled by comparison. Not only was this true of the nation as a whole in respect to the plutocracy, but there was an inner plutocracy in every community and every profession that aroused the same vague resentment: "The most curious factor," he found, in the almost universal American antagonism toward the plutocracy, was "that an increasing bitterness is felt by a majority which is not worse but better off than before. This majority suffers not an absolute decline but a relatively slower growth. It objects that the plutocracy grows too fast; that in growing so rapidly it squeezes its growing neighbors. Growth is right and proper, but there is, it is alleged, a rate of growth which is positively immoral.... To a considerable extent the plutocracy is hated not for what it does but for what it is.... It is the mere existence of a plutocracy, the mere 'being' of our wealthy contemporaries, that is the main offense. Our over-moneyed neighbors cause a relative deflation of our personalities. Of course, in the consumption of wealth, as in its production, there exist 'noncompetitive groups,' and a two-thousand-dollar-a-year-man need not spend like a Gould or a Guggenheim. Everywhere, however, we meet the millionaire's good and evil works, and we seem to resent the one as much as the other. Our jogging horses are passed by their high-power automobiles. We are obliged to take their dust.

"By setting the pace for a frantic competitive consumption, our infinite gradations in wealth (with which gradations the plutocracy is inevitably associated) increase the general social friction and produce an acute social irritation.... We are developing new types of destitutes—the automobileless, the yachtless, the Newport-cottageless. The subtlest of luxuries becomes necessities, and their loss is bitterly resented. The discontent of today reaches very high in the social scale....

"For this reason the plutocracy is charged with having ended our old-time equality.... Our industrial development (of which the trust is but one phase) has been towards a sharpening of the angle of progression. Our eminences have become higher and more dazzling; the goal has been raised and narrowed. Although lawyers, doctors, engineers, architects, and professional men generally, make larger salaries than ever before, the earning of one hundred thousand dollars a year by one lawyer impoverishes by comparison the thousands of lawyers who scrape along on a thousand a year. The widening of the competitive field has widened the variation and has sharpened the contrast between success and failure, with resulting inequality and discontent."

Whenever an important change takes place in modern society, large sections of the intellectuals, the professional and opinion-making classes, see the drift of events and throw their weight on the side of what they feel is progress and reform. In few historical movements have these classes played a more striking role than in Progressivism. While those intellectuals and professional men who supported Progressive causes no doubt did so in part for reasons that they shared with other members of the middle classes, their view of things was also influenced by marked changes within the professions themselves and by changes in their social position brought about by the growing complexity of society and by the status revolution.

In the previous era, during the industrial and political conflicts of the 1870's and 1880's, the respectable opinion-making classes had given almost unqualified support to the extreme conservative position on most issues. The Protestant ministry, for instance, was "a massive, almost unbroken front in its defense of the status quo." Most college professors preached the great truths of *laissez-faire* and the conservative apologetics of social Darwinism, and thundered away at labor unions and social reformers. Lawyers, except for a rare small-town spokesman of agrarian unrest or little business, were complacent. And while an occasional newspaper editor launched an occasional crusade, usually on a local issue, the press was almost as unruffled.

Beginning slowly in the 1890's and increasingly in the next two decades, members of these professions deserted the stand-pat conservatism of the post-Civil War era to join the main stream of liberal dissent and to give it both moral and intellectual leadership. The reasons for this reversal are complex. But if the professional groups changed their ideas and took on new loyalties, it was not in simple response to changes in the nature of the country's problems—indeed, in many ways the problems of American life were actually less acute after 1897—but rather because they had become disposed to see things they had previously ignored and to agitate themselves about things that had previously left them unconcerned. What interests me here is not the changed external condition of American society, but the inward social and psychological position of the professionals themselves that made so many of them become the advisers and the gadflies of reform movements. The alienation of the professionals was in fact a product of many developments, but among these the effects of the status revolution must be given an important place. Conditions varied from profession to profession, but all groups with claims to learning and skill shared a common sense of humiliation and common grievances against the plutocracy.

The contrast between the attitude of the clergy in the 1870's and that of the 1890's measures the change. When the hard times following the panic of 1873 resulted in widespread labor unrest, culminating in the railway strikes of 1877, the Protestant religious press was bloodthirsty in its reaction. The laborers were described as "wild beasts" and "reckless desperados," and some of the religious papers suggested that if they could not be clubbed into submission they should be mowed down with cannon and Gatling guns. During the social conflicts of the 1880's, ministers expressed an attitude only slightly less hysterical. By the 1890's a liberal minority was beginning to express a far milder view of strikes, though the chief religious papers were still completely hostile, for instance, to the American Railway Union in the Pullman strike of 1894. By this time, however, a substantial reversal of opinion was under way, and the ideas of social Christianity and the social gospel had profoundly modified the outlook of many ministers in the major denominations. From 1895 through the Progressive era "the doctrines developed by the [early social-gospel] generation . . . increasingly dominated the most articulate sections of American Protestantism."

The clergy were probably the most conspicuous losers from the status revolution. They not only lost ground in all the outward ways, as most middle-class elements did, but were also hard hit in their capacity as moral and intellectual leaders by the considerable secularization that took place in American society and intellectual life in the last three decades of the nineteenth century. On one hand, they were offended and at times antagonized by the attitudes of some of the rich men in their congregations. On the other, they saw the churches losing the support of the working class on a large and ominous scale. Everywhere their judgments seemed to carry less weight. Religion itself seemed less important year by year, and even in their capacity as moral and intellectual leaders of the community the ministers now had to share a place with the scientists and the social scientists. In the pre-Civil War days, for example, they had had a prominent place in the control of higher education. Now they were being replaced on boards of trustees by businessmen, bankers, and lawyers, and the newer, more secular universities that were being founded with the money of the great business lords brought with them social scientists whose word began to appropriate some of the authority that the clergy had once held. University learning, in many fields, carried with it the fresh and growing authority of evolutionary science, while the ministers seemed to be preaching nothing but old creeds.

The general decline in deference to the ministerial role was shown nowhere more clearly than in the failure of the lay governors of Protestant congregations to maintain the standard of living of their pastors under the complex conditions of urban life and the rising price level of the period after 1897. Not only were the clergy less regarded as molders of opinion, but they were expected to carry on the arduous work of their pastorates with means that were increasingly inadequate and to defer meekly to far more affluent vestrymen.

In the light of this situation, it may not be unfair to attribute the turning of the clergy toward reform and social criticism not solely to their disinterested perception of social problems and their earnest desire to improve the world, but also to the fact that as men who were in their own way suffering from the incidence of the status revolution they were able to understand and sympathize with the problems of other disinherited groups. The increasingly vigorous interest in the social gospel, so clearly manifested by the clergy after 1890, was in many respects an attempt to restore through secular leadership some of the spiritual influence and authority and social prestige that clergymen had lost through the upheaval in the system of status and the secularization of society.

That the liberal clergy succeeded in restoring some of their prestige by making themselves a strong force in the Progressive ranks no student of the history of American social Christianity is likely to deny. As practical participants and as ideologists and exhorters the clergy made themselves prominent, and a great deal of the influence of Progressivism as well as some of its facile optimism and naïveté may be charged to their place in its councils. Indeed, Progressivism can be considered from this standpoint as a phase in the history of the Protestant conscience, a latter-day Protestant revival. Liberal politics as well as liberal theology were both inherent in the response of religion to the secularization of society. No other major movement in American political history (unless one classifies abolitionism or prohibitionism as a major movement) had ever received so much clerical sanction. Jeffersonianism had taken the field against powerful clerical opposition; Jacksonianism had won its triumphs without benefit of clergy; but the new-model army of Progressivism had its full complement of chaplains.

The situation of the professors is in striking contrast to that of the clergy—and yet the academic man arrived by a different path at the same end as the cleric. While the clergy were being in a considerable measure dispossessed, the professors were rising. The challenge they made to the *status quo* around the turn of the century, especially in the social sciences, was a challenge offered by an advancing group, growing year by year in numbers, confidence, and professional standing. Modern students of social psychology have suggested that certain social-psychological tensions are heightened both in social groups that are rising in the social scale and in those that are falling; and this may explain why two groups with fortunes as varied as the professoriat and the clergy gave so much common and similar support to reform ideologies.

Unlike the clergy, academic men in America before 1870 had had no broad public influence, no professional traditions nor self-awareness, hardly even any very serious professional standards. The sudden emergence of the modern university, however, transformed American scholarship during the last three decades of the century. Where there had been only a number of denominational colleges, there were now large universities with adequate libraries, laboratories, huge endowments, graduate schools, professional schools, and advancing salaries. The professoriat was growing immensely in numbers, improving in professional standards, gaining in compensation and security, and acquiring a measure of influence and prestige in and out of the classroom that their predecessors of the old college era would never have dreamed of. And yet there was a pervasive discontent. To overestimate the measure of radicalism in the academic community is a convention that has little truth. In the Progressive era the primary function of the academic community was still to rationalize, uphold, and conserve the existing order of things. But what was significant in that era was the presence of a large creative minority that set itself up as a sort of informal brain trust to the Progressive movement. To call the roll of the distinguished social scientists of the Progressive era is to read a list of men prominent in their criticism of vested interests or in their support for reform causes—John R. Commons, Richard T. Ely, E. R. A. Seligman, and Thorstein Veblen in economics, Charles A. Beard, Arthur F. Bentley and J. Allen Smith in political science, E. A. Ross and Lester Ward in sociology, John Dewey in philosophy, and (for all his formal conservatism) Roscoe Pound in law. The professors had their intimate experience with and resentments of the plutocracy—which illustrates Walter Weyl's apt remark that the benefactions of the millionaires aroused almost as much hostility as their evil works. Professors in America had always had the stauts of hired men, but they had never had enough professional pride to express anything more than a rare momentary protest against this condition. Now, even though their professional situation was improving, they found in themselves the resources to complain against their position; not the least of their grievances was the fact that their professional affairs were under the control of the plutocracy, since boards of trustees were often composed of those very businessmen who in other areas of life were becoming suspect for their predatory and immoral lives. Further, academic men in the social sciences found themselves under pressure to trim their sails ideologically; and caste self-consciousness was heightened by a series of academic-freedom cases involving in some instances the more eminent members of the emerging social sciences—Richart T. Ely, Edward A. Ross, J. Allen Smith, and others. In 1915 this rising self-consciousness found expression in the formation of the American Association of University Professors.

If the professors had motives of their own for social resentment, the social scientists among them had special reason for a positive interest in the reform movements. The development of regulative and humane legislation required the skills of lawyers and economists, sociologists and political scientists, in the writing of laws and the staffing of administrative and regulative bodies. Controversy over such issues created a new market for the books and magazine articles of the experts and engendered a new respect for their specialized knowledge. Reform brought with it the brain trust. In Wisconsin even before the turn of the century there was an intimate union between the La Follette regime and the state university at Madison that foreshadowed all later brain trusts. National recognition of the importance of the academic scholar came in 1918 under Woodrow Wilson, himself an ex-professor, when the President took with him as counselors to Paris that grand conclave of expert advisers from several fields of knowledge which was known to contemporaries as The Inquiry.

The legal profession, which stands in a more regular and intimate relation with American politics than any other profession or occupation, affords a good example of the changing position of the middle-class professional in the development of corporate society. The ambiguous situation of many lawyers, which often involved both profitable subservience to and personal alienation from corporate business, contributed significantly to the cast of Progressive thought and the recruitment of Progressive leaders. While many lawyers could participate in Progressive politics in the spirit of good counselors caring for their constituents, many also felt the impact of the common demand for reform as a response to changes in their own profession.

In the opening decades of the century the American legal profession was troubled by an internal crisis, a crisis in self-respect precipitated by the conflict between the image of legal practice inherited from an earlier age of more independent professionalism and the realities of modern commercial practice. Historically the American legal profession had had four outstanding characteristics. Where it was practiced at its best in the most settled communities, it had the position of a learned profession with its own standards of inquiry and criticism, its own body of ideas and ethics. A lawyer's reputation and fortune had been based upon courtroom advocacy, forensic skill, learning, and presence. It was, secondly, a professional group of exceptional public influence and power. Tocqueville's famous observation that in the absence of a fixed and venerable class of rich men the closest thing to an American aristocracy was to be found in the bench and bar may have been somewhat exaggerated, but it does justice to the mid-nineteenth-century position of this professional group —the nursery of most American statesmen and of the rank and file of practicing politicians. Thirdly, a sense of public responsibility had been present in the moral and intellectual traditions of the bar—a feeling embodied in the notion that the lawyer was not simply an agent of some litigant but also by nature an "officer of the court," a public servant. Finally, law had been, preeminently in the United States, one of the smoothest avenues along which a man who started with only moderate social advantages might, without capital, rise upward through the ranks to a position of wealth or power. Democratic access to the bar had been jealously protected— so much so that a peculiar notion of the "natural right" to practice law had developed and many professional leaders felt that the standards of admission to the profession had been set far too low.

At the turn of the century lawyers as a group were far less homogeneous than they had been fifty years before. The large, successful firms, which were beginning even then to be called "legal factories," were headed by the wealthy, influential, and normally very conservative minority of the profession that tended to be most conspicuous in the Bar Associations. In their firms were many talented young lawyers, serving their time as cheap labor. There was a second echelon of lawyers in small but well-established offices of the kind that flourished in smaller cities; lawyers of this sort, who were commonly attached to and often shared the outlook of new enterprisers or small businessmen, frequently staffed and conducted local politics. A third echelon, consisting for the most part of small partnerships or individual practitioners, usually carried on a catch-as-catch-can practice and eked out modest livings. As the situation of the independent practitioners deteriorated, they often drifted into ambulance-chasing and taking contingent fees. Much of the talk in Bar Associations about improving legal ethics represented the unsympathetic efforts of the richer lawyers with corporate connections to improve the reputation of the profession as a whole at the expense of their weaker colleagues.

A body of professional teachers of law, outside the ranks of practicing lawyers, was also developing as an independent force within the profession. The most effective type of legal education, then becoming dominant in the best university law schools, was Langdell's case method. It had been a part of Langdell's conception that the proper training for the teaching of law was not law practice but law study. As the part-time practicing lawyer became less conspicuous in legal education and the full-time *teaching* lawyer replaced him, the independent and professional consciousness of the guild was once again reinforced. Lawyers who were most attracted by the more intellectual and professional aspects of their field tended to go into teaching, just as those most interested in public service went into politics or administration. Young Charles Evans Hughes, for instance, temporarily deserted an extremely promising career in metropolitan practice for a relatively ill-paid job as a professor in Cornell's law school. In the movement for broader conceptions of professional service, for new legal concepts and procedural reforms, for deeper professional responsibility, for criticism of the courts, the teaching side of the profession now became important. The teachers became the keepers of the professional conscience and helped implant a social view of their functions in the young men who graduated from good law schools.

With the rise of corporate industrialism and finance capitalism, the law, particularly in the urban centers where the most enviable prizes were to be had, was becoming a captive profession. Lawyers kept saying that the law had lost much of its distinctly professional character and had become a business. Exactly how much truth lay in their laments cannot be ascertained until we know more about the history of the profession; but whether or not their conclusions were founded upon a false sentimentalization of an earlier era, many lawyers were convinced that their profession had declined in its intellectual standards and in its moral and social position. Around the turn of the century, the professional talents of courtroom advocacy and brief-making were referred to again and again as "lost arts," as the occupation of the successful lawyer centered more and more upon counseling clients and offering business advice. General and versatile talent, less needed than in the old days, was replaced by specialized practice and the division of labor within law firms. The firms themselves grew larger; the process of concentration and combination in business, which limited profitable counseling to fewer and larger firms, engendered a like concentration in the law. Metropolitan law firms, as they grew larger and more profitable, moved into closer relationships with and became "house counsel" of the large investment houses, banks, or industrial firms that provided them with most of their business. But the relation that was the source of profit brought with it a loss of independence to the great practitioners. The smaller independent practitioner was affected in another, still more serious way: much of his work was taken from him by real-estate, trust, and insurance companies, collection agencies, and banks, which took upon themselves larger and larger amounts of what had once been entirely legal business. A speaker at the meeting of the Baltimore Bar Association in 1911 estimated that 70 per cent of the members of the profession were not making a suitable living. "Corporations doing our business are working . . . to our detriment," he said. "Slowly, but with persistence, the corporations are pushing the lawyer to the wall. They advertise, solicit, and by their corporate influence and wealth monopolize the legal field."

That the dignity and professional independence of the bar had been greatly impaired became a commonplace among lawyers and well-informed laymen. "How often we hear," declared an eminent lawyer in an address before the Chicago Bar Association in 1904, "that the profession is commercialized; that the lawyer today does not enjoy the position and influence that belonged to the lawyer of seventy-five or a hundred years ago. . . ." He went on to deny—what many lawyers did not deny—that the alleged commercialization was serious; but he conceded that the lawyer had indeed suffered from what he called "the changed social and industrial conditions." These conditions, he observed, had "taken from the lawyer some of his eminence and influence in other than legal matters" and had also, for that matter, *"in the same way and in no less degree affected the other learned professions, and indeed all educated or exceptional men."* Several years later another lawyer put it somewhat more sharply in an essay entitled "The Passing of the Legal Profession": "The lawyer's former place in society as an economical factor has been superseded by [the corporation] this artificial creature of his own genius, for whom he is now simply a clerk on a salary."

Lord Bryce, in comparing the America of 1885 with the America of Tocqueville, had concluded that "the bar counts for less as a guiding and restraining power, tempering the crudity or haste of democracy by its attachment to rule and precedent, than it did." Shortly after the turn of the century he remarked that lawyers "are less than formerly the students of a particular kind of learning, the practitioners of a particular art. And they do not seem to be so much of a distinct professional class." Commenting in 1905 on Bryce's observations, Louis D. Brandeis said that the lawyer no longer held as high a position with the people as he had held seventy-five or indeed fifty years before; but the reason, he asserted, was not lack of opportunity, but the failure to maintain an independent moral focus. "Instead of holding a position of independence, between the wealthy and the people, prepared to curb the excesses of either, able lawyers have, to a large extent, allowed themselves to become adjuncts of great corporations and have neglected the obligation to use their powers for the protection of the people. We hear much of the 'corporation lawyer,' and far too little of the 'people's lawyer.' "

Thus internal conditions, as well as those outward events

which any lawyer, as a citizen, could see, disposed a large portion of this politically decisive profession to understand the impulse toward change.

For Further Reading

Louis Filler, *Crusaders for American Liberalism* (1939), and C. C. Regier, *The Era of the Muckrakers* (1932), are both useful studies but should be supplemented with some primary reading. Recommended is Lincoln Steffens, *The Shame of the Cities* (1904); David Graham Phillips, *The Treason of the Senate* (1906); Ray Stannard Baker, *Following the Color Line* (1908); Richard Hofstadter, ed., *The Progressive Movement, 1900–1915* (1963), and Arthur and Lila Weinberg, eds., *The Muckrakers: An Anthology* (1961). Indispensable for the theory of the progressive movement is Herbert Croly, *The Promise of American Life* (1909); but see also Woodrow Wilson, *The New Freedom* (1913), which understandably views Progressivism through Democratic lenses.

The idea of a status revolution first appeared in George Mowry, *The California Progressives* (1951), and the same author has produced an excellent recent interpretation in *The Era of Theodore Roosevelt, 1900–1912* (1958), a volume in the New American Nation series which complements Arthur S. Link, *Woodrow Wilson and the Progressive Era, 1900–1917* (1954). Also of high quality is Benjamin DeWitt, *The Progressive Movement* (1915). John Chamberlain's *Farewell to Reform* (1932) is a critical study written from a Marxist viewpoint and describing Progressivism as a typical example of liberal failure. In *Rendezvous with Destiny: A History of Modern American Reform* (1952), Eric Goldman sees "reform Darwinism" as the intellectual basis for Progressivism. Russell B. Nye in *Midwestern Progressive Politics* (1951) argues that in the Midwest at least, the progressive movement was a "lineal descendant" of Populism. The role of the immigrant leaders is stressed in Arthur Mann, *Yankee Reformers in an Urban Age* (1954), and in J. Joseph Huthmacher's "Urban Liberalism and the Age of Reform," *Mississippi Valley Historical Review*, XLIX (September, 1962).

Concerned primarily with the intellectual history of the era are Daniel Aaron, *Men of Good Hope* (1961), which pictures Theodore Roosevelt as a pseudo-progressive, and Henry F. May, *The End of America Innocence* (1959). See also the pertinent sections in Louis Hartz, *The Liberal Tradition in America* (1954), and Arthur Ekirch, *The Decline of American Liberalism* (1956); and two volumes by Harold U. Faulkner, *The Quest for Social Justice 1897–1917* (1931) and *The Decline of Laissez-Faire, 1898–1914* (1931).

Roosevelt versus Taft–1912

Mark Sullivan

Rarely has there been a more exciting year in American politics than 1912. The presidential election saw the progressive movement reach its zenith as the three professed liberal reform candidates, the Democratic victor, Woodrow Wilson, the Progressive Party's nominee, Theodore Roosevelt, and the Socialist Eugene V. Debs polled eleven million of the fifteen million ballots cast. Over three quarters of the electorate thus indicated their endorsement of reforming change. Moreover, the fourth candidate, Republican William Howard Taft, although classified as conservative, often displayed his conservatism in a way which William McKinley would have considered strange. Ideologically the campaign had centered on how the federal government could best deal with the trusts. Wilson, in a program described as the New Freedom, stressed the need to restore competition by strengthening antitrust legislation. The government should break up the great trusts, eliminate special privileges, and restore a true free enterprise

Source: Mark Sullivan, *Our Times: The United States, 1900–1925* (4 vols.; New York: Charles Scribner's Sons, 1926–1932); Vol. IV, *The War Begins, 1909–1914* (1932), pp. 487–540. Copyright 1932 by Charles Scribner's Sons; renewed © 1960 by Mark Sullivan, Jr. Reprinted by permission of the publisher.

system. Roosevelt, despite his reputation as a "trust-buster," contended that the large corporations were an asset to the nation. The function of the government, in his plan which he called the New Nationalism, was to regulate the giant corporations, to make them servants, not masters, of the people. The overwhelming majority of the electorate probably did not follow this debate closely. Most people voted according to traditional party loyalties or responded to personalities, and a split in the Republican Party insured Wilson's election.

Roosevelt, in a moment of exuberance following his election in 1904, had praised the "wise custom which limits the President to two terms" and had declared that under no circumstances would he be candidate for or accept another nomination. Undoubtedly he came to regret this impulsive decision; it not only weakened his bargaining position as President in his second term but made it difficult for him to defend his candidacy in 1912. The erstwhile Rough Rider had left the White House in 1909 after arranging the succession of Taft, his longtime friend and Secretary of War. In retrospect, the break between the ex-President and his protégé appears almost inevitable, but it developed slowly. Taft truly desired to carry on in the progressive tradition established by his predecessor. For his part, Roosevelt helped Taft in his attempt to create a distinct identity for his administration by embarking on a fifteen-month tour of Africa and Europe following Taft's inauguration. To his dismay, when he returned he found the Republican Party in turmoil and disarray. Taft had proved to be politically inept. His judicial temperament was not suited to the rough-and-tumble, give-and-take atmosphere of practical politics. In addition, in spite of some considerable accomplishments in trust-busting, he remained basically conservative; he particularly distrusted the group of Republican progressives led by Senators Robert M. LaFollette of Wisconsin and Albert J. Breveridge of Iowa. These men and other insurgent Republicans had been successively pleased, then dumbfounded, and finally outraged when Taft early in 1909 called a special session of Congress to revise the tariff downward in line with pledges made in the Republican platform, then proceeded to not only accept the Payne-Aldrich Tariff which actually increased rates but to defend it as the best tariff bill the Republican Party had ever passed. Progressives came to regard Taft's renomination as out of the question when he failed to support the ultimately successful attempt by insurgents in the House of Representatives to reduce the dictatorial powers wielded by the reactionary Speaker "Uncle Joe" Cannon.

To insure the selection of a progressive candidate in 1912, the insurgents early in 1911 organized the National Progressive Republican League. Many of the founders hoped Roosevelt would accept the leadership of the movement, but at that point he was reluctant to precipitate an open fight with Taft. In October 1911, a conference of the League endorsed LaFollette for the presidency. Only a few months later, however, Roosevelt, in a characteristic mixture of modern and Victorian idiom, announced, "My hat is in the ring, the fight is on and I am stripped to the buff." What prompted Roosevelt to challenge the President instead of letting Taft go down to what appeared inevitable defeat in 1912 and then accept the party's nomination in 1916 was the administration's decision to institute an antitrust suit against the United States Steel Corporation. Roosevelt's philosophy toward the trusts favored regulation and opposed dissolution; but more to the point, the chief charge against the steel combine was its acquisition of the Tennessee Coal and Iron Company during the panic of 1907, an act which had Roosevelt's specific approval. Taft's action seemed to imply that his predecessor had been duped. When Roosevelt entered the race, LaFollette charged betrayal, asserting that Roosevelt had promised to support his candidacy. This has never been proved. In any case, the chances of the Wisconsin senator had begun to diminish even before Roosevelt's entry into the race, when he had collapsed after giving an incoherent and repetitious speech. As might be expected, Roosevelt's entry generated an enormous interest in the nation's press. One of the journalists covering the campaign was Mark Sullivan (1874–1952). This onetime muckraker, whose exposé of the patent-medicine racket in a series of articles in the *Ladies' Home Journal* earned him a share of the credit for the passage of the Pure Food and Drug Act of 1906, was editor of *Collier's Magazine* in 1912. Having grown increasingly conservative over the years, Sullivan made no secret of his disgust with Roosevelt's eventual bolt from the G.O.P., which handed the White House to the Democrats. But his colorful prose, replete with many pungent epigrams, comes very close to capturing the excitement as Roosevelt's challenge to Taft reached its climax at the Republican National Convention in Chicago.

*R*oosevelt's fight against Taft, the cleavage in the Republican party it precipitated, divided brother from brother, father from son, friend from friend. More than the Civil War—because that was sectional—the Roosevelt-Taft feud drove its rending force into the hearts of communities, churches, clubs, families. Of the friendships sundered, the most exalted, next to that between the principals themselves, was between Roosevelt and Lodge, Lodge who had been Roosevelt's intimate more than thirty years, who had talked with him at least once a day whenever both were in Washington, and written him when they were separated at least once a week on the average, letters which on Lodge's side began "Dear Theodore" and on Roosevelt's side "Dear Cabot"; letters ending, "Give my love to Nannie [Lodge]" or "to Edith [Roosevelt]." Now was parting. Publicly, in the austere spirit of New England, Lodge announced, within forty-eight hours after Roosevelt's Columbus speech: "I am opposed to the constitutional changes advocated by Colonel Roosevelt." Privately he wrote to Roosevelt: "I have had my share of mishaps in politics but I never thought that any situation could arise which would have made me so miserably unhappy. . . . There is very little of the Roman in me toward those I love best."

Gaily Roosevelt replied: "I don't know whether to be most touched by your letter or most inclined to laugh over it. My dear fellow, you could not do anything that would make me lose my warm personal affection for you. . . . Now don't you ever think of this matter again. Tell Nannie how delighted I was to see John and Mary. . . . Ever affectionately, Theodore Roosevelt."

Roosevelt, by his present fight, had added wholly new groups to the host that had criticized him while President. To the stodgy conservatives, who during his Presidency had hated him merely because he held a club over big business, were added a group of old-time sentimental Republicans, whose personal memories ran far back toward the Civil War, to whom the Republican party was really something a little sacred, and who now saw the ark of the covenant soiled by an attack upon a Republican President and an attempt to deprive him of the renomination to which by custom he was entitled; and another group, shocked to the bone at the notion of the recall of judicial decisions; and another group to whom the rule against a third term was a sanctified thing, and who now saw, as they viewed it, Roosevelt trying to violate that rule by attempting a third term, as they considered, for himself; and yet another group whose distaste for Roosevelt arose out of what they regarded as his lack of loyalty to his friend Taft, coupled with the lack of sportsmanship inherent in his fighting a President whom he himself had placed in office; and yet another group who were repelled by Roosevelt's violence; and by still another one whose attitude toward the show was one of cynical amusement. From all these, with their various reasons for opposing Roosevelt, through their several media of editorial, cartoon, or speech, came upon Roosevelt's head a tornado of assault, a rain of epithet, a biting sleet of satire. The assaults on Roosevelt took in many cases the direction of two assumptions: one, that Roosevelt was crazy—crazy was the word, no euphemism like "unbalanced"; the other, that he aimed at a life tenure in the Presidency and, thereafter, hereditary succession. "Does any sane person believe," asked the Philadelphia *Evening Telegraph,* "that if Theodore Roosevelt is nominated and elected in November, he will ever quit the Presidency alive? . . . An election in 1912 will be equivalent to an election for life and hereditary succession." Colonel Henry Watterson's Louisville *Courier-Journal* managed to compress both caustic assumptions, insanity and ambition for life tenure, into a double-barbed sentence: "Unless he breaks down under the strain and is taken to a lunatic asylum . . . there can be in his name and person but one issue, life tenure in the executive office."

There erupted, of course, accusations of inconsistency, violation of pledge—the charge was put with characteristic succinctness and force in an editorial which the New York *Sun* printed on March 6, 1912, and kept repeating with iterative emphasis throughout the campaign:

THE DEADLIEST OF ALL PARALLELS

| President Roosevelt's Decision on November 8, 1904: "Under no circumstances will I be a candidate for or accept another nomination." | Ex-President Roosevelt's Decision on February 25, 1912: "I will accept the nomination for President if it is tendered to me." |

To this, necessarily foreseen by Roosevelt, he replied:

My position on the third term is perfectly simple. I said I would not accept a nomination for a third term under any circumstances, meaning of course a third consecutive term. . . . The precedent which forbids a third term has reference solely to a third consecutive term. A President of the United

States can, if he knows how to use the machinery at his disposal, renominate himself even though the majority of the party is against him. But after he has been out of office for a term he has lost control of that machinery. He is in the position absolutely of any private citizen.

All of which was put by the sedate *Outlook* into a homely parable: "When a man says at breakfast in the morning 'No, thank you, I will not take any more coffee,' it does not mean that he will not take any more coffee to-morrow morning, or next week, or next month, or next year."

Above the thunders about the third term tradition, the solemn warnings of threatened dictatorship, played the American sense of humor—expressed in the Brooklyn *Eagle*'s "No place feels like home after you have once lived in the White House," and the *Ohio State Journal*'s "There is a fairly well-grounded impression that Colonel Roosevelt also favors the recall of former Presidents," and the *Wall Street Journal*'s "Those most enthusiastic over the recall of judicial decisions are prevented by prison rules from working for the Colonel," and *Life*'s "The popular demand for Colonel Roosevelt is increasing; but however great the demand may become, it can never be as great as the supply." Even *Life*, however, found it not easy to be funny. Its deeper emotion was expressed in a passage: "The cold chills race up and down our spine. . . . The Roosevelt Presidency was one of the most interesting national moving picture films that was ever unrolled before us. We haven't a single regret for the time and money we spent upon it. But to have to sit through it again!"

Roosevelt in his formal announcement of his candidacy had said, in a shrewd combination of high principle with the best advantage of himself:

> One of the chief principles for which I have stood is the genuine rule of the people. I hope that the people may be given the chance, through direct primaries, to express their preference as to who shall be the nominee.

There had been, under way, as an incident of the Insurgent uprising—as, indeed, perhaps the main detail of their programme—a movement for "Presidential primaries," to be substituted for conventions as the mechanism for selecting (and instructing) delegates to national conventions. The movement up to now had had no marked success—about as much, let us say, as would reflect the momentum of the early Insurgent leader, LaFollette, as a candidate for the Republican Presidential nomination.

With Roosevelt's announcement of his candidacy, the comparatively few who had been tepidly interested in direct primaries as a cause were now joined by the very many who were ardently interested in Roosevelt as a hero, who knew that the conventions would be controlled by Standpatters and office-holders, and who saw in the presidential primary Roosevelt's only chance.

Immediately "Presidential primaries," from a sluggishly moving cause, became a torrential crusade. "GET THE DIRECT PRIMARY FOR YOUR STATE," cried a fierce young eagle of the press of that day, Mark Sullivan, ardent for Roosevelt. Vividly he explained what the new device was: "The Presidential primary means that you can go to the polls (if you are a Republican) and say whether you want Taft or Roosevelt. If you don't do the choosing the bosses will." With emphasis of reiteration he amplified: "The Republican nominee will be Roosevelt or Taft; the choice between these two will be made in one of two ways, either by bosses in back rooms or by the people at primary elections. Which is the more desirable?" "Do you," he asked of "every Republican voter," paying his reader the compliment of italicized type:

> Do *you* have an opinion as to whether Taft or Roosevelt ought to be the nominee? Do you believe you ought to have a right to express your opinion at the polls? With Presidential primaries you will have the chance; without them, the choice between Taft and Roosevelt will be made by the bosses.

Evangelically he supplied his readers with arguments to heckle the politicians:

> Ask the Republican politicians this question: If the plain voter is capable of choosing between Taft and Wilson, assuming they should be the candidates, why isn't he also capable of choosing between Taft and Roosevelt?

Urgently he stirred his readers to act:

> Get the Presidential primary for your State. Don't let the politicians tell you it is too late. The politicians in Michigan refused it a long time but they called a special session of the legislature last Monday to pass the law. The Presidential primary can be got for every State if the people demand it vigorously enough. Don't let the politicians dodge this issue. GET THE DIRECT PRIMARY FOR YOUR STATE.

Under such hectic urging, in a spirit almost of national emergency, Presidential primary laws were adopted by special or regular sessions of the legislatures in Massachusetts, Pennsylvania, Illinois, Maryland, Ohio, and South Dakota. In Illinois, when the Governor demurred to calling a special session of the Legislature to enact a primary law, the Chicago *Tribune,* ardent for Roosevelt and ardent for the direct primary as a means of helping Roosevelt, forced the Governor's hand by obtaining signatures from more than a majority of the Legislature.

Roosevelt won and got the delegates in practically every State in which the direct primary method was used. He carried Illinois by 139,436; he carried New Jersey by 17,213; he carried Pennsylvania by 105,899; he carried California by 69,218; he carried Nebraska by 16,769 more than Taft and LaFollette together; he carried Taft's own State, Ohio, by 47,447. In thirteen States that had primaries, there were 388 delegates—Roosevelt got 281, Taft 71, LaFollette 36.

From that showing the inference was indisputable: the people, the rank and file of Republican voters, wanted Roosevelt. But if Roosevelt got substantially all the delegates from the Presidential primary States, he got relatively few from the States in which the old convention system prevailed. And of these there were rather too many.

The outcome was clouded by the fact that in several States the election of the delegates (either by convention or primary) was not conclusive; contesting delegations were sent to the convention, in some cases by Roosevelt partisans, in some others by Taft's. The number of contests was 252 out of a total of 1,078 delegates in the convention. The settlement of these contests would determine whether Roosevelt or Taft would have a majority in the convention.

The contests would be tried and decided, in the first instance, by the Republican National Committee. In that fact lay Roosevelt's weakness. The National Committee in 1912 (and in every Presidential year) is made up four years before —the method is fixed by long custom. At the national convention four years before, in 1908, the delegates from each State had selected the State's member of the National Committee, and the forty-eight thus selected remained in power until the succeeding convention in 1912. It was these forty-eight who would now try the contests. They reflected a convention four years before which had nominated Taft; they held over from a time when there were no Presidential primaries; they belonged prevailingly to the old, standpat wing of the party; they were, as a body, loyal to Taft.

To try the contests (in the first instance) the National Committee met in Chicago twelve days before the convention itself. The only chance Roosevelt would have to influence their decision must be by focusing publicity upon them. To do this, Roosevelt retired to Oyster Bay, whence twice a day went out to the country a barrage of protest, appeal and miscellaneous excitants to public emotion.

With the primaries over and the State conventions all held, with the processes of producing delegations (and contesting delegations) completed, Roosevelt remained at Oyster Bay, but decidedly not in retirement. Through countless messages to lieutenants over the long distance telephone (then still somewhat a novelty) to Chicago, and through a private telegraph wire with one end in the attic at Sagamore Hill and the other in the bedroom of his manager at Chicago, Senator Joseph M. Dixon of Montana; through verbal messages carried by friends who raced from Oyster Bay to take the Twentieth Century Limited westward; through inspiration poured into the eager ears of subordinates who on their way to Chicago stopped at Oyster Bay for contact with the master, Roosevelt directed the preliminary moves at Chicago.

With equal energy and adeptness he executed the other of the two functions that were important at this time, the fighting of that part of the battle of which the field was the public mind. Through the avenues of publicity eagerly opened to him and through other mechanisms that his resourcefulness laid hold upon, he cheered his followers, subtly insinuated discord among his opponents, pleaded with the "in betweens." With charge and reply to charge (though not often the latter), now with satire, now with furious denunciation; with solemnity, with gaiety, and always with vitality, Roosevelt kept the public eye upon the Chicago battlefield, the public mind upon the issues, the public emotions at mounting fever heat.

To the reporters who twice each day trudged the mile of hill from their headquarters at Oyster Bay to Roosevelt's front porch, he exclaimed, on May 31, "Fake, pure fake," as his comment on a rumor that he would go to Chicago. "I may alter my plans," he added, with a second thought of throwing a menace in the general direction of his opponents, "if circumstances demand, of course I'll go." On June 1, he demanded that the contests over rival delegations at Chicago be open to the press, and complained that the Republican

National Committee, in its distribution of seats, was denying a fair share to his supporters, indicating, he said, "a deliberate purpose to use ten thousand tickets to stuff the gallery with shouters who would try to overawe the convention." June 2 being a Sunday, Roosevelt, following family custom and deferring to the old American feeling about how the Sabbath should be observed, remained in seclusion, silent.

June 3, when the National Committee, which had charge of convention details and was partial to Taft, revealed an intention of making Elihu Root permanent chairman of the coming convention, Roosevelt took a notice which had to be carefully phrased. Of Root, who had been Roosevelt's Secretary of State and Secretary of War; of Root, whom he had described as the "ablest statesman on either side of the Atlantic Ocean in my time" and of whom he had said: "I would rather see [him] in the White House than any other man now possible, I would walk on my hands and knees from the White House to the Capitol to see Root made President"; of Root who during Roosevelt's Presidency had been flint to his steel, Damon to his Pythias, safety-valve to his multitubular boiler— of Root, now in the camp opposed to him, Roosevelt had to say something condemnatory, something castigatory of his present activities. Roosevelt must, in a word, picture Root as a horrible example of a good man gone wrong. "In the past," began Roosevelt's curious indictment, "Mr. Root has rendered distinguished services as Secretary of State and Secretary of War." "But in this contest," began the philippic part of Roosevelt's comment, "Mr. Root stands as the representative of reaction. He is put forward by the bosses and the representatives of special privilege. He has ranged himself against the men who stand for progressive principles within the Republican party; that is, against men who stand for making the Republican party what it was in the days of Abraham Lincoln" —the sum of which turgidity merely amounted to Roosevelt saying "Root is against ME!"

On June 4, when the Ohio Republican convention gave

the eight "at large" delegates to Taft, although in the direct primary Roosevelt had carried the State by 47,000, he cried, "political brigandage," "frank and cynical defiance of the emphatic action of the people"—adding to a reporter who asked him, as he handed out his statement, whether he had "hit hard," "This is no time for excited utterances. I prefer to underestimate and understate facts and conditions and make as conservative a statement as possible." "That's bully," he said on June 5, grinning jovially as he told of receiving a telegram from South Dakota. "Why," he chuckled, "my vote there was larger than that of Taft and LaFollette put together. They are running very close." "Stuff and nonsense of the most tawdry description," he said on the same day, of a report that Wall Street interests offended by Taft's anti-trust suit had raised a fifteen million dollar fund for Roosevelt. June 6, he received at Oyster Bay a hard-boiled Pittsburgher, William Flinn, who had temporarily ousted Penrose as boss of Pennsylvania. "I am sending Flinn to Chicago," said Roosevelt to the newspaper men, creating the impression that if at Chicago strong-arm tactics were to be resorted to, champions would not be lacking on the Roosevelt side. June 7, spending the day at his *Outlook* office in New York, Roosevelt received in a corridor outside his office and therefore peculiarly publicly, Director Samuel McCune Lindsay, Director of the New York School of Philanthropy, John A. Kingsbury, of the New York Association for Improving the Condition of the Poor, and Secretary Homer Folks, of the Charities Aid Society; whom he permitted to state, for the newspapers: "We called on Colonel Roosevelt to submit planks for the national Republican platform, to give definite form to the conception of social and industrial justice, which Colonel Roosevelt has made the dominant issue in his campaign"—Roosevelt knew well the persuasive publicity value of the concatenation of altruistic affiliations and implications.

In reply to a question by a newspaper man picturing a parallel between the 1912 Republican convention and the one of 1880, Roosevelt said: "If they act honestly, there will be no occasion for any one to bolt." June 8, receiving from Chicago news of a decision adverse to him, he said that "again and again we have sent to the penitentiary election officials for deeds not one whit worse than what was done by the National Committee at Chicago yesterday." June 9, another Sabbath, contributed no emanation from Oyster Bay. June 10, asked if it was true a special train was waiting to take him to Chicago, he snapped, "Nonsense!" June 11, Roosevelt, in his rôle of Contributing Editor of the *Outlook,* erstwhile decorous and polite journal of opinion, denounced the seating of certain of Taft's delegates at Chicago as "a fraud as vulgar, as brazen, and as cynically open as any ever committed by the Tweed régime in New York forty years ago." In this editorial he brought into use a new and not entirely pat adjective of combat: "The contest for the Republican nomination has now narrowed down to a naked issue of right and wrong; for the issue is simply whether or not we shall permit a system of naked fraud, of naked theft from the people, to triumph"— causing Roosevelt's sly enemy, the New York *Sun,* to mimic him: "So much for the naked issue, now for the naked truth . . ." June 11, he denounced an action of the Republican National Committee at Chicago as "dangerously near being treason," and continued: "To whom does the Republican party belong? I hold that it belongs to the plain people. Mr. Taft, through his lieutenants, acts on the belief that the party belongs to the bosses." Roosevelt defined the issue as being "simply whether the people have the right to nominate whomever they wish for the highest office in their gift, or whether by deliberate theft and fraud certain machine leaders, acting in the interest of special privilege, are to be permitted to deprive the people of this right." June 12, Roosevelt denounced the acts of Taft's men at Chicago: "There is no form of rascality which the Taft men had not resorted to."

The whole of the Colonel's objurgations, denunciations,

accusations, calumniations, and miscellaneous fulminations causing the indispensable "Mr. Dooley" to remark:

> I had no idee it was so bad. I wint to bed last night thinkin' th' counthry was safe, so I put out th' cat, locked th' dure, counted th' cash, said me prayers, wound th' clock, an' pulled into th' siding f'r th' night. Whin I got up I had a feelin' that somethin' was burnin', th' same as I had th' mornin' iv th' big fire. But I cudden't find annything wrong till I opened up th' pa-apers an', much to me relief, found that it was not me pants but th' republic that was on fire. Yes, sir; th' republic is doomed to desthruction again.

For response or counter-attack to Roosevelt's barrage of denunciations from Oyster Bay, Taft in the White House was impotent by temperament, handicapped by his office or his sense of the dignity of it. The news coming out of the White House dealt practically wholly with Taft's official duties—at the moment rather onerous. Almost the only news emanating from Taft that had to do even faintly with the fight was a despatch saying that Taft had chosen, to make his nominating speech, an Ohio Republican, a "fluent speaker with a strong voice"—his name was Warren G. Harding. On June 14 he was quoted as saying: "All the information I get is that I will be nominated on the first ballot."

If Taft himself was inept and otherwise barred from the sort of repartee that Roosevelt's barrage called for, Taft's lieutenants, while willing, were hardly a match for the Colonel. When the Roosevelt forces charged the National Committee with refusing to give Roosevelt's friends an adequate supply of tickets for the convention gallery, the Committee chairman, Harry S. New, retorted that the Roosevelt manager was a "pettifogging falsifier,"—anemic verbal shadow of the Colonel's robustious "shorter and uglier word." When a Roosevelt man telegraphed the National Committee's sergeant at arms, William F. Stone, asking for tickets, Stone wired back, "Not a damned ticket to any Roosevelt man." The retort, while forceful, somehow lacked the public appeal of the Roosevelt method. On June 9, the Taft managers decided to "draw a contrast between themselves and the Roosevelt headquarters," and in that purpose "not to answer the Colonel's charges," to "give the Roosevelt forces a monopoly of the publicity"—an abnegation of which the virtue lay in recognition of inferiority, somewhat like the rabbit, in a contest with the porcupine, preferring weapons other than quills.

If Taft was unwilling, and his managers unskilled, in the arts of vocal barrage, their deficiency was abundantly supplied by volunteers from the sidelines. The most effective missiles came from the New York *Sun,* in the form of satire. On June 13, *The Sun,* in a pseudo concern for Roosevelt's place in history, advised him to quit. He had already had honors enough, *The Sun* said, listing them:

> For a man whose feet have already surmounted almost every pinnacle of human ambition; who has been statesman, ruler, philosopher, warrior, reformer, preacher, historian, faunal naturalist, autobiographer, sage, idol, instructor of the other nations of the earth and swayer of the minds of millions of his own fellow countrymen by sheer personal force; who has figured not only as the maker of peace between two of the greatest of world powers engaged in one of the most tremendous conflicts in military annals, but has himself taken the sword against a formidable European antagonist and charged on horseback up San Juan hill in a picture by Frederic Remington, and, if we are not mistaken, in another picture by Vasili Verestchagin; who has not only held for two terms the most exalted office in the world but has also won uncounted minor triumphs with pen, mouth, elephant rifle, boxing gloves and epigrams—for such a man... not much is left to be desired.

For which reasons *The Sun* slyly urged that Roosevelt abandon his present ambition, and particularly that he should not go to Chicago in person.

At Oyster Bay June 14, Roosevelt arose early, breakfasted early. In a flurry of instructions to servants and good-byes to neighbors who had come to wish him luck, he climbed into the tonneau of an open car and, with Mrs. Roosevelt, started for New York, forty miles away. It was noticed by the little group who saw him off that the Colonel's afflatus suggested more militancy, more snap and crackle, than usual, due, in part, to the new hat he was wearing, a hat among hats, big, tan, with a deep crown and a wide brim, having a sombrero effect; the hat of a soldier, of a Rough Rider.

Just before noon Roosevelt reached his office in *The Outlook*. In the corridor outside his door were jammed hundreds of people, through whom Roosevelt shouldered a way, smiling, responding to greetings. As he reached his door, a newspaper man asked a question. Roosevelt turned around, waited for silence: "When am I going to Chicago? I do not know yet. I may return to Oyster Bay this afternoon. But sometimes things move quickly these days." Grinning, he pushed open the door, backed through, and closed it.

In the corridor the hum of excitement went on. Inside, Roosevelt talked over the telephone with his aides in Chicago. The Convention was only two days away.

Presently Roosevelt came out, handed around copies of a statement—he was going to Chicago. Reporters rushed to telephones. In the afternoon Roosevelt started.

At Chicago, police had made preparations to control the crowd at the railroad station. The plan, from the moment Roosevelt appeared, evaporated. The sight of the Colonel, teeth agleam, romantic headgear, burly arms waving greetings, was catalytic. A mob, shouting, laughing, cheering, shoving, engulfed the police and took Roosevelt to its bosom. The drive to the hotel was through lines of sensation-mad people, "who greeted him as they might have greeted a successful Roman general returning from the wars." They followed him into the hotel, jammed the lobby, almost crushed the breath from his body. Finally he escaped to an elevator and thence to his headquarters, and ten minutes later emerged onto a balcony and gave a short talk: "It is a naked fight against theft, and the thieves will not win." The crowds in Michigan Avenue and Grant Park roared back, "Soak 'em, Teddy! Give it to 'em!"

To a reporter who asked him a commonplace question about his health and spirits, Roosevelt achieved—in this case without planning it—one of the most potent for effect of all the striking phrases that sparkled along the path of his career. "I'm feeling," he said, using a quite artless simile that came to his mind from his hunting experiences, "like a bull moose" —bringing it about that BULL MOOSE should stalk in heavy black letters across the front pages of 10,000 newspapers (conveying, one wonders, what mystic significance, to a nation in which not one of a hundred had ever seen an antlered animal, or could know how a bull moose feels under any set of circumstances). Crudely drawn pictures of the animal appeared in immense posters on the walls of hotels and as placards at the head of improvised parades, the biological details giving some pain, doubtless, to the curator of the Field Museum on Michigan Avenue, but the spirit adequately grasped by Roosevelt's exalted followers. Manufacturers of campaign buttons telegraphed frantically to their factories, where harried artists made unaccustomed demands on local libraries for a picture of *"Alces Americana."* The name, "Bull Moose," the idea, the spirit, was taken into the national consciousness, became an established thing, a symbol universally understood. Roosevelt's political following was the "Bull Moose Party," a partisan of him was a "Bull-mooser."

The spirit into which Roosevelt at Oyster Bay had whipped the scene and which rose to surround him as he arrived on the field in person, was not what might have been expected from the angry epithets which Roosevelt had been using to stimulate his followers. It was a fighting spirit, of course—it could hardly have avoided that, but the kind of fighting spirit that is described as martial, and the precise shade of martial which verges into religious. Due to the presence of women in large numbers in Roosevelt's ranks, entering into politics for the first time and taking it with exalted seriousness; due to the implications, vague but always elevated, of the phrase Roosevelt had made a slogan, "social justice"; and due perhaps to a certain solemnity, a fatefulness in the fact that the Republican party, then still remembered as having fought the Civil War and saved the Union, was now in its own grapple of life and death—due to these and whatever causes, the emotion Roosevelt inspired expressed itself in what had already begun to be sung and what became the practically official and universally used battle songs of Roosevelt's party,

> Onward Christian soldiers
> Marching as to war...

and the "Battle-Hymn of the Republic":

> Mine eyes have seen the glory of the coming of the Lord,
> He is trampling out the vintage where the grapes of wrath are stored.
> Glory, glory hallelujah!
> Glory, glory hallelujah!
> Glory, glory hallelujah,
> His truth is marching on.

Even the arguments, the most violent of them, were expressed in symbols of religion, Biblical quotations. The Chicago *Tribune,* earnest Roosevelt organ, as an appeal to the National Committee for justice to the Roosevelt delegations, printed in large type across the entire page, and on all the pages of its issue of June 18:

> THE EIGHTH COMMANDMENT: THOU SHALT NOT STEAL

Solemnly, with utter seriousness, almost reverently, *The Tribune* said of the convention hall that "the coliseum is the temple at Gaza and Samson is between the pillars."

In that spirit, on the night preceding the opening of the convention, Monday, June 17, Roosevelt made perhaps the most moving speech of his career. The Auditorium would hold 5,000—four times that many struggled to enter. Roosevelt began on a high note: "Disaster is ahead of us if we trust to the leadership of men whose souls are seared and whose eyes are blinded, men of cold heart and narrow mind, who believe we can find safety in dull timidity and dull inaction." As for his own fortunes, he offered himself in the spirit of utter sacrifice: "What happens to me is not of the slightest consequence. I am to be used, as in a doubtful battle any man is used, to his hurt or not, so long as he is useful, and is then cast aside or left to die. I wish you to feel this and I shall need no sympathy when you are through with me, for this fight is far too great to permit us to concern ourselves about any man's welfare." In his peroration he achieved a climax which in emotional intensity equalled Bryan's "crown of thorns, cross of gold," which was comparable to the most elevated oratory in the language—and which made a very old word newly familiar to an America that was beginning to lose acquaintance with its Bible:

> We fight in honorable fashion for the good of mankind; fearless of the future, unheeding of our individual fates, with unflinching hearts and undimmed eyes; we stand at Armageddon, and we battle for the Lord.

Something about the word "Armageddon," an implication at once mystic and martial, made it overnight part of the language of the street. Embattled righteousness was the meaning commonly ascribed to it; its pronunciation varied with individual preference. Scores of songs and poems were inspired by it:

> We stand at Armageddon, and we battle for the Lord,
> And all we ask to stead us is a blessing on each sword;
> And tribes and factions mingle in one great fighting clan,
> Who issue forth to battle behind a fighting man.

Not all that "Armageddon" inspired was reverent, not all took either the word or its discoverer seriously. The New York *Sun* found in it material for jeering wit.

In spite of some hesitancies of pronunciation the brethren got a holy joy out of "Armageddon." There is a mystic wonderful charm to it; it is like "Abracadabra" or "parallelopipedon," a word of might with magic in the vowels and the bowels of it. Seth Bullock believes it to be a township in Oklahoma. The Hon. Angelo Perkins is positive that it is Welsh. Medill McCormick holds that it was an early skirmish in the Revolution....

Of all the satires and ironies that arose out of the religious flavor which Roosevelt's 1912 crusade took on, the most penetrating came from one unknown to the present historian, or, I suspect, to any other. His performance was of a sort that does not get itself into the official records, nor even into the newspapers. His name is forgotten, if indeed it was ever known. Only the thing he did is recalled. But I can visualize him. A homely philosopher he must have been, one, I imagine, with some small income, sufficient to save his cerebration from being dissipated in the pursuit of livelihood, one having a bent for reading and able to indulge it, having a bent also for observation of mankind and above all one with capacity to reflect fruitfully upon what he read and observed. A sense of humor he must have had, yet I suspect the thing he did was not so much in the spirit of humor as of adequacy—it seemed called for and he did it.

I can visualize him strolling down the quieter side of Michigan Avenue, the Park side. I can imagine him pausing to observe the Colonel going by, and the crowds that followed. He noticed the rapt quality of them, the visionary gleam in their eyes, the frenzy in some. Seeing it he recalled from his reading the age-long disposition of men to set up heroes, to expect Messiahs. Seeing and reflecting, it occurred to him that the scene called for a comment on mankind and his incredible ways. Being a laconic person, his comment took the form of action. Waiting until the crowd had hurried by, he crossed the street, sought a small printer, had a brief order filled, and employed some small boys, with the result that throughout Chicago's streets were scattered thousands of dodgers reading:

> *At Three o'Clock*
> *Thursday Afternoon*
> THEODORE ROOSEVELT
> WILL WALK
> on the
> WATERS OF
> LAKE MICHIGAN

The official for the formality of opening the convention was Victor Rosewater, whose gentleness of voice, paleness of face, and slightness of figure were apt for the status he had in private life, editor of the Omaha (Neb.) *Bee,* and would have been appropriate for a musician or a Hebraic poet—might, indeed, have marked him for almost any possible rôle before that of presenting his frail breast to a political tornado. Rosewater, his shortness of stature emphasized by the length of the gavel he now grasped, and the height of the reading desk behind which he stood, his thinness of voice almost grotesquely in contrast with the hoarse passions raging in the hall, his manner that of a man whose certainty that bombs will strike near him is accentuated by anxious uncertainty whether they will fall to right or to left, to front or to rear, or, as happened, on all sides at once—Rosewater had quiet for just two perfunctory acts. Without interruption from the floor he was allowed to introduce the clergyman—whose invocation ventured only so far into the faint umbra of the matters on hand as to ask God to "direct all our actions by

Thy holy inspiration"—and then retreated to the safe neutrality of repeating the Lord's Prayer. Upon the heels of the "Amen," Rosewater, who had a manner of nervous hurry, directed the Secretary to read the routine call for the convention; and hardly had the closing syllable dropped from the Secretary's lips when the first thunder of the storm broke out.

The National Committee had made up, as usual, the "temporary roll" of delegates and had placed upon it the 72 Taft delegates when the Committee a few days before had adjudged winners of the contests. This roll, the Roosevelt forces now challenged, denouncing the 72 as "not honestly elected" and moving that in place of them there be substituted the "seventy-two [Roosevelt] delegates who have been elected by the honest votes of the Republican voters"—that, in short, as it was expressed again and again by the Roosevelt spokesmen, with no attempt at delicacy, "the roll be purged of fraud." To this motion the Taft forces interposed a parliamentary objection, on the ground that "no business of any character is in order until after the Convention shall have been properly organized."

Rosewater, facing the necessity of deciding whether or not the Roosevelt motion was in order, rather timorously disavowed personal responsibility for the decision he was about to make, saying that he had apprehended the question would come up, that therefore he had had it "under advisement for several days," that he had "had advice upon it from many distinguished gentlemen more learned in parliamentary law than myself," that he was greatly indebted to these gentlemen" for "elucidating the question" for him, and that he would have the clerk "read a statement" containing the arguments, precedents, and conclusions with which his advisers had provided him. The statement, of course, reached the conclusion that the motion of the Roosevelt leaders was "out of order," that the 72 contested Taft delegates should remain on the temporary roll. With that decision announced, Rosewater, with the eager manner of hurrying toward an end to his disquieting responsibilities, went on with his one remaining function, the election of a permanent chairman to preside over the coming and certain-to-be-stormy session. With that, the convention passed into its tensest phase, for it was known to every delegate, to every spectator in the galleries—not "every spectator," rather "every partisan," for there was no spectator who was not a partisan—and to every citizen waiting tensely before newspaper bulletin boards in every corner of the country, that the election of the permanent chairman would be the first test, that whichever side mustered a majority in that test would, if its ranks held and its determination endured, have the same majority (substantially) for the nomination of the Presidential candidate. Whichever side won the permanent chairmanship would win the Presidential nomination.

The Roosevelt candidate for permanent chairman was Francis E. McGovern, put in nomination by a Wisconsin delegate as "the brilliant, the able, the impartial, and the fearless Governor of my commonwealth."

McGovern did not really live up to all those adjectives. He was chosen by the Roosevelt forces as their candidate for permanent chairman partly with the shrewd notion that they thereby could muster the maximum number of votes against the Taft candidate. All the Roosevelt delegates would (and did) vote for McGovern as a matter of course; the Roosevelt forces hoped that the little group of 26 Wisconsin delegates, who were not for Roosevelt but for LaFollette, would, on the vote for chairman, be led by state pride to support McGovern. But the Roosevelt leaders did not know, as the country did later, LaFollette's limitless intransigence. LaFollette, speaking through one of his delegates (Walter L. Houser), coldly informed the convention that McGovern was not his candidate, that McGovern did "not represent the interests of LaFollette."

The candidate of the Taft forces for permanent chairman was Elihu Root. To put his name before the convention, they relied upon the speech-making talent and other versatile abilities of a New York delegate, Job E. Hedges, who was the one man in the Taft forces equipped with, or able to retain in this moment, any qualities of poise and humor. With irony, with serenity; with the capacity, as occasion arose, for what a later generation would have called "a snappy come-back," this proposer of Root won an opening trick in the forensic game by quoting a panegyric about Root which had been uttered by Roosevelt himself a few short years before—"Elihu Root is the ablest man that has appeared in the public life of any country in any position in my time." When, upon this quotation being read, cheers broke out more for Roosevelt than for Root, Hedges urbanely assured the Roosevelt rooters that "you need not hesitate to cheer Roosevelt in my presence; I cheered him seven years. . . . Elihu Root was good enough for Roosevelt and he is good enough for me."

There followed, on both sides, a welter of seconding speeches which, heard and seen as a whole, including the cross-fire among the delegates and the frequent remarks from the galleries, had the effect of a lake of fiery lava on the surface of which erupted detonating bombs of anger and malediction, humor and irony.

A good many of the seconders of McGovern forgot McGovern and talked about Roosevelt—or, in another spirit, about Root. Francis J. Heney of California, in a long speech seconding McGovern (on the rare occasions when he thought of it), reviewed the history "of the conduct of the national committee" in a vocabulary and a spirit with which Heney had become familiar through his practice as prosecutor in the criminal courts. Scornfully he designated a Taft leader with a term from the argot of the underworld, "Big Steve of Colorado." Shockingly pointing his finger at the victim of his acid words, he said, of this Taft leader, that he "differs from Abe Ruef of California only in the fact that Abe Ruef was in the penitentiary last week while Big Steve was helping to make this temporary roll"—leading to a demonstration which the official stenographer embalmed for history, rather mildly, as "disorder and confusion in the hall." To permit the 72 disputed Taft delegates to vote on the question of chairman when they "have no legal, moral, or ethical right to be in this convention," was, Heney said, simply "the proposition that a corrupt judge shall sit in his own case." "You may as well hear me out," he continued, "because you are going to hear me if it takes all summer."

A delegate from West Virginia, William Seymour Edwards, rising to second McGovern, began in the manner of Rome and Shakespeare: "Gentlemen and fellow-delegates: Give me your ears"—but quickly, upon hearing unpropitious sounds from the gallery, changed his tempo to something more consistent with the present occasion, saying, in the next sentence, "Boys, give me a chance."

When a Kentucky Senator, W. O. Bradley, undertook to second Root with a tribute of the conventional sort, a Roosevelt delegate, recalling a not universally admired episode in Bradley's senatorial career, called out, with effective irrelevancy, "You voted for Lorimer." This interpolation into the proceedings of a happening rather far removed from the matter of electing a chairman of the convention, was greeted with manifest satisfaction and approval by the Roosevelt delegates, who with good heart and ample lung-power united in a chant, "Lorimer! Lorimer! Lorimer!" Bradley, exasperatedly resigning himself to the change of theme forced upon him by the Roosevelt partisans, singled out a conspicuous Roosevelt delegate from California, and addressed him in a shout of such volume as to be heard above the tumult: "Yes, I voted for Lorimer and when I did I voted for a man ten thousand times better than you. . . . I want to say that the time will never come when the great State of Kentucky will be so low and degraded as to accept moral advice from Francis J. Heney."

Bradley, his creative spirit pleased at having invented so apt a retort, swung back into his panegyric of Root, and as he approached his conclusion found himself in a mood sufficiently charitable to say, "I want to thank you gentlemen for your decorous and courteous attention." To which the Roosevelt delegates, in ungracious repudiation of the virtues Bradley had attributed to them, repeated their chorus, "Lorimer! Lorimer! Lorimer!" Whereupon Bradley, with a quick change of tempo into both the mood and the melody, the lilt of the precise moment, retorted "Liar! Liar! Liar!"

Finally, the oratory of seconding the nominees for permanent chairman exhausted itself, the calling of the roll began. At each point where the name of a contested Taft delegate was called, shrill protest arose from the Roosevelt leaders, expressed in forms that did not always take the trouble to adhere strictly to the ceremonious locutions of parliamentary procedure. When the Secretary called the name of a Taft delegate from Pennsylvania, Roosevelt-leader Flinn of that State challenged the vote. When the chair declined to entertain the protest, Flinn expressed his appeal from the decision of the chair by a simple affirmation, "Steal! Thief! You are a pack of thieves." When the chair seemed not disposed to entertain this form of appeal and proceeded with the calling of the roll, Flinn informed the chairman, the convention, and the world that "You'll have a happy time calling any roll here this afternoon unless you give us justice; we are going to be heard in this convention or you are not going to have any roll call." "Do you want me," he added, "to come up [on the platform] where I can talk to you?" Flinn had a reputation that gave validity to his threat, gave substance to the innuendo which the chair saw in his words, and justified the apprehension, plain in the chair's manner, that if Flinn should come up on that platform his processes of persuasion might not be confined to talk.

Finally, when Flinn's and all other protests had been ignored, the roll call was completed and the chair announced that "a majority of the delegates have voted for Senator Root." As Root took the chair, the outraged Flinn made his so-to-speak minority report in a simple epithet. To the very face of Root, to the former Secretary of State of the United States, to one of the half-dozen leading statesmen of the world, Flinn exclaimed: "Receiver of stolen goods." He was informally seconded by another Roosevelt delegate who, with an attempt at fine discrimination, reduced the charge to "Protector of stolen goods." Whereupon the listening Chicago chief of police, out of a criteria of violence including the Great Conflagration, the Haymarket riots, the Pullman strike, and the daily alarums in the stockyards district, expressed juridical condemnation, in a voice loud enough to be heard and included by the stenographer in the permanent record: "This is a plain breach of the peace."

To all this Root's cool response was to enter calmly upon the delivery of his prepared address, consisting chiefly of a laudatory review, in the usual form and spirit, of the achievements of Taft's administration. Root concluded, climactically, with a tribute to "the courts, state and federal . . . Their judges will not be punished for honest decisions; their judgments will be respected and obeyed. The keystone established by our fathers will not be shattered by Republican hands. 'For there is no liberty where the power of judging be not separate from the legislative and judicial powers.' 'To what purpose are powers limited, and to what purpose is that limitation committed to writing, if these limitations may at any time be passed by those intended to be restrained?' "

By which every one understood that Root was putting the emphasis of the climax of his speech not, according to the tradition of Republican convention keynote oratory, upon the wickedness of Democrats but upon that of a Republican; that Root was subtly creating an effect upon the convention and the country by recalling, and condemning, Roosevelt's fatal phrase "the recall of judicial decisions."

The vote for permanent chairman had been Root 558, McGovern 501. Had the 72 contested Taft delegates been prevented from voting, Root would have had less than a majority, Roosevelt's candidate for chairman would have been elected, Roosevelt's friends would control the convention, Roosevelt would be nominated. Unless these 72, or an appreciable proportion of them, could be unseated, Roosevelt's cause was lost. To the unseating of those delegates, therefore, or to successfully indicting their right to vote, the Roosevelt leaders now proceeded to devote their parliamentary battle.

Governor Hadley of Missouri, floor leader of the Roosevelt forces, had already at the opening of the convention moved that the 72 Taft delegates, against whom contests had been made, be removed, and that there be substituted the 72 Roosevelt delegates on whose behalf the contest had been made. This motion the chair had ruled out of order. Now Hadley renewed it as the opening move in a long parliamentary battle, in the course of which his motion became standardized, that "List 1," the 72 Taft delegates, be stricken off, and "List 2," the 72 Roosevelt delegates, be substituted.

When the Roosevelt forces realized that the motion in this form would be lost, they modified it, to the effect that the 72 contested Taft delegates as a group should not be permitted to vote in any matter affecting their titles as a group to their seats. Shrewdly, by iteration, Hadley emphasized that a contested delegate voting upon his own title to the seat he claimed was as being defendant and juror in the same case. "It is written in the law of England," said Hadley, quoting a classic of jurisprudence, "that no man shall be a judge of his own case." The same axiom, expressed in less classic words, was on the banner which the California delegation jiggled up and down in the face of the delegates every time this question was before them: "We refuse to try title to property before the thief who stole it."

To which Root as presiding officer made a distinction between an individual voting on the title to his own individual seat, and a group voting on questions affecting the title of the whole group to their several seats. Root conceded that "no man can be permitted to vote upon the question of his own right to his seat" but held, and quoted the parliamentary manual of the House of Representatives to sustain him, that "the disqualifying interest must be such as affects the member directly, and not as one of a class." The rule does not disqualify any delegate whose name is upon the roll from voting upon the contest of any other man's right. "Otherwise," Root pointed out, "any minority could secure control of a deliberative body by grouping a sufficient number of their opponents in one motion, and by thus disqualifying them, turn the minority into a majority, without any decision upon the merits of the motion."

The Roosevelt forces lost their motion by 567 to 507. Then as the separate cases of contesting State and district delegations were brought up, Hadley each time moved that the Taft delegates be unseated, the Roosevelt delegates substituted. Each time, the Roosevelt forces lost, by 569 to 499, by 564 to 497, and votes closely similar in numbers. The nearest the Roosevelt forces came to winning any contest was in the case of two California delegates, when the Roosevelt forces had 529 to the triumphant 542 of the Taft forces.

It was clear, and had been since the vote on permanent chairman, that the Taft forces had control of the convention.

Those of the Roosevelt leaders who had had hard-boiled experience, either political or parliamentary, knew well that once the Taft forces had secured control of the convention (through the action of the National Committee in deciding in favor of Taft contesting delegates) there was no parliamentary means by which they could be unseated. "The national committee," conceded an ardent Roosevelt partisan, George Ade, "fixed things so that they couldn't be unfixed by anything short of an earthquake."

But the hope of the Roosevelt forces did not depend wholly, or even, at this stage of the contest, greatly, on their delegate strength or on success in unseating contested Taft delegates. Indeed, fully half the Roosevelt hope and objective, fully half the Roosevelt method of battle, was to convince the Taft leaders and especially the officials of the National Committee and the other custodians of the destinies of the Republican party, that Taft was the weaker candidate, Roosevelt the stronger one; that Taft if nominated could not win the election, that only Roosevelt could; that in the circumstances under which the contest had developed and in the pitch to which it had now come, millions of Republicans would vote for a Democrat rather than for Taft; that, as it was put, in effect, again and again, "you can nominate Taft, but only the people can elect him, and the people won't." Hadley, in the very midst of his technical legal argument against the right of the contested Taft delegates to their seats, interjected an irrelevance, not so much in deliberate shrewdness as in naïve expression of what was in his mind:

> I do not know whether a majority of this Convention agrees with me that Theodore Roosevelt ought to be our candidate for President, but there can be no difference upon the proposition that he can command the support of more people, and he can lead a larger number of American voters in a cause for which he fights, than any other man.

Only to a slight extent, however, did the Roosevelt leaders make this appeal in formal argument to the Taft forces. They did not need to. The appeal, the proof of Roosevelt's greater popularity, and of the disapprobation into which Taft sank deeper each day came in spontaneous demonstrations from the crowds in the gallery, from the milling masses in Chicago outside the convention walls, from every corner of the country. It came in the infinitely varied forms to which spontaneity gives birth; and the whole of it composed a characteristic picture of the American spirit, expressing itself at one moment in deeply earnest devotion to something the crowd vaguely understood to be the "Spirit of Social and Industrial Justice," the next moment in such a fecund gamut of humor and good-natured jeering as only the American spirit produces. The crowd had taken the fancy that the operations of the Taft political machine, in the stolid impassiveness with which it had gone about the business of seating Taft delegates and casting out Roosevelt ones, had a resemblance to a steam-roller. "Steam-roller," therefore, the management of the convention became, with Root in the rôle of driver. Every time he rose to make a decision, from a thousand vocal cords, bass and tenor, alto and soprano, came a myriad imitations, each with its individual over-tone of irony, of a steam-roller getting under way, "toot, toot," followed, as the week went on, by an imitation of steam escaping from a laboring engine, achieved by rubbing two pieces of sand-paper together—by the end of the convention there could hardly have been a square inch of sand-paper left in any Chicago shop. Whenever Root made a decision unpleasing to the Roosevelt partisans, their comment took a vocal form which would have led a visitor from Mars to assume that some ten thousand persons had suddenly suffered a simultaneous and universal stomach-ache. When Chairman Rosewater announced that the photograph of the convention was about to be taken, and that the photographer would be pleased if the crowd would look pleasant, a delegate expressed the loud opinion that it would be the first and last time. When Rabbi Joseph Stolz prayed that "the counsel of righteousness and truth of the everlasting God prevail over the waves of passion and the tumult of voices," an audible titter through the hall indicated lack of faith in the power of prayer. From time to time rumors went about that Roosevelt in person would come to the convention, that he would address the convention, that he would march down the aisles at the head of his followers and seize the convention by force, that he would grasp a moment when the hall was empty—three o'clock in the morning was the hour commonly assigned by this rumor—and would, with his followers, take possession of the hall, the platform, the gavel, and the other symbols, forms, and insignia of the Republican party. That particular one of the rumors caused the nervous managers of the Republican party to ask for an extra detail of police—additional to the 500 already employed—to guard the hall at times when its only occupants were the rats in the basement.

Once the crowd, or the nine-tenths of it that was for Roosevelt, merged itself into a remarkable mass demonstration, in which the precipitant was a young woman in the galleries, destined to be described minutely later by the newspapers as wearing a suit of cream-colored linen, a blue straw turban hat, and a bouquet of sweet peas, and as having a "radiant and infectious smile." She had been, during the morning, merely a face in the gallery, no more noticed than any other of the thousands of women who, in the genteel restraint of that day, confined their expressions of Roosevelt emotion mainly to decorous waving of their handkerchiefs. At one point, however, Mrs. Davis, moved by some incident to an exceptional exaltation, seized a poster of Roosevelt, leaned with it far over the edge of the gallery, and waved it in time with music the band happened to be playing. The crowd began to turn toward her; she, stimulated by the crowd, rose to a rare height and ingenuity of emotional leadership. Holding the Roosevelt poster at arm's length in one hand, she greeted it with her handkerchief in the other. In pantomime she coaxed the Taft leaders to be fair to her hero, holding out her hands in mute appeal, and expressing in her mobile features a gamut of appropriate manifestations of feminine winsomeness. By this time, the delegates, the crowd, and the band had turned to her leadership. Roosevelt delegates from California, bearing an immense golden bear that served at once as the State's emblem and as a Teddy-bear, went to the gallery, placed themselves behind Mrs. Davis, marched her up the aisles of the main floor with the Roosevelt State delegations and placards falling in line, and thrust her on an elevation occupied by the press. Under her spell the hall passed into an orgy of Roosevelt cheering that lasted forty-two minutes, throughout which by no means the least interesting spectacle was the features and manner of Mr. Root, and of his associates on the platform, faced with a development of political conventions not provided against by any paragraph in Jefferson's manual of parliamentary procedure. William Jennings Bryan, occupying a seat with the reporters, recorded in the following day's newspapers, that "It is only fair to the Taft delegates to say that they preserved a proper decorum during the entire performance, their faces wearing an expression suited to the occasion."

From the Roosevelt point-of-view, all was vain, and had been since the first parliamentary decision against them. Parliamentarily, the Taft forces controlled. As for persuasion or intimidation, neither beautiful women in the galleries nor catcalls from the crowd, neither hint of bolt nor certainty of Roosevelt's greater popularity could move the Standpatter forces. They would rather lose the election, even destroy the Republican party, than let Roosevelt have the nomination. It was in terms of political death that all had come to think —death for the Republican party and for the two principals, Taft and Roosevelt. "The only question now," said Chauncey M. Depew, "is which corpse gets the most flowers."

Roosevelt, when he realized he could not win, announced through Henry Allen of Kansas that the Roosevelt delegates would continue to sit in the convention but not vote nor otherwise participate. When the convention ended he called an informal meeting of his followers, announced a new party, the Progressives, and perfected the organization of it at a new convention two months later. In the election he carried six States to Taft's two, got 4,117,813 votes to Taft's 3,486,316.

But the Democratic candidate, Woodrow Wilson, carried forty States, got 6,294,293 votes, and became President.

What was it all about? Apart from the personal aspect, apart from the wish of Roosevelt to be in the White House again and the wish of millions of Americans to have him there, what was the meaning of the Progressive party? What was the fundamental difference, in terms of governmental policy, between the old Republican party and the new Progressive one? What, aside from the emotion generated by the angry epithets —"Socialist" hurled by one side, "reactionary" by the other— what differences of principle separated the two? What was decided when the Republicans controlled the convention, and what when the Progressives had the larger popular vote? And what would have been decided had the Republicans under Taft won the Presidency, or the Progressives under Roosevelt? And what was decided when the Democrats actually won it?

Only to a comparatively slight extent did the average man think of the conflict in terms of principle at all; he saw it mainly as a duel between personalities, Roosevelt on the one side, Taft on the other. More accurately, the issue was pro-Roosevelt and anti-Roosevelt; for Taft as a personality had no great magnetism, did not attract any large personal following—Taft's rôle in the fight was largely as a symbol for those who hated Roosevelt, or the smaller number who merely deplored him. The average man, indeed, did not so much *think* about any theories of government involved as *feel* the emotions stirred up by the slogans: those of odium, "standpatism," "Cannonism," "Aldrichism"; or those of altruism, "social and industrial justice." The average man in the mass, the whole of the America of that day, was divided—mainly by temperament, by differing responsiveness to certain appeals— into two groups; those whose eyes became rapt in the thrill of singing "Onward, Christian Soldiers" behind the banner of Roosevelt; and those who were indifferent to Roosevelt or were moved to acute distaste by his actions and utterances.

Most of the shouting and tumult was emotion and little more. By far the greater amount of the Roosevelt and Progressive speech-making and hymn-singing proceeded from and was aimed at those areas of the cerebellum where spinal tremors originate. Those portions of Senator Beveridge's keynote speech at the Progressive National Convention that were most effective in inspiring cheers—a delirious salvo at each semicolon —would have been difficult to parse in the austere terms of political economy or social philosophy: "We stand for a nobler America; we stand for an undivided Nation; we stand for a broader liberty, a fuller justice; we stand for social brotherhood as against savage individualism; we stand for intelligent co-operation instead of a reckless competition; we stand for mutual helpfulness instead of mutual hatred; we stand for equal rights as a fact of life instead of a catch-word of politics; we stand for the rule of the people as a practical truth instead of a meaningless pretense; we stand for a representative government that represents the people; we battle for the actual rights of man."

Just what did those eloquent affirmations mean in terms of concrete legislation? And when Roosevelt electrified the nation with his "We stand at Armageddon and we battle for the Lord," just what did the average man assume would be the consequence of winning the battle or losing it—other than that in one case Roosevelt would be in the White House and the air would sparkle, while in the other Roosevelt would be at Oyster Bay and the world would be drab?

One clear difference of fundamental principle there was: The Progressive party and Roosevelt stood for the universal participation of all men and women in all the mechanisms of government (with very slight exceptions, if any). That was new, and far-reaching. Between that and the representative form of government supported by the Republicans, the difference was wide and deep, and the question of national policy thus laid before the country may possibly have been, as the excited disputants on both sides heatedly declared, the most important since the Civil War.

Direct popular government, as expressed in Roosevelt's sequence of "I believe's" in his "Charter of Democracy," embraced: direct primaries for the nomination of all party candidates for all offices, including, as respects candidates for President, direct preferential primaries in which the voter should instruct delegates as to the voter's choice; direct election of United States Senators by vote of the people—as distinct from the historic method of election by State legislatures; the initiative, whereby the people by petition could initiate laws, could, in effect, command the legislature to enact laws; and the referendum, whereby the people could pass upon laws enacted by the legislature; and the recall, whereby the people could by popular vote remove from office any official, including judges, regardless of the length of term for which he had been elected.

As against that, the Republicans in their platform, with a manner of declining to dignify these upstart innovations by mentioning them, stood firm for the old way: "We believe in our self-controlled representative democracy."

One other deep-reaching difference of principle there was. Roosevelt and the Progressives believed in the "recall of judicial decisions"—that was Roosevelt's phrase in his Charter of Democracy speech. It is doubtful if any political term since "nullification" had so startled the nation. In part the shock was due to popular misunderstanding. When newspapers carried the phrase in headlines, great numbers of people understood Roosevelt to mean that immediately after any judicial decision in any sort of case, criminal trial for murder or civil case of trespass, the public would have the right immediately to act as a court of appeal. As the deeply shocked New York *Sun* put it: "Roosevelt proposed to establish on the street corners a higher court of law, the Court of Crowd, with supreme jurisdiction—the craziest proposal that ever emanated either from himself or from any other statesman. . . ."

Actually, Roosevelt meant only that in cases involving judicial interpretation of the Constitution the people should have a right to pass upon the decision: "I very earnestly ask you clearly to provide means which will permit the people themselves, by popular vote, after due deliberation and discussion, but finally and without appeal, to settle what the proper construction of any constitutional point is. When a judge decides a constitutional question, when he decides what the people as a whole can or cannot do, the people should have the right to recall that decision if they think it wrong."

Roosevelt's limited, actual meaning, as expressed in the text of his Charter of Democracy speech in February, was never able to catch up with the broader, incorrect meaning inferred by the public from the early newspaper headlines. After trying to make his meaning clear, and succeeding only in intensifying the opprobrium of the idea, he resigned himself to the rueful conclusion that it is a major error for a man in public life to fail to make himself clear; by the time the Progressives were ready to write their platform in August they were careful to state the idea with meticulous exactness —and with avoidance of the fatal phrase:

> The Progressive party demands such restriction of the power of the courts as shall leave to the people the ultimate authority to determine fundamental questions of social welfare and public policy. To secure this end, it pledges itself to provide:
> That when an act passed under the police power of the state is held unconstitutional under the state constitution by the courts, the people, after an ample interval for deliberation, shall have an opportunity to vote on the question whether they desire the act to become law, notwithstanding such decision.

Against that the Republicans, in their platform, affirmed their unqualified support of

> An untrammelled and independent judiciary.... The Republican party reaffirms its intention to uphold at all times the authority and integrity of the courts, both state and federal, and it will ever insist that their powers to enforce their process and to protect life, liberty, and property shall be preserved inviolate.... We regard the recall of judges as unnecessary and unwise.

There was yet another difference: The Republicans in their platform—though most of them hated to do it—endorsed the Sherman law making all trusts criminal, pointed with pride to having originated the law in 1889, congratulated themselves —with some polemic license—upon having "consistently and successfully" enforced it. The Progressives presented the country with a new attitude, advocating, not dissolution by prosecution but rather fostering through regulation:

> We demand a strong national regulation of interstate corporations. We insist that [commercial power] shall be exercised openly, under public supervision and regulation of the most efficient sort which will preserve its good while eradicating and preventing its ill. To that end we urge the establishment of a strong federal administrative commission of high standing which shall maintain permanent active supervision over industrial corporations engaged in interstate commerce.

Those three tenets of Progressive doctrine, direct participation of all voters in the processes of government, a check by the people upon judicial interpretation of constitutions, and "constructive regulation of trusts instead of destructive litigation," would presumably have made progress had Roosevelt and the Progressives won the election of 1912. Yet it is by no means certain the public was strongly determined upon any or all; actually, during twenty years following, direct primaries made no progress but rather some recession, the recall of judicial decisions acquired no foothold whatever, and trusts in 1932 were treated the same as in 1912. And it is fairly certain that whatever change Roosevelt, had he been elected, might have made along any of these lines would have been unimportant compared to the consequences of his directing the country with respect to the Great War.

The War, lurking just ahead in the corridor of years, utterly unanticipated in 1912, gave a new tangent to everything, making it impossible to say and futile to guess what might have been the future of the Progressive movement in a normal world.

For Further Reading

The contest of 1912 may be most conveniently studied through biography. A good one to begin with is Arthur S. Link, *Wilson, Road to the White House* (1947). This is the first volume of what promises to be the standard life. For Taft, Henry F. Pringle, *The Life and Times of William Howard Taft* (1939), although uncritical, is still the best study. Pringle has also authored *Theodore Roosevelt: A Biography* (1931), an excellent, readable life which is, perhaps, overly critical. For a more favorable assessment of the Rough Rider, see John Morton Blum, *The Republican Roosevelt* (1954). There is as yet no adequate biography of LaFollette but some useful material can be found in Bela Case LaFollette and Fola LaFollette, *Robert M. LaFollette* (1953). Ray Ginger, *The Bending Cross: A Biography of Eugene Victor Debs* (1949), is first rate on the Socialist leader. Other important biographies include Claude G. Bowers, *Beveridge and the Progressive Era* (1932); John A. Garraty, *Henry Cabot Lodge* (1953); Alpheus T. Mason, *Brandeis* (1946); and Merlo J. Pusey, *Charles Evans Hughes* (1951).

Memoirs and autobiographies of the 1912 campaign include William Allen White, *The Autobiography of William Allen White* (1946); William Jennings Bryan, *A Tale of Two Conventions* (1912), in which "the Peerless Leader" compares the Democratic convention at Baltimore and the Republican convention at Chicago; Robert M. LaFollette, *LaFollette's Autobiography* (1913); William F. McCombs, *Making Woodrow Wilson President* (1921); and Henry L. Stoddard, *As I Knew Them* (1927).

For the conflicts of the Taft administration and the insurgent revolt, see Kenneth W. Hechler, *Insurgency: Personalities and Politics of the Taft Era* (1940); George Mowry, *Theodore Roosevelt and the Progressive Movement* (1946); Alpheus T. Mason, *Bureaucracy Convicts Itself: The Ballinger-Pinchot Controversy of 1910* (1941); and Ida Tarbell, *The Tariff in Our Time* (1911). Informal but very readable is William Manners, *TR and Will: The Friendship that Split the Republican Party* (1970).

Different trends in progressive political thought are illustrated by Theodore Roosevelt, *The New Nationalism* (1910); Woodrow Wilson, *The New Freedom* (1913); Herbert Croly, *The Promise of American Life* (1909); and Walter Lippmann, *Drift and Mastery* (1914).

Entry into World War I

Arthur S. Link

*I*n the late summer of 1935, shortly after Mussolini's Italy had declared war on Ethiopia, the United States Congress passed the Neutrality Act of 1935. The legislation warned Americans that they traveled at their own risk on the ships of belligerent nations, and gave the President the power to prevent the sale or transportation of munitions to belligerents once he had proclaimed the existence of a state of war. One editorial aptly referred to the statute as an act designed to keep the country out of the war of 1914. About the same time, Representative Louis Ludlow of Indiana proposed an amendment to the federal constitution stating that except in the event of invasion of the United States or its territorial possessions, the authority of Congress to declare war should not become effective until confirmed by a majority vote in a nationwide referendum.

The Neutrality Act and Ludlow Amendment reflected a then popular phobia against international involvement. The public opinion polls of the middle 1920's consistently showed a large majority who believed American participation in World War I had been a mistake. Most

Source: Arthur S. Link, *Wilson: Campaigns for Progressivism and Peace, 1916–1917* (5 vols.; Princeton: Princeton University Press, 1965), V, 372–377, 390–415. Copyright © 1965. Reprinted by permission of Princeton University Press.

respondents agreed with the conclusions of the Special Senate Committee to Investigate the Munitions Industry, the famous Nye Committee, to the effect that bankers and munition makers, "merchants of death," had made large profits by supplying the Allies in the neutrality years between 1914 and 1917. This close economic liaison —"ties that bind"—the Nye Committee contended, had been the chief cause of the entry of the United States into the war. This narrow, simplistic theory replaced in popular acceptance another single-cause theory of our intervention: barbarous submarine warfare waged by Germany. Accounts written during or immediately after the war had stressed the frightfulness of the "Huns" and their "inhuman engines of destruction." Universally pro-Wilson and interventionist, contemporary writers also immersed themselves in the rhetoric of the President's war message and developed the idea of "a war to end wars." United States participation had given direction to the world's progress and had assured the triumph of democracy over aristocracy. But the publication in the decade and a half after the war of a series of books that effectively challenged the view of German barbarity, even of Germany's responsibility for starting the war, together with a growing disillusionment with our former Allies, brought to an end interpretations of the war as a moral crusade. Nonetheless, advocates of the submarine thesis continued to insist on its validity. Charles Seymour, editor of the papers of Colonel Edward House and author of the first scholarly study of American foreign policy during World War I, categorically declared: "There is every evidence that the sole factor that could have driven Wilson from neutrality in the spring of 1917 was the resumption of the submarine campaign."

Equally critical of the submarine thesis and of the findings of the Nye Committee, which he accused of propagating "a devil theory of war," the best-known American historian of his day, Charles A. Beard, writing in 1936, professed himself to be a multi-causationist, and thought it impossible for the historian to accurately measure the degree of influence exerted by any one factor. Yet a careful analysis of his work contains, as Edward N. Saveth has observed, a kind of backstairs argument that places heavy stress upon the Wilson loan policy as bringing about involvement. His research ultimately led Beard into the camp of the revisionists, the term used to describe the growing group of historians who believed that the United States should not have intervened in 1917.

Revisionism reached flood tide in 1938 with the publication of Charles C. Tansill's *America Goes to War*, which emphasized the pro-Ally bias of President Wilson, who surrounded himself with advisers eager for war. Tansill charged the Wilson administration with overlooking Allied violations of American neutrality while holding the Germans to strict accountability. He relied on Nye Committee testimony to contend that business interests profiting from the war at least indirectly influenced the decision for war. Tansill's book received almost unanimous popular and critical acclaim. In retrospect much of the praise is probably attributable to the pervasive mood of disillusionment and isolationism of the times. For example, the eminent intellectual historian Henry Steele Commager described the book as "the most valuable contribution" to the history of intervention. In addition, it was a "warning and guidepost for the present" in tracing "the missteps which carried the United States along the road to war."

After World War II a new round of interpretation commenced. The distinguished diplomat and historian George F. Kennan, studying American diplomacy during the first half of the twentieth century, saw the United States as primarily concerned with remaining neutral after 1914, while maintaining neutral rights. As the war progressed, however, a situation involving national security developed as it became evident that an Allied defeat would be detrimental to American interests. Wilson erred in basing his case on morality and legalisms instead of emphasizing the dangers of a German victory. The President had been right in bringing the country into the war, Kennan claimed, but had given the wrong reasons. Before long this concept of intervention to maintain a beneficent balance of power appeared in the writings of most historians concerned with the question of intervention, including the scholar universally acknowledged as the preeminent authority on Wilson, Professor Arthur S. Link (b. 1920). In *Wilson the Diplomatist,* Link discussed "Wilson's apparent fear that the threat of a German victory imperiled the balance of power and all his hopes for the future reconstruction of the world," and his belief that "a German victory meant a peace of domination and conquest; it meant the end of all of Wilson's dreams of helping to build a secure future." But Link could find no evidence that Wilson thought a German victory would seriously endanger American security. In the following selection taken from the fifth volume of what surely will be the definitive biography of the twenty-eighth President, Link now concludes that Wilson did not in any sense accept belligerency because he thought the Allies in danger of losing the war and he dreaded a German triumph. He had become convinced that American interests, to say nothing of the interests of mankind, would best be served by a draw in Europe. In the following selection, Link presents an interpretation of intervention that is the product of years of study and research on the problem.

Wilson . . . following adjournment of the Sixty-fourth Congress, had given virtually all his thought to the problem of arming American merchantmen. There seemed to be no doubt that Congress and the vast majority of Americans wanted action. Even many of the antiwar leaders had said and were saying that armed neutrality was the proper response to the German submarine threat. More important, there was now no doubt whatsoever that armed neutrality offered the only hope of maintaining and defending American commerce on the high seas. The German Admiralty announced on March 2 that the period of grace for neutral ships in the Atlantic had expired, and that submarines would hereafter sink *all* ships, armed and unarmed, belligerent and neutral, without warning.

Wilson on March 5 asked Attorney General Gregory to examine the statutes, particularly the piracy statute of 1819, to determine whether there were legal impediments, and to report within twenty-four hours. The Attorney General replied, apparently orally, the following morning that he did not think that the piracy statute applied to the present situation. Wilson went to the State Department at 3:15 in the afternoon and discussed the legal issues with Lansing. The Secretary of State argued emphatically that the statute of 1819 did not limit the President's power in present circumstances. He asserted with equal forcefulness that the government should place armed guards on merchantmen so long as the German government menaced American lives by refusing to obey elementary international law. Wilson next visited Daniels in his office to inquire about plans to speed naval construction and ask him to prepare a memorandum on arming merchant ships.

Lansing came to the White House on the following morning, March 7, for an hour's conference presumably about armament for merchantmen. Doctor Grayson put the President to bed that afternoon with a heavy cold that he had caught standing in the wind on inaugural day. The memorandum from Daniels, explaining three policies that might be followed in armed neutrality, arrived on the following day, March 8, and Wilson had the head usher call the Secretary to the White House. He had decided to arm American ships, Wilson told Daniels, but he did not like certain features of the regulations that the Navy Department had proposed. Daniels returned to his office for further conferences. He sent a revised memorandum and a long letter to the White House on the following morning, March 9.

Daniels began his letter by reporting that Admiral William S. Benson, Chief of Naval Operations, had conferred with P. A. S. Franklin of the American Line and others in New York City on the preceding night. The important question, Daniels went on, was the best policy to follow in executing armed neutrality. His memorandum of March 8, the Secretary added, had outlined three possible policies as follows:

First, to reply to the German threat by permitting armed American merchantmen to shoot on sight at German submarines encountered anywhere, on the assumption that submarines would attack all American ships without warning.

Second, to permit armed American merchantmen to shoot on sight at German submarines only in the war zones, and to require armed American merchant ships to grant German submarines the right of visit and search in all other areas of the high seas.

Third, to require armed American merchantmen to submit to visit and search by German submarines everywhere, but to permit merchantmen to resist certain unlawful acts of submarines.

He was, Daniels continued, enclosing a new draft of the memorandum, recommending adoption of the second policy. It had the disadvantages, Daniels warned, of making the United States a party to transportation of contraband, which was an act of war, and of being difficult to enforce because merchant vessels would tend to use their armament outside proscribed zones. Germany, Daniels went on in his letter, might say that the United States was denying her the belligerent right to visit and search ships anywhere on the high seas. The American government could reply that Germany's notice of intention to sink all ships without warning in certain areas fully justified such action.

Admiral Benson, Daniels continued, strongly believed that the American government should forthwith notify Germany that it intended to arm its ships for protection on account of the German declaration of ruthless undersea warfare. Benson thought that it was barely possible that such warning might prevent execution of the German threat. "If we deny the right of visit," the Secretary went on, "Germany would declare that to be a warlike act, and that we were responsible for bringing on war. It is entirely probable that the next step would be war. If we must enter it to protect our rights and the lives of our people, I have felt we ought to do nothing to put the responsibility for this step upon our government." He had conferred last night, Daniels continued, with Rear Admiral Leigh C. Palmer of the Bureau of Navigation about crews to man the guns. Palmer had just written to make it clear that Germany would probably regard the presence of American armed forces on merchant ships as an act of war, that German submarines would probably attack American armed merchantmen without warning, and that armed merchantmen would necessarily fire at submarines on sight.

"The question arises, too," Daniels added, "whether it would not be wisest to state that you had reached the conclusion that you had a right to arm the ships and would do so, making no statement as to the time or the method. I cannot resist the feeling that this would be the best course and meet public approval. If Germany wants war, she will try to sink in any event. If she wishes to avert war with us, there would be time to modify her orders to Naval commanders so they would not commit the overt act. . . . The protection of our ships and their reaching ports in safety raises so many difficult questions, and the consequences are so grave, that I am trying to present them to you before the final order to arm is given, though, of course, they have been present in your mind during the whole controversy."

Wilson sent Daniels's letter and revised memorandum to Lansing for his comment in the late morning (of March 9), asking him to reply as quickly as possible since he, Wilson, wanted to issue orders that day. The Secretary of State replied that afternoon, saying emphatically that he preferred the second policy, but with addition of instructions permitting armed guards to resist illegal attack outside the war zones. A confidential message from Page arrived at the State Department at this very time. It read:

"For the President and the Secretary only. In reporting on the general feeling here I find that continued delay in sending out American ships, especially American liners, is producing an increasingly unfavorable impression. In spite of all explanations, which are imperfectly understood here, delay is taken to mean the submission of our Government to the German blockade. This is the view of the public and of most of the press. There is a tendency even in high government circles to regard the reasons for delay which are published here as technicalities which a national crisis should sweep aside. British opinion couples the delay of our ships with the sinking of the *Laconia* and the Z[immermann] telegram and seems to be reaching the conclusion that our Government will not be able to take positive action under any provocation. The feeling which the newspaper despatches from the United States produce on the British mind is that our Government is holding back our people until the blockade of our ships, the Z telegram, and the *Laconia* shall be forgotten and until the British Navy shall overcome the German submarines. There is danger that this feeling [will] harden into a conviction and interfere with any influence that we might otherwise have when peace comes.

"So friendly a man as Viscount Grey of Fallodon writes me privately from his retirement: 'I do not see how the United States can sit still while neutral shipping is swept off the sea. If no action is taken, it will be like a great blot in history or a failure that must grievously depress the future history of America.'"

The President probably saw this message soon after it arrived, but it is not likely that it had any decisive effect. Wilson had decided as early as February 16 to arm merchantmen as soon as it was apparent that the Germans meant what they said about attacking neutral ships without warning. He had waited for clear proof both of German intention and congressional and public opinion. There was no longer any doubt on either score. He also knew that armed neutrality carried heavy risks of war. Germany might well declare war if armed American merchantmen began shooting at submarines on sight, and it might be impossible to restrain congressional and public demands for a declaration of war if fighting on the seas went on very long. Wilson was surely aware of these hazards.

There simply did not seem to be any alternative but complete withdrawal and submission to the German threat. Wilson had earlier said that he would submit if that was necessary to avoid American belligerency and it was right to avoid war. Had the rising, overwhelming demand for armed neutrality caused his change of mind? Perhaps it had had its effect without Wilson's knowing it fully. The Zimmermann telegram and the sinking of the *Laconia* had also made their important contributions. Wilson had decided to go to armed neutrality *if the Germans committed overt acts against American shipping* before public opinion at home was aroused, the Zimmermann dispatch was disclosed, and the *Laconia* went to the bottom of the Irish Sea. But he had apparently made this decision without full realization of the risks of war that it involved. We can conclude, therefore, that these developments confirmed in Wilson's mind the necessity and wisdom of the decision for armed neutrality even though the Germans had not yet committed an overt act against American commerce and he now realized that armed neutrality would probably lead to hostilities and a declaration of war.

Wilson announced from his sick bed in the late afternoon of March 9 that he was instructing the navy to put guns and gun crews on liners and merchantmen. He also issued a proclamation calling Congress into special session on April 16 and a special statement to the country, as follows: "Secretary Tumulty stated in connection with the President's call for an extra session of Congress that the President is convinced that he has the power to arm American merchant ships and is free to exercise it at once. But so much necessary legislation is pressing for consideration that he is convinced that it is for the best interests of the country to have an early session of the Sixty-fifth Congress, whose support he will also need in all matters collateral to the defense of our merchant marine."

Work on orders to ship captains and gun crews went forward in the State and Navy Departments while senators in Washington and editors throughout the country were applauding the President's announcement. Daniels discussed the proposed regulations with Wilson on March 10 and Lansing on March 10, and the Secretary of the Navy sent a draft to the Secretary of State on the following day. Lansing must have gone over this paper with the President when he visited him in his bedroom between 9:45 and 10:25 on March 11. Lansing then prepared a memorandum to serve as a basis for revision of these orders and handed it to Daniels in the afternoon of March 12. The Secretary of State on the same day sent formal notices to foreign governments that the United States Government had decided to place armed guards on all American merchant vessels entering the war zones delimited in the German decree of January 31, 1917. Daniels issued the final orders on March 13. They permitted ship captains and naval officers commanding gun crews to shoot on sight at submarines if they came within torpedo range in the war zones. But the orders forbade American ships to pursue or search out submarines or to engage in any aggressive warfare against them anywhere. They also forbade offensive action against submarines outside the proscribed zones unless the U-boat was submerged or guilty of unlawful acts that jeopardized the safety of the ship.

Naval crews installed guns on the *Manchuria*, a cargo liner of the Atlantic Transport Line, on March 13, and work proceeded on other vessels immediately afterward. Wilson, still recovering from his cold, stayed in his private apartment on

March 13 and 14 and saw only intimate members of his family. One of the documents that he read most intently was a memorandum that Walter Lippmann had prepared after a conversation with Colonel House and left at the White House on March 12. It argued that the American government was resisting German assaults on American neutral rights mainly because it believed that the Reich was "fighting for a victory subversive of the world system in which America lives." The memorandum went on:

"The only victory in this war that could compensate mankind for its horrors is the victory of international order over national aggression. Whatever measures America takes will always be adapted to that end. It has no designs on Germany's life or her legitimate national development. It does not seek to humiliate the German people. It does not even propose to return upon them the grievous injuries inflicted by their government upon us.

"But it does propose to resist the aggression which is touching America. It will not commit itself to any aggression upon Germany or her allies. It will reserve freedom of action for itself, and whenever Germany is ready to abandon aggression and enter a league of nations, America will be ready to discuss the matter through open diplomacy."

Lippmann added in a covering letter that Herbert Croly and he believed that the Germans were making much impression in the United States with their plea that the American government was enforcing its rights against Germany and ignoring British infringements. The President, Lippmann went on, needed to educate Americans to the truth that the fundamental issue with Germany was not legal or commercial but one arising out of America's vital interest in a just and lasting peace. Wilson, by reviving his proposal for a league of nations, would capture liberal sentiment in Allied countries, encourage German radicals to force a statement of German terms, and warn American jingoes that American belligerency would remain subordinate to liberal policy and objectives.

Wilson did not comment or reply, probably because he saw at once that Lippmann was seeking to lead him to commitment to belligerency. Events soon afterward, on March 14, revealed that he was still far from ready to admit that war was inevitable. There was a report at noon that day from the American Consul in Plymouth, England, that a German submarine had sunk the American steamer *Algonquin* by shell fire without warning and without loss of life on March 12. It was the first case of unwarned sinking of an American ship since the German announcement of January 31, 1917. Nothing in the incident, said a report that could only have been inspired by the White House, changed the situation between the United States and Germany. The American government, this report added, had already done everything short of war to meet German assaults on American shipping. Wilson saw Ambassador Gerard—the first person outside the White House circle he had seen since March 12—on the following day, March 15. "He was in a most serious mood," Gerard afterward wrote. "He said that he had done everything to preserve peace and even yet he hoped that the Germans would abandon the ruthless submarine war."

Public opinion, even after the sinking of the *Algonquin*, was more quiescent than it had been at any time since the armed ship fight in Congress. Theodore Roosevelt's editorial spokesman, *The Outlook*, called for a declaration of war in its issue of March 14. The American Rights Committee was working to stimulate other such demands, and an overwhelming majority of the members of the New York Federation of Churches indicated in a poll completed on March 11 that they favored extreme measures for protection of American lives and commerce. The paucity of such expressions only emphasized that enthusiasm for full-fledged involvement had considerably diminished since the excitement engendered by the Zimmermann telegram, the sinking of the *Laconia*, and the armed ship fight.

"More than a month and a half has passed since we broke relations with Germany," Elihu Root lamented, "and we have done nothing but talk, and print interviews, and fill the papers with headlines, while we have carefully avoided doing one single thing to prepare to fight." Roosevelt agreed, writing: "I regard Wilson as far more blameworthy than the 'willful' Senators. I am as yet holding in; but if he does not go to war with Germany I shall skin him alive. To think of Hughes' folly, and the folly of those who nominated Hughes, having cursed the country with the really hideous misfortune of four years more of Wilson in this great and terrible world crisis!" And Page wrote in his diary about Wilson: "He shut himself up ... and engaged in what he called 'thought.' The air currents of the world never ventilated his mind.... He has not breathed a spirit into the people: he has encouraged them to supineness. He is *not* a leader, but rather a stubborn phrasemaker. His chief counsel is with—House, as timid a dependent-in-thought as one man ever found in another."

News of two momentous events came to Wilson in his seclusion on March 15 and 16. The first was a report from the Hotel Biltmore in New York City that the National Conference Committee of the Railways and the brotherhood chieftains, who had been discussing the demand of the brotherhoods that the railroads put the eight-hour day into effect forthwith, even before the Supreme Court ruled on the Adamson Act, had come to total impasse, and that railroad workers would begin a progressive strike at seven p.m. on March 17. Wilson, a White House correspondent said, was amazed at the news. "If a strike should start at this time," Tumulty warned the President on the following morning, "God only knows how it might spread."

The crisis brought the President from his sick room, prematurely, Grayson said, at noon on March 16. He held a brief Cabinet meeting at two-thirty. Then he dispatched a telegram to the Conference Committee and the brotherhood presidents, urging them to accept the mediation of a special committee of the Council of National Defense. "A general interruption of the railway traffic of the country at this time," he added, "would entail a danger to the nation against which I have the right to enter my most solemn and earnest protest. It is now the duty of every patriotic man to bring matters of this sort to immediate accommodation. The safety of the country against manifest perils affecting its own peace and the peace of the whole world makes accommodation absolutely imperative and seems to me to render any other choice or action inconceivable."

The brotherhood presidents responded by postponing the strike for forty-eight hours and warning that this was absolutely their last concession. "I am exceedingly glad," Wilson wrote in a telegram to the conferees in New York on March 17, "that the conferences have been reopened and that the prospect of a settlement looks brighter. I hope most earnestly for the sake of all concerned and most of all for the sake of the nation, that the two parties will continue to draw closer together and that a little further conference will lead to the result the whole country hopes for and expects." The mediators from the Council of National Defense—Secretary Lane, Secretary William B. Wilson, Samuel Gompers, and Daniel Willard, president of the Baltimore & Ohio Railroad—worked with both sides in the Hotel Biltmore all through March 18, but to no avail. Lane telephoned the discouraging news to the White House at about midnight, and Wilson responded with a dire warning that he was determined to prevent a strike at all costs. The railroad managers caved in thirty minutes later and authorized the mediators to grant whatever demands were necessary to prevent the walkout. The brotherhood presidents revoked the strike order a short time later.

Both sides signed an agreement early in the morning of March 19 giving brotherhood members ten hours' pay for eight hours' work and overtime pro rata, regardless of the

Supreme Court's verdict on the Adamson Act. Chief Justice White, speaking for a bare majority of the Court a few hours later, upheld the Adamson Act in sweeping language.

The second report on March 15, much amplified and clarified during the following two days, thrilled the President and country as much as news of the impending railroad strike frightened them. It was word from Petrograd, confirmed definitively on March 17, that a liberal group representing a majority in the Russian parliament had deposed the Czar, formed a provisional government, and promised to establish a new constitutional order and carry on the war for democratic aims. The liberation of the Russian people from Romanov despotism seemed also to herald the end of Prussian autocracy. Bethmann Hollweg, speaking as Minister President in the Prussian House of Lords on March 15, announced a "new orientation" in German political history—a movement after the war to democratize Prussian political institutions. "Woe to the statesman," he said with great emotion, "who does not recognize the signs of the times and who, after this catastrophe, the like of which the world has never seen, believes that he can take up his work at the same point at which it was interrupted."

It seemed incontrovertible that autocracy was doomed everywhere in Europe. "What the Russians have done," exclaimed the New York *World,* "the Germans and the Austrians and Hungarians can do if they will. They at last are masters of their own destiny so far as the character of their Government is concerned." Added the *New York Evening Post*: "Not since August 1, 1914, has anything come out of Europe to stir the pulse and fire imagination like the news from Russia." Americans who believed that the Allies on the whole represented the cause of European democracy were particularly heartened. As the New York *Nation* put it in the most incisive contemporary comment:

"With a single gesture the Russian people has won its own freedom and lifted a heavy burden from the shoulders of the Entente. The democratic nations of Western Europe have been emancipated from the handicap of Czarism and have won a new ally—democratic Russia. To the nations engaged in the defence of public law against the power of the mailed fist, and of the right of the little peoples against the ambitions of *Weltmacht,* it has been from the beginning a pain and a drag that their necessary partner should be the Russia of Polish oppression and Kishineff massacres, the Russia of corrupt and stupid bureaucrats, of witch-doctors and bribe-takers and Black Hundreds. . . . The revolution at Petrograd has enormously enriched the issues for which the Allies are contending, to such an extent as almost to make one forget the original objects of the war. . . . The preservation and extension of the liberties so rapidly won in Russia are now inextricably bound up with the success of the Allies. A German victory now would mean the collapse of free Russia."

Wilson left no evidence of his first reactions. It seems reasonable to assume that he shared the general American enthusiasm for what seemed to be a momentous triumph for human liberty, and, more important, that he interpreted the Russian Revolution and German reactions as further evidence that the war was entering its final apocalyptic stage of death grapple between despotism and democracy. It must be said with some emphasis that there is no evidence that events in Petrograd had any direct influence on his later decision for war with Germany. The most that can be said is that the Russian Revolution might possibly have facilitated his final decision.

Lansing sent to the President on March 16 a long telegram from Samuel N. Harper, the leading American authority on Russia, saying that Harper was convinced that the liberal element was in control and Russia would henceforth be better able to prosecute her war effort. Colonel House urged the President on March 17 to recognize the new Russian government, adding, "I am not too sure that the present outcome in Russia is not due largely to your influence."

Wilson needed no prodding. He had decided to recognize the provisional Russian government, he told the French Ambassador on about March 19, in order to encourage the effort of this great democracy. Everyone could see that the men now in power in Petrograd were honorable; and the fact that the new government's position was precarious was all the more reason for giving it diplomatic support. The old order of things, Wilson added, has no chance of being reestablished. Therefore, let us recognize the new immediately. Lansing sent instructions to Ambassador David R. Francis in Petrograd on March 20; he granted formal recognition to Foreign Minister Paul Milyukov at eleven a.m. on March 22.

Washington was rocked on Sunday, March 18, by news that German submarines had just destroyed three American ships—*City of Memphis,* sunk with no casualties off the Irish coast on March 17 after warning and evacuation of crew; *Illinois,* sent to the bottom by gunfire without warning off Alderney on March 18, one member of the crew being wounded; and *Vigilancia,* torpedoed without warning west of Bishop on March 16, with fifteen members of the crew being drowned while launching the lifeboats.

The President and Mrs. Wilson stayed in their private quarters all morning and then had lunch with Wilson's cousin, James Woodrow. Wilson received the Attorney General at 2:15 for a brief conference and then went motoring with Mrs. Wilson for the balance of the afternoon. Excitement, stimulated by newspaper reports and editorials and a statement by Theodore Roosevelt demanding an immediate declaration of war, was spreading over the country by the time that Lansing, responding to the President's summons, went to the White House at a little after eleven o'clock on Monday morning, March 19. "For an hour," Lansing noted in his diary, "the President and I sat in his study and debated the course of action which should be followed. The President said that he did not see that we could do more than we were doing in the way of protecting our vessels as already three of the American Line steamships had sailed for Europe with armed guards, each carrying four guns and forty men. I argued that war was inevitable, that I had felt so for months, and that the sooner we openly admitted the fact so much stronger our position would be with our own people and before the world. I left the President without a definite impression as to what his decision would be."

"I have just returned from a conference with the President," Lansing wrote to Colonel House as soon as he returned to his office. "He is disposed not to summon Congress as a result of the sinking of these vessels. He feels that all he could ask would be powers to do what he is already doing. I suggested that he might call them to consider declaring war, and urged the present was the psychological moment in view of the Russian revolution and the anti-Prussian spirit in Germany, and that to throw our moral influence in the scale at this time would aid the Russian liberals and might even cause revolution in Germany. He indicated to me the fear he had of the queries and investigations of a Congress which could not be depended upon because of the out-and-out pacifists and the other group of men like Senator Stone. If you agree with me that we should act now, will you not please put your shoulder to the wheel?" Lansing also talked to Polk, and he called House twice to urge him to come to Washington and stir the President from his inertia.

Wilson was going through considerably greater agony of spirit than he revealed to his Secretary of State. The only alternative to armed neutrality was war, and he was not yet prepared to drink that cup. He had lunch alone with Mrs. Wilson and then walked over to the Navy Department to talk to Secretary Daniels. "Wished everything possible done in addition to Armed Guards to protect American shipping, hoping this would meet the ends we have in view," Daniels wrote in his diary. "He had been urged to call Congress and to declare war. He still hoped to avoid it and wished no cost & no effort spared to protect shipping." He returned to the

White House and received Frank Cobb, editor of the New York *World*, at three-thirty. Cobb's recollection of their conversation follows in part:

"He said he couldn't see any alternative, that he had tried every way he knew to avoid war. 'I think I know what war means,' he said, and he added that if there were any possibility of avoiding war he wanted to try it. 'What else can I do?' he asked. 'Is there anything else I can do?'

"I told him his hand had been forced by Germany, that so far as I could see we couldn't keep out.

" 'Yes,' he said, 'but do you know what that means?' He said that war would overturn the world we had known; that so long as we remained out there was a preponderance of neutrality, but that if we joined with the Allies the world would be off the peace basis and onto a war basis.

"It would mean that we should lose our heads along with the rest and stop weighing right and wrong. It would mean that a majority of people in this hemisphere would go war-mad, quit thinking and devote their energies to destruction. The President said a declaration of war would mean that Germany would be beaten and so badly beaten that there would be a dictated peace, a victorious peace.

" 'It means,' he said, 'an attempt to reconstruct a peace-time civilization with war standards, and at the end of the war there will be no bystanders with sufficient power to influence the terms. There won't be any peace standards left to work with. There will be only war standards.'

"The President said that such a basis was what the Allies thought they wanted, and that they would have their way in the very thing America had hoped against and struggled against. . . . He had the whole panorama in his mind. He went on to say that so far as he knew he had considered every loophole of escape and as fast as they were discovered Germany deliberately blocked them with some new outrage.

"Then he began to talk about the consequences to the

United States. He had no illusions about the fashion in which we were likely to fight the war.

"He said that when a war got going it was just war and there weren't two kinds of it. It required illiberalism at home to reinforce the men at the front. We couldn't fight Germany and maintain the ideals of Government that all thinking men shared. He said we would try it but it would be too much for us.

" 'Once lead this people into war,' he said, 'and they'll forget there ever was such a thing as tolerance. To fight you must be brutal and ruthless, and the spirit of ruthless brutality will enter into the very fibre of our national life, infecting Congress, the courts, the policeman on the beat, the man in the street.' Conformity would be the only virtue, said the President, and every man who refused to conform would have to pay the penalty.

"He thought the Constitution would not survive it; that free speech and the right of assembly would go. He said a nation couldn't put its strength into a war and keep its head level; it had never been done.

" 'If there is any alternative, for God's sake, let's take it,' he exclaimed. Well I couldn't see any, and I told him so."

Representative William C. Adamson, who talked with Wilson several times during this period, later testified that these were indeed some of Wilson's fundamental concerns. As Adamson remembered these conversations:

"He stressed elaborately and most earnestly his aversion to being drawn into the war, urging many reasons therefor. . . . Time and again he told the writer that in addition to the disorganization of business and expenditure of treasure and the possible loss of life in the field, he dreaded the general disorganization consequent upon war and conditions inevitably connected therewith and produced thereby. He said that a state of war suspended the law, and legal and moral restraints being relaxed, there not only ensues an era of recklessness and crime, but also the disregard of commercial integrity and a saturnalia of exploitation, profiteering and robbery. Men who in time of peace deport themselves decently, in times of war regard it as no robbery to extort anything obtainable from fellow citizens, friend or foe. Industry would be so demoralized, profiteering run rampant, robbery would become the order of the hour and prices would soar so high that even after peace should be restored, it would require a generation to restore normal conditions."

Cobb left in the late afternoon, and Wilson had dinner with Mrs. Wilson and members of the Bolling family and saw no other persons during the evening. Lansing went to the Japanese Embassy for dinner and returned home at eleven o'clock. Between eleven and one in the morning he put down in a letter to the President all the conclusions that had taken form in his mind since their conversation of the preceding morning. He now agreed, Lansing began, that the sinking of the three ships was no good reason for a declaration of war. But war would come soon, just as soon as there was fighting between an armed American merchantman and a German submarine. The advantage of waiting to recognize that a state of war existed would seem to be that Germany might herself declare war after an encounter on the high seas. Still, Lansing went on, he was convinced that the German government would not declare war in any circumstances. It would prefer to profit from the submarine blockade without adding the United States to its enemies.

If war *was* inevitable, Lansing went on, then there were certainly many reasons for immediate American participation. It would greatly encourage the new Russian government and put heart into the democratic element in Germany. It would give great moral support to the Allies, already encouraged by recent military successes, and tend to shorten the conflict. It would gratify the American people, who were bitterly critical of the administration's failure to act. Finally, America's future influence in world affairs would be greatly enhanced by action in favor of democracy and against absolutism. "This would be first shown in the peace negotiations and in the general readjustment of international relations. It is my belief that the longer we delay in declaring against the military absolutism which menaces the rule of liberty and justice in the world, so much the less will be our influence in the days when Germany will need a merciful and unselfish foe."

"I have written my views with great frankness," Lansing concluded, "as I am sure you would wish me to do, and I trust that you will understand my views are in no way influenced by any bitterness of feeling toward Germany or by any conscious emotion awakened by recent events. I have tried to view the situation coldly, dispassionately and justly."

Lansing's lofty sentiments were no doubt genuine. None the less, he had not been entirely artless in making the case for a war declaration on the only grounds that Wilson could approve.

Wilson played golf with Grayson from nine until ten forty-five on the following morning, March 20. He then went to his office where he found, among other things, Lansing's letter. We may be sure that he read it carefully. He had lunch with Mrs. Wilson and then went to the Cabinet meeting. The following memorandum from the Lansing diary tells the story in a moving narrative:

> The Cabinet Meeting of today I consider the most momentous and, therefore, the most historic of any of those which have been held since I became Secretary of State, since it involved, unless a miracle occurs, the question of war with Germany....
>
> [Here Lansing describes events of Sunday, March 18, to Tuesday, March 20, and recounts his conversation with Wilson on the morning of March 19.]
>
> From Sunday noon until Tuesday noon there was intense public excitement. Many of the newspapers clamored for war and inveighed bitterly at the President's failure to act. There was a general feeling that, if war did not come at once, it

would come shortly, and that there was no valid reason for waiting for another outrage. I myself shared this feeling and was prepared to urge immediate action at the meeting of the Cabinet.

The corridors of the State Department and the Executive Office swarmed with press correspondents seeking to get some inkling of what would be done from passing officials. It was through these eager crowds of news-gatherers that I forced my way at half past two Tuesday afternoon under a bombardment of questions, to which I made no reply, and entered the Cabinet room where all the other members had arrived.

Three minutes later the President came in and passed to his place at the head of the table shaking hands with each member and smiling as genially and composedly as if nothing of importance was to be considered. Composure is a marked characteristic of the President. Nothing ruffles the calmness of his manner or address. It has a sobering effect on all who sit with him in council. Excitement would seem very much out of place at the Cabinet table with Woodrow Wilson presiding.

After felicitating Secretaries Lane and Wilson on the success of their efforts at mediation between the railroad managers and the "Four Brotherhoods," the President said that he desired advice from the Cabinet on our relations with Germany and the course which should be pursued. He began with a review of his actions up to the present time pointing out that he had said to Congress on February 3rd that, while the announced policy had compelled the severance of diplomatic relations, he could not bring himself to believe that the German Government would carry it out against American vessels, but that, if an "overt act" occurred, he would come before them again and ask means to protect Americans on the high seas even though he thought he possessed the constitutional power to act without Congress. He said that the situation compelled him to do this on February 23rd and Congress had desired to adopt the measures which he sought, but had been prevented, and that he had then acted on his own authority and placed armed guards on American vessels intending to proceed to the German barred zone.

He went on to say that he did not see from a practical

point of view what else could be done to safeguard American vessels more than had already been done unless we declared war or declared that a state of war existed, which was the same thing; and that the power to do this lay with Congress.

He said that the two questions as to which he wished to be advised were—

Should he summon Congress to meet at an earlier date than April 16th, for which he had already issued a call?

Second. What should he lay before Congress when it did assemble?

He then spoke in general terms of the political situations in the belligerent countries, particularly in Russia where the revolution against the autocracy had been successful, and in Germany where the liberal element in the Prusssian Diet was grumbling loudly against their rulers. He also spoke of the situation in this country, of the indignation and bitterness in the East and the apparent apathy of the Middle West.

After the President had finished McAdoo was the first to speak. He said that war seemed to him a certainty and he could see no reason for delay in saying so and acting accordingly; that we might just as well face the issue and come out squarely in opposition to Germany, whose Government represented every evil in history; that, if we did not do so at once, the American people would compel action and we would be in the position of being pushed forward instead of leading, which would be humiliating and unwise. He further said that he believed that we could best aid the Allies against Germany by standing back of their credit, by underwriting their loans, and that they were sorely in need of such aid. He felt, however, that we could do little else, and doubted whether we could furnish men.

McAdoo spoke with great positiveness in advocating an immediate call of Congress. His voice was low and his utterance deliberate, but he gave the impression of great earnestness.

Houston, who followed, said that he agreed with McAdoo that it would create a most unfortunate, if not disasterous [sic], impression on the American public as well as in Europe if we waited any longer to take a firm stand now that Germany had shown her hand. He said that he doubted whether we should plan to do more than to use our navy and to give financial aid to the Allies; that to equip an army of any size would divert the production of our industrial plants and so cut off from the Allies much needed supplies; and he thought that we ought to be very careful about interfering with their efficiency. He concluded by urging the President to summon Congress at once because he felt that a state of war already existed and should be declared.

Redfield followed Houston with his usual certainty of manner and vigor of expression. He was for declaring war and doing everything possible to aid in bringing the Kaiser to his knees. He made no points which particularly impressed me; and, as he had so often shown his strong pro-ally sentiments, I was sure his words made little impression upon the President.

Baker was the next to express an opinion and he did so with the wonderful clearness of diction of which he is master. He said that he considered the state of affairs called for drastic action with as little delay as possible, and that he believed Congress should meet before April 16th. He said that the recent German outrages showed that the Germans did not intend to modify in the least degree their policy of inhumanity and lawlessness, and that such act could mean only one thing, and that was war.

Since we were now forced into the struggle he favored entering into it with all our vigor. He advocated preparing an army at once to be sent to Europe in case the Allies became straightened [sic] in the number of their men. He said that he believed the very knowledge of our preparations would force the Central Powers to realize that their cause was hopeless. He went on to discuss the details of raising, equipping and training a large force.

I followed Baker and can very naturally remember what I said better and more fully than I can the remarks of others.

I began with the statement that in my opinion an actual state of war existed today between this country and Germany, but that, as the acknowledgement of such a state officially amounted to a declaration of war, I doubted the wisdom as well as the constitutional power of the President to announce such fact or to act upon it; that I thought that the facts should be laid before Congress and that they should be asked to declare the existence of a state of war and to enact the laws necessary to meet the exigencies of the case. I pointed out that many things could be done under our present statutes which seriously menaced our national safety and that the Executive was powerless to prevent their being done. I referred in some detail to the exodus of Germans from this country to Mexico and Cuba since we severed diplomatic relations, to the activities of German agents here, to the transference of funds by Germans to Latin American countries, to the uncensored use of the telegraph and the mails, etc.

For the foregoing reasons I said that I felt that there should be no delay in calling Congress together and securing these necessary powers.

In addition to these reasons which so vitally affected our domestic situation I said that the revolution in Russia, which appeared to be successful, had removed the one objection to affirming that the European war was a war between Democracy and Absolutism; that the only hope of a permanent peace between all nations depended upon the establishment of democratic institutions throughout the world; that no League of Peace would be of value if a powerful autocracy was a member, and that no League of Peace would be necessary if all nations were democratic; and that in going into the war at this time we could do more to advance the cause of Democracy than if we failed to show sympathy with the democratic powers in their struggle against the autocratic government of Germany.

I said that the present time seemed to me especially propitious for action by us because it would have a great moral influence in Russia, because it would encourage the democratic movement in Germany, because it would put new spirit in the Allies already flushed with recent military successes, and because it would put an end to the charges of vacillation and hesitation, which were becoming general, and bring the people solidly behind the President.

"The time for delay and inaction," I said, "has passed. Only a definite, vigorous and uncompromising policy will satisfy or ought to satisfy the American people. Of this I am convinced. We are at war now. Why not say so without faltering? Silence will be interpreted abroad as weakness, at home as indecision. I believe that the people long for a strong and sure leadership. They are ready to go through to the very end. If we enter this war, and there is not the slightest doubt but that we will enter[,] if not today then tomorrow, the Government will lose ground which it can never regain by acting as if it was uncertain of its duty or afraid to perform that duty, a duty which seems to me very plain."

I said a good deal more in the same vein and urged the propriety of taking the advantage of the aroused sentiment of the people since it would have a tremendous influence in keeping Congress in line. I said that I would not permit my judgment to be swayed by this sentiment but that as a matter of expediency in affecting congressional action it ought to be used. I must have spoken with vehemence because the President asked me to lower my voice so that no one in the corridor could hear.

The President said that he did not see how he could speak of a war for Democracy or of Russia's revolution in addressing Congress. I replied that I did not perceive any objection but in any event I was sure that he could do so indirectly by attacking the character of the autocratic government of Germany as manifested by its deeds of inhumanity, by its broken promises, and by its plots and conspiracies against this country.

To this the President only answered "Possibly."

[Another Cabinet member wrote in his diary: "The President said that the principal things which had occurred since he had last addressed Congress which differed, except in degree, from what had been discussed, were the Russian Revolution, the talk of more liberal institutions in Germany, and the continued reluctance of our ships to sail. If our entering the war would hasten and fix the movements in Russia and Germany, it would be a marked gain to the world and would tend to give additional justification for the whole struggle, but he could not assign these things as reasons for calling Congress at an earlier date. The justification would have to rest on the conduct of Germany, the clear need of protecting our rights, of getting ready, and of safeguarding civilization against the domination of Prussian militarism."]

Whether the President was impressed with the idea of a general indictment of the German Government I do not know. I felt strongly that to go to war solely because American ships had been sunk and Americans killed would cause debate, and that the sounder basis was the duty of this and every other democratic nation to suppress an autocratic government like the German because of its atrocious character and because it was a menace to the national safety of this country and of all other countries with liberal systems of government. Such an arraignment would appeal to every liberty-loving man the world over. This I said during the discussion, but just when I do not remember.

When I had finished, Secretary Wilson in his usual slow but emphatic way said: "Mr. President, I think we must recognize the fact that Germany has made war upon this country and, therefore, I am for calling Congress together as soon as possible. I have reached this conviction with very great reluctance, but having reached it I feel that we should enter the war with the determination to employ all our resources to put an end to Prussian rule over Germany which menaces human liberty and peace all over the world. I do not believe we should employ half-measures or do it half-heartedly."

In view of the fact that Wilson had on previous occasions shown a disposition to temporize with the German Government and had opposed war because of submarine attacks, I was surprised at his frank assertion in favor of radical measures. There is this to be said of Secretary Wilson, he never speaks at hap-hazard; he is slow to express an opinion but very firm in it when it is once declared. When I have disagreed with him I have always had to acknowledge the soundness of his reasoning unless the subject was Labor, as to that he is biased. I consider him a valuable adviser because he is equipped with an abundance of common sense.

Gregory, who had been listening with much attention although on account of his deafness I am sure only heard his neighbors at the table, gave it as his opinion that it was useless to delay longer, that the possibility of peace with Germany was a thing of the past, and that he was in favor of assembling Congress as soon as possible, of enacting all necessary legislation, and of pursuing as aggressive action toward Germany as we were able. He went on to speak of German intrigues here, of the departure of German reservists and of the helplessness of his Department under existing laws. He said that every day's delay increased the danger and Congress ought to be called on to act at once.

After Gregory had given his views the President said, "We have not yet heard from Burleson and Daniels."

Burleson spoke up immediately and said: "Mr. President, I am in favor of calling Congress together and declaring war; and when we do that I want it to be understood that we are in the war to the end, that we will do everything we can to aid the Allies and weaken Germany with money, munitions, ships and men, so that those Prussians will realize that, when they made war on this country, they woke up a giant which will surely defeat them. I would authorize the issue of five billions in bonds and go the limit." He stopped a moment and then added, "There are many personal reasons why I regret this step, but there is no other way. It must be carried through to the bitter end."

The President then turned his head towards Daniels who sat opposite Burleson and said: "Well, Daniels?" Daniels hesitated a moment as if weighing his words and then spoke in a voice which was low and trembled with emotion. His eyes were suffused with tears. He said that he saw no other course than to enter the war, that do what we would it seemed bound to come, and that, therefore, he was in favor of summoning Congress as soon as possible and getting their support for active measures against Germany.

Burleson had at previous meetings resisted an aggressive policy toward Germany, and he had, as late as the Cabinet meeting on Friday, the 16th, advocated very earnestly taking a radical stand against Great Britain on account of detention of the mails. Whenever I had called attention to the illegal acts of Germany he would speak of British wrong-doings. I felt sure that he did this to cause a diversion of attention from the German violations of law. Possibly I misjudged him, and there was no such motive. His words at this meeting indicated hostility to Germany and a desire for drastic action, so I may have been mistaken.

As for Daniels his pacifist tendencies and personal devotion to Mr. Bryan and his ideas were well known. It was, therefore, a surprise to us all when he announced himself to be in favor of war. I could not but wonder whether he spoke from conviction or because he lacked strength of mind to stand out against the united opinion of his colleagues. I prefer to believe the former reason, though I am not sure.

The President said, as Daniels ceased speaking: "Everybody has spoken but you, Lane."

Lane answered that he had nothing to add to what had been said by the other members of the Cabinet, with whom he entirely agreed as to the necessity of summoning Congress, declaring war and obtaining powers. He reviewed some of the things which had been said but contributed no new thought. He emphasized particularly the intensity of public indignation against the Germans and said that he felt that the people would force us to act even if we were unwilling to do so.

Knowing the President's mental attitude as to the idea of being forced to do *anything* by popular opinion, these remarks of Lane seemed to me unwise and dangerous to the policy which he advocated. I could almost feel the President stiffen as to resist and see his powerful jaw set as Lane spoke. Fortunately before the President had time to comment Lane kept on in his cool and placid way drifting into another phase of the subject which was more to the President's taste since it appealed to his conception that he must be guided by the principle of right and by his duty to this country and to all mankind. Thus what might have been a dangerous incident was avoided.

The foregoing is a brief outline of the debate which occupied over two hours and which frequently was diverted into other channels such as the effectiveness of armed guards on merchant ships, the use of patrol boats, German plots in Latin America, the danger of riots and vandalism in this country, the moving of interned vessels, the need of censors, etc., etc.

When at last every Cabinet officer had spoken and all had

expressed the opinion that war was inevitable and that Congress ought to be called in extraordinary session as soon as possible, the President [said] in his cool, unemotional way: "Well, gentlemen, I think that there is no doubt as to what your advice is. I thank you." . . .

Thus ended a Cabinet meeting the influence of which may change the course of history and determine the destinies of the United States and possibly of the world. The possible results are almost inconceivably great. I am sure that every member of the Cabinet felt the vital importance of the occasion and spoke with a full realization of the grave responsibility which rested upon him as he advised the President to adopt a course which if followed can only mean open and vigorous war against the Kaiser and his Government. The solemnity of the occasion as one after another spoke was increasingly impressive and showed in every man's face as he rose from the council table and prepared to leave the room. Lane, Houston and Redfield, however, did not hide their gratification, and I believe we all felt a deep sense of relief that not a dissenting voice had been raised to break the unanimity of opinion that there should be no further parley or delay. The ten councillors of the President had spoken as one, and he—well, no one could be sure that he would echo the same opinion and act accordingly.

Wilson asked Lansing and Burleson, after the other Cabinet members had left, how long it would take to prepare the necessary legislation for submission to Congress in the event that a state of war was declared. They agreed that more than a week would be required, and that it would not be wise to call Congress to meet before April 2. Wilson issued the call on March 21, requesting Congress to meet in special session on April 2 "to receive a communication concerning grave matters of national policy."

This meant, as the Washington correspondents noted at the time, that Wilson made the decision for war either during or immediately following the Cabinet meeting of March 20. It was apparently a firm decision, even though he disclosed it to no one for a week. White House correspondents reported on March 22 that the President was assembling materials for his war message on that date. He asked Daniels after the Cabinet meeting on March 20 to discuss the submarine menace with the General Board. And when Daniels reported that the General Board had said that there was no effective defense against submarines, Wilson instructed the Secretary to establish confidential liaison immediately, "until the Congress has acted," with the British Admiralty and work out some plan of cooperation. "As yet," he added, "sufficient attention has not been given, it seems to me, by the authorities on the other side of the water to the routes to be followed or to plans by which the safest possible approach may be made to the British ports. As few ports as possible should be used, for one thing, and every possible precaution thought out. Can we not set this afoot at once and save all the time possible?" Daniels, on March 26, instructed Rear Admiral William S. Sims, soon to be appointed commander of American naval operations in European waters, to come to Washington, preparatory to going to London to establish liaison with British naval authorities.

Other actions left no doubt about Wilson's intentions. He called the Council of National Defense to meet on March 23; ordered Brand Whitlock, Minister to Belgium, and American members of the Belgian Relief Commission on March 24 to withdraw from Belgian territory; increased the enlisted strength of the Navy and Marine Corps and mobilized certain units of National Guard on March 25 and 26; and suspended the mustering out of National Guard units still on the Mexican border on March 27. The Cabinet discussed these and more far-reaching plans on March 23 and 27. Baker, consequently, submitted a new army bill on March 29. It increased the Regular Army to war strength, called the entire National Guard into federal service, and authorized the raising of a "first unit," 500,000 men strong, of a new national army "exclusively by selective draft." The idea of laying down terms to the Allies for American participation never seemed to have occurred to Wilson at this time.

The abundant evidence of Wilson's reactions and thought does not leave much doubt, as we have already seen, why he decided to break relations with Germany and adopt a policy of armed neutrality. The only troubling question at this later point is why he decided to abandon armed neutrality without really giving it a try and accept the decision for full-fledged belligerency that his Cabinet advisers pressed upon him on March 20. The evidence on this crucial point is neither definitive nor absolutely revealing.

We can be more confident of our ground in saying why he did not make the fateful decision. For one thing, he did not accept belligerency because he thought that the Allies were in danger of losing the war and a German victory would imperil American national interests. We now know that the Allies were in desperate straits if not in danger of defeat. The French had begun to draw upon their last manpower and were already in the midst of what they called their "crisis of reserves." The submarine campaign was succeeding, actually beyond the expectations of the German Admiralty. Nearly 600,000 tons of Allied and neutral shipping were sunk during March, and the toll would reach the staggering figure of nearly 900,000 tons in April. The British and French faced an exchange problem that seemed insoluble.

But Wilson and his advisers knew virtually none of these facts. The French guarded the secret of their "crisis of reserves" so carefully that the American Embassy in Paris did not discover it until about March 23, and officials in Washington did not learn the frightening news until after the United States was in the war. There had been some recent Allied successes on the western front, and American leaders thought, as the Cabinet discussions of March 20 revealed, that they heralded a great Allied offensive in the spring, as, indeed, they did. Few persons in America (or Europe, either, for that matter) thought that the Russian Revolution would soon lead to Russian withdrawal from the war. On the contrary, virtually everyone assumed that the new Russian government would wage war more efficiently and enthusiastically than the old, as, indeed, it tried to do. American officials could have been only vaguely aware of the staggering effect of the submarine campaign on the British economy. Wilson and other leaders in Washington did know, as we have seen, something about the dimensions of the exchange crisis, but no one thought that a solution depended upon American belligerency.

All the evidence of Wilson's thinking since the summer of 1916 about long-range American national interests in the outcome in Europe leads to the conclusion that he believed that American interests, to say nothing of the interests of mankind, would be best served by a draw in Europe. He not only thought that a peace without victory offered the best hope for the right reconstruction of the world order, but he also now feared destruction of German power and an absolute Anglo-French-Russian military hegemony in Europe.

We can say with some assurance, in the second place, that Wilson did not accept the decision for war because he thought that the Allies were fighting altogether for worthy objectives and the Germans altogether for unworthy ones. There is no need to review the evidence in this volume and the preceding two on Wilson's thinking about the issues of the European war. It must suffice to say that his views had become increasingly sophisticated and detached once the shock of the war's outbreak wore off in the autumn of 1914. He certainly had no illusions about Allied objectives by the end of 1916; if anything, he tended to give the British less credit for idealism and generous motives than they deserved. His suspicion accounts in large part for his decision, once the United States had entered the war, not to join the Allies in any political commitments but to maintain a free hand to conclude peace once American objectives were attained.

It is equally clear that Wilson was not pushed into war by an aroused public opinion. There was an authentic demand for a declaration of war, reflected largely in the big-city newspapers and the Senate, from the moment that the Zimmermann telegram was published. It grew louder after news on March 18 of the sinking of the three American ships. But it was still far from being obviously a great, overwhelming, and irresistible national demand when Wilson made his own decision for belligerency on March 20 or 21. One is entitled to doubt that Wilson in any event would have chosen belligerency only because public opinion demanded it.

It is almost abundantly clear that Wilson simply concluded that there was no alternative to full-fledged belligerency. The United States was a great power. It could not submit to Germany's flagrant—so it seemed to Wilson and his contemporaries—assault on American sovereignty without yielding its honor and destroying its influence for constructive work in the world. Wilson's first response was of course armed neutrality. But he soon concluded that armed neutrality was neither a feasible nor a sufficient response. He fortunately explained, at least partially, why he came to this conclusion in an exchange of letters before he went to Congress on April 2. John P. Gavit of the *New York Evening Post*, Senator Joseph I. France of Maryland, Matthew Hale, and Senator Hitchcock wrote between March 25 and March 29 urging Wilson to stand firm in armed neutrality and saying, further, that this was the most sensible way to protect maritime rights and the great majority of Americans did not want full-fledged participation. Wilson replied most explicitly to Hale, as follows:

"I value your letter of March twenty-eighth and find that it has stirred many sympathetic thoughts in me.

"I would be inclined to adopt the third course you mention [continuance of armed neutrality, at least until Germany declared war], indeed, as you know, I had already adopted it, but this is the difficulty: To defend our rights upon the seas, we must fight submarines. From the point of view of international law, they are when used as Germany has used them against merchantmen in effect outlaws to begin with. Merchantmen cannot defend themselves against them in the way which international law has regarded as consistent with neutrality. They must be attacked on sight and to attack them is practically to commit an act of war if they are attacked before showing an intention themselves to attack. Germany has intimated that she would regard the only sort of warfare that is possible against her submarines as an act of war and would treat any person who fell into her hands from the ships that attacked her submarines as beyond the pale of law. Apparently, to make even the measures of defense legitimate we must obtain the status of belligerents, and if we do that, we have taken the second of the three courses that you mention."

Wilson was not altogether using a technicality to mask a deeper motive. The problem he described was a serious one, giving the assumption that well-defined international law should govern the relations of nations. Naval advisers, as we have seen, had already warned that, legally speaking, armed neutrality was war in the circumstances created by use of submarines as commerce destroyers. Therefore, war between the United States and Germany would most probably ensue. Once he accepted this conclusion, Wilson must have been very greatly moved by the argument of some Cabinet members that it would be difficult to fight even a limited war on the seas unless the government enjoyed the advantages and privileges that accompanied formal belligerency.

Even so, Wilson knew, as Lansing had been frank enough to say in his letter of March 19, that there was a good chance that Germany would prefer American armed neutrality to belligerency and refrain both from declaring war in the event of hostilities between an armed ship and a submarine and mistreating American seamen if a submarine captured any after such an engagement. We now have good evidence that

Wilson thought that the "piracy talk" was absurd, that is, that it was nonsense to believe that the Germans would deal with the captured crews of armed American merchantmen as if they were pirates. Wilson, in any event, did not wait and see what the Germans would do. Thus it has to be said that to some degree he chose war, even though the issue had obviously been forced upon him.

He chose war over a risky and ambiguous armed neutrality in part, certainly, because he had lost all confidence in the Imperial German Government on account of its assault upon American shipping and the Zimmermann telegram. He was not indiscriminate in his indictment, but events had convinced him that militarists and extreme nationalists were now in the saddle in Berlin, and that he simply could not do business with them or hope for any lasting peace so long as they were in control of German policy. It is also difficult to see how Wilson could have failed to be impressed by the fact that his Cabinet advisers, to say nothing of many others in the second rank of officialdom, were now united in the belief that circumstances left no alternative to belligerency. Wilson would almost surely have stood his ground, as he did in the later struggle over ratification of the Versailles Treaty, if duty had spoken unmistakably. But duty did not speak so clearly in 1917. Wilson said over and over that he was struggling for right policy and unsure of his ground. In such a situation the united advice of counselors must have weighed heavily in his thinking.

It is this writer's opinion that the most important reason for Wilson's decision was his conviction that American belligerency now offered the surest hope for early peace and the reconstruction of the international community. Wilson, we may be reasonably confident, believed that the European conflict was in its final stages. Perhaps he thought that it would end after Germany had shot her submarine bolt and the Allies had tried one last offensive in the spring and summer of 1917. In any event, he certainly believed that American participation, as decisive as possible, would hasten the end of the ghastly carnage, if not end it quickly. American entry would spell Germany's inevitable defeat, or at least frustration of German plans. The German people, or their leaders in the Reichstag, might take control as liberals had done in Russia and refuse to fight for imperialistic ends.

Then there was a final tempting thought. It was that American belligerency would enhance his own ability to force an early settlement. He would continue as a neutral to be frustrated by both sides in his efforts for peace. He would have more influence with the Allies as a belligerent and, finally, some bargaining power with Germany. American belligerency would assure American guarantee of the peace settlement and membership in a postwar league of nations. This knowledge might make the English and French willing to negotiate a reasonable settlement. And when the great day did come he would have a seat at the peace table, not a stool outside the conference room. Jane Addams, who visited the White House with other members of the Emergency Peace Federation on February 28, later remembered that Wilson said that "as head of a nation participating in the war, the President of the United States would have a seat at the Peace Table, but that if he remained the representative of a neutral country he could at best only 'call through a crack in the door.'"

Colonel House almost certainly spoke accurately for the President when he told Whitehouse on March 30 and April 5:

"The President was going into this war to fight against Junkerism in every country. We had it in England but in England it would disappear after the war. He was convinced that no real peace was possible so long as the Prussian ideals remained. But the President was not going into the war for the obscure reasons that might actuate the Allies, nor was he going to be bound by an[y] treaty with them, and he was going to reach the end of it at the earliest possible moment. . . .

"House wished me specially to tell the members of the House of Commons who took a moderate view on the war that the President was entirely democratic in his sympathies, and his aim was to bring the war to an end at the earliest possible moment. He would certainly not sign the Allies agreement about a separate peace and would preserve his freedom to act as a mediating influence still. He had a profound disbelief in secret diplomacy and in the way it had been practiced in Europe by all countries including England. He was going to try to set another example. . . .

"The question of peace terms would now take a new form with America in the war. England would now have the guarantees for the future which she desired as America would be a party to whatever settlement was arrived at. The objections to England going into a conference in the future would be removed."

All this has been said with no intention of suggesting that Wilson ever wanted war. He had continued to hope to the very end that the Germans would yield the single thing that he demanded, observance of the rules of cruiser warfare in dealing with American merchantmen, and presumably safeguarding of human life on passenger liners. His agony was great as he passed through the dark valley of his doubts. He saw the dangers of intervention, to both his own people and the world, with wonderful clarity. But he could see no alternative, and he set aside his doubts in the hope that acting as a belligerent he could erect and achieve objectives to justify the decision he had made.

It would surely be superfluous to discourse on the significance of the decision, except perhaps to recall Winston Churchill's words: "Writing with every sense of respect, it seems no exaggeration to pronounce that the action of the United States with its repercussions on the history of the world depended, during the awful period of Armageddon, upon the workings of this man's mind and spirit to the exclusion of almost every other factor; and that he played a part in the fate of nations incomparably more direct and personal than any other man."

For Further Reading

In addition to the volume from which the preceding selection has been taken, Link traces the course of Wilson's diplomacy in detail in *Wilson: The Struggle for Neutrality 1914–1915* (1960) and *Wilson: Confusions and Crisis 1915–1916* (1964), Volumes III and IV of his magisterial biography. See also his *Wilson the Diplomatist: A Look at His Major Foreign Policies* (1957). Two helpful collections are Edward H. Beuhrig, ed., *Wilson's Foreign Policy in Perspective* (1957), and Arthur P. Dudden, ed., *Woodrow Wilson and the World of Today* (1957).

Charles Seymour, *American Diplomacy During the World War* (1934) and *American Neutrality, 1914–1917* (1935), justify intervention on the basis of the submarine warfare alone as does Harley Notter, *The Origins of the Foreign Policy of Woodrow Wilson* (1937).

The most important of the revisionist accounts are C. Hartley Grattan, *Why We Fought* (1929), which delivers less of an explanation than its title promises; a most readable shorter work by Walter Millis, *Road to War: America 1914–1917* (1935), and the more complete study of Charles C. Tansill, *America Goes to War* (1938). Also revisionist, but emphasizing one particular aspect of intervention are H. C. Peterson, *Propaganda for War: The Campaign Against American Neutrality, 1914–1917* (1939), and Edwin Borchard and William P. Lage, *Neutrality for the United States* (1937), which stresses the legal aspects of neutrality. Charles A. Beard, *The Devil Theory of War* (1937), attributes intervention to economic factors.

In addition to George Kennan, *American Diplomacy, 1900–1950* (1951), the thesis that we went to war to preserve national security is presented in Walter Lippmann, *United States Foreign Policy: Shield of the Republic* (1943), Edward H. Beuhrig, *Woodrow Wilson and the Balance of Power* (1955), and Ernest R. May, *The World War and American Isolation 1914–1917* (1959), but the latter work also reaffirms Wilson's hope for a better postwar world as a crucial element in his thinking.

The Supreme Infanticide

Thomas A. Bailey

*I*t is now generally agreed that the failure of the U.S. Senate to ratify the Treaty of Versailles and approve American entry into the League of Nations accurately reflected popular disenchantment with the Wilsonian peace program. At the time of the Armistice and through the first half of 1919, the public consensus, as reflected in newspapers and periodicals and in Congressional correspondence, showed overwhelming support for the peace program enunciated by President Wilson in his Fourteen Points and supplemental addresses. A poll of almost fourteen hundred newspaper editors taken by the *Literary Digest* showed a pro-League majority in every section of the country with only 181 papers unconditionally opposed. The soon-to-be leading critic of Mr. Wilson's peace, Senator Henry Cabot Lodge, complained of widespread support for the League of Nations to the country's foremost isolationist, Senator William E. Borah: "What are you going to do? It's hopeless. All the newspapers in my state are for it."

Yet by November when the Senate rejected the treaty

Source: Thomas A. Bailey, *Woodrow Wilson and the Great Betrayal* (New York: The Macmillan Company, 1945), pp. 271–287, 356–369. Copyright 1945 by The Macmillan Company. Reprinted by permission of the publisher.

for the first time, public opinion had apparently shifted to approval of American participation in the League only with reservations which would safeguard the special interests of the U.S. When the Senate took its second and final vote on ratification in March 1920, the treaty commanded a simple majority but fell short of the necessary two-thirds vote. Informed that only a treaty with reservations could garner the necessary votes, Wilson nonetheless refused to compromise. Instead he appealed to the American people to indicate their support for his proposals by making the presidential election of 1920 "a solemn referendum" on the League of Nations. History has demonstrated the unsuitability of a presidential canvass for determining opinion on a single issue; other elements are certain to intrude. The year 1920 was no exception. As one critic of Wilson's appeal had predicted, the solemn referendum turned out to be a great and solemn muddle. To be sure, the Democratic candidate James M. Cox forthrightly endorsed the League, but the Republican standard-bearer Warren G. Harding equivocated with enough success to win the support of both pro- and anti-League factions within his party. Nonetheless, Harding's smashing victory—he polled sixteen million votes to Cox's nine million—was widely interpreted as a repudiation of the League. Two days after the election the President-elect accurately described the League as "deceased."

The defeat of the Versailles Treaty did not insure World War II, as has sometimes been charged, but it certainly did enlarge the possibility of war and for this reason was a genuine tragedy. Who was responsible? According to more than one historian, Senator Lodge, the Republican leader in the Senate and chairman of the Foreign Relations Committee, deserves most of the blame. His decision to hold lengthy hearings on the treaty and his successful effort to add reservations to the original covenant of the League were not, in the opinion of his critics, sincere efforts to improve the treaty, but merely tactics adopted to insure its eventual rejection. Some go so far as to portray Lodge as an irreconcilable, a term applied to those senators who refused to accept American participation in the world organization under any conditions. Thomas A. Bailey (b. 1902) disagrees. A prominent diplomatic historian and the author of a two-volume study on peacemaking in 1919–20, Bailey locates the failure of the treaty in the intransigence of Woodrow Wilson. He does not fully absolve Lodge, who admittedly had a deep personal rancor against Wilson, the man who had taken from him the title "the scholar in politics." Lodge, at a critical point, placed the interests of his party above the interests of the nation, but Bailey contends that Lodge was making a genuine effort to get the treaty approved prior to the second rejection. In the following selection, Bailey presents a severe indictment of Wilson and his stubborn insistence on ratification on his terms alone. Even Wilson's admirers have admitted the force of his arguments. It would not do, however, to assign responsibility to personalities alone. A large share of the blame for this failure in American statesmanship must fall on the nation's liberals who condemned the treaty for its failure to fully realize the Fourteen Points. They protested the severity of the terms imposed upon Germany and accepted as their bible of the peace conference *The Economic Consequences of Peace,* a polemical account written by the young British economist John Maynard Keynes. His thesis that the European diplomats had "bamboozled" the naïve American President and had ignored the economic realities of 1919 to indulge their ancient hatreds was adopted by liberal journals such as the *Nation* and the *New Republic.* In addition, ethnic groups, such as the Irish, German, and Italian-Americans, resentful over the way Wilson had dealt with their mother countries, added strident criticisms. Politicians dependent upon the votes of immigrant blocs found support of the League a risky business. In 1920 many of these normally Democratic groups delivered a huge protest vote against Wilsonian candidates. Much of the isolationist opposition to the League emanated from progressives fearful that overseas commitments would retard the achievement of domestic reforms, but other isolationists catered to popular prejudices and nationalistic biases with emotional and irrational attacks on "world super governments." Finally, a sense of disillusionment had come over the country by 1920. The war to end wars and to make the world safe for democracy had proved to have been no such thing. As Professor Bailey has observed, if the sovereign people had truly desired the League of Nations they almost certainly would have had their way: "A treaty without reservations, or with a few reservations acceptable to Wilson, doubtless would have slipped through the Senate. But the American people were one war short of accepting the leadership in a world organization for peace, which, as Wilson's vision perceived, had become a necessity for the safety and welfare of mankind."

The treaty was now dead, as far as America was concerned. Who had killed it?

The vital role of the loyal Democrats must be reemphasized. If all of them who professed to want the treaty had voted "Yea," it would have passed with more than a dozen votes to spare. If the strait-jacket of party loyalty had not been involved, the necessary two-thirds could easily have been mustered.

In the previous November, the Democrats might have voted against the treaty (as they did) even without White House pressure. But this time pressure had to be applied to force them into line, and even in the face of Wilsonian wrath almost half of them bolted. On the day of the final balloting the newsmen observed that two Cabinet members (Burleson and Daniels), possibly acting at the President's direction, were on the floor of the Senate, buttonholing waverers. The day after the fateful voting Hitchcock wrote Wilson that it had required the "most energetic efforts" on his part *to prevent a majority of the Democrats from surrendering to Lodge.* Desertion of the President, as we have seen, is no light offense in the political world, especially when he has declared himself emphatically. Senators do not ordinarily court political suicide. Wilson still had the patronage bludgeon in his hands, and having more than a trace of vindictiveness, he could oppose renegade senators when they ran again, and in fact did so.

Many of the loyal Democrats were up for reelection in 1920. They certainly were aware of the effects of party treachery on their political fortunes. They knew—or many of them knew— that they were killing the treaty; they made no real effort to revive it; they must have wanted it killed—at least until after the November election.

One striking fact stands out like a lighthouse. With the exception of Hitchcock of Nebraska, Johnson of South Dakota, and Thomas of Colorado, *every single one of the twenty-three senators who stood loyally with Wilson in March came from south of the Mason and Dixon line.* Only four of the "disloyal" twenty-one represented states that had seceded in 1860–1861. At the polls, as well as on the floor of the Senate, decent southern Democrats voted "the way their fathers shot." As between bothersome world responsibility on the one hand, and loyalty to President, party, section, and race on the other, there was but one choice. Perhaps world leadership would come eventually anyhow.

Democratic senators like Walsh of Montana and Ashurst of Arizona were not from the South. When the issue was clearly drawn between loyalty to party and loyalty to country, their consciences bade them choose the greater good. Ashurst had gone down the line in supporting Wilson; but several days before the final vote he declared, "I am just as much opposed to a White House irreconcilable as I am to a Lodge irreconcilable."

A word now about public opinion.

In March, as in November, more than 80 per cent of the senators professed to favor the treaty with some kind of reservations. All the polls and other studies indicate that this was roughly the sentiment of the country. Yet the senators were unable to scrape together a two-thirds vote for any one set of reservations.

The reaction of many newspaper editors, as before, was to cry out against the shame of it all—this indictment of the "capacity of our democracy to do business." We had astonished the world by our ability to make war; we now astonished the world with our "imbecility" in trying to make peace. How could we blame other countries for thinking us "a nation of boobs and bigots"? The Louisville *Courier-Journal* (Democrat), referring to our broken promises to the Allies, cried that we stood betrayed as "cravens and crooks," "hypocrites and liars."

Partisan Republican newspapers loudly blamed the stiff-backed Wilson and his "me-too" senators. Two wings of "irreconcilables"—the Wilsonites and the "bitter-enders"—had closed in to execute a successful pincers movement against the treaty. The New York *Tribune* (Independent Republican) condemned the "inefficiency, all-sufficiency and self-sufficiency of our self-named only negotiator," Woodrow Wilson. If the treaty died, said the *Tribune,* the handle of the dagger that pierced its heart would bear the "initials 'W. W.' "

If Republicans scolded Democrats, Democrats scolded Republicans. Lodge and his cheap political tricks were roundly condemned, and the general conclusion was that "the blood of the Treaty stains the floor of the Republican wigwam." A few of the less partisan Democratic journals openly conceded that Wilson's obstinacy had something to do with the final result. William Jennings Bryan asserted from the platform that this "most colossal crime against our nation and the civilized world in all history" made his "blood boil." He began a vigorous campaign against the two-thirds rule in the Senate. "A majority of Congress can declare war," he cried; "it ought to be as easy to end a war as to begin it."

The leading liberal journals, as before, were sadly happy. They rejoiced that the result would clear the way for a renovation of the treaty, but they regretted that the pact had been defeated as a result of partisanship rather than as a result of the betrayal of Wilson's promises.

An impressive number of the more discerning editors deplored the fact that the issue was now in the dirty hands of politicians. An electoral referendum, it was felt, would merely confuse the issue; such a canvass could not possibly reveal anything more than was already known, namely, that *an overwhelming majority of the people wanted the treaty with some kind of reservations.*

Is it true that the invalid in the White House really strangled the treaty to death with his own enfeebled hands?

It is seldom that statesmen have a second chance—a second guess. They decide on a course of action, and the swift current of events bears them downstream from the starting point. Only rarely does the stream reverse itself and carry them back.

In November, Wilson had decided that he wanted deadlock, because he reasoned that deadlock would arouse public opinion and force the Senate to do his bidding. The tidal wave of public opinion did surge in, and Wilson got his second chance. But he threw it away, first by spurning compromise (except on his terms), and then by spurning the Lodge reservations.

There had been much more justification for Wilson's course in November than in March. In November he was sick, secluded, was fed censored news, and was convinced by Hitchcock that the strategy of deadlock was sound. In March, he was much improved in health, far less secluded, more in touch with the press and with the currents of opinion, though probably still not enough. He consulted even less with the Senate, presumably because he had made up his mind in advance to oppose the Lodge reservations. In November, there was a fair possibility of reconsideration; in March, it was clear that the only possibility lay in making the League an issue in the coming campaign. Wilson, with his broad knowledge of government and politics, should have seen that this hope was largely if not completely illusory. Perhaps he would have seen it had he not been blinded by his feeling for Lodge.

The evidence is convincing that Wilson wanted the issue cast into the hurly-burly of politics. He could not accept Lodge's terms; Lodge would not accept his terms. The only possible chance of beating the senator—and this was slim indeed—was to win a resounding mandate in 1920.

Yet this strategy, as already noted, meant further delay. At Paris, the feeling at times had been, "Better a bad treaty today than a good treaty four months hence." Europe was still in chaos, and increasingly in need of America's helping hand. Well might the Europeans cry, "Better a treaty with the Lodge reservations today than a probable treaty without reservations after the election." Or as Dr. Frank Crane wrote in *Current Opinion,* "It is vastly more needful that some sort of League be formed, *any sort,* than that it be formed *perfectly.*" (Italics Crane's.)

Yet Wilson, for the reasons indicated, could not see all this clearly. Four days after the fatal vote he wrote Hitchcock, praising him for having done all in his power to protect the honor of the nation and the peace of the world against the Republican majority.

Mrs. Wilson, no doubt reflecting her husband's views, later wrote, "My conviction is that Mr. Lodge put the world back fifty years, and that at his door lies the wreckage of human hopes and the peril to human lives that afflict mankind today."

To the very end Wilson was a fighter. When the Scotch-Irish in him became aroused, he would nail his colors to the mast. He said in 1916 that he was "playing for the verdict of mankind." His conception of duty as he saw it was overpowering. He once remarked that if he were a judge, and it became his duty to sentence his own brother to the gallows, he would do so—and afterwards die of a broken heart.

It is well to have principles; it is well to have a noble conception of duty. But Wilson, as he became warmed up in a fight, tended to get things out of focus and to lose a proper sense of values.

The basic issue in 1920 was the Hitchcock reservations or the Lodge reservations. Wilson accepted those of Hitchcock while rejecting those of Lodge, which, he said, completely nullified the treaty and betrayed his promises to the Allies and to the American dead.

This, as we have seen, was a gross exaggeration. Minds no less acute than Wilson's, and less clouded with sickness and pride, denied that the Lodge reservations completely nullified the treaty. To the man in the street—in so far as he gave the dispute thought—there was little discernible difference between the two sets of reservations. How could one decry statements which merely reaffirmed the basic principles of the Constitution and of our foreign policy? To a vast number of Americans the Lodge reservations, far from nullifying the treaty, actually improved it. This was so apparent to even the most loyal Democrats in the Senate that Wilson could barely keep them in line.

In the final analysis the treaty was slain in the house of its friends rather than in the house of its enemies. In the final analysis it was not the two-thirds rule, or the "irreconcilables," or Lodge, or the "strong" and "mild reservationists," but Wilson and his docile following who delivered the fatal stab. If the President had been permitted to vote he would have sided with Borah, Brandegee, Johnson, and the other "bitter-enders"—though for entirely different reasons.

Wilson had said that the reservation to Article X was a knife thrust at the heart of the Covenant. Ironically, he parried this knife thrust, and stuck his own dagger, not into the heart of the Covenant, but into the entire treaty.

This was the supreme act of infanticide. With his own sickly hands Wilson slew his own brain child—or the one to which he had contributed so much.

This was the supreme paradox. He who had forced the Allies to write the League into the treaty, unwrote it; he who had done more than any other man to make the Covenant, unmade it—at least so far as America was concerned. And by his action, he contributed powerfully to the ultimate undoing of the League, and with it the high hopes of himself and mankind for an organization to prevent World War II.

The preceding dogmatic observations are of course qualified by the phrase, "in the last analysis."

Many elements enter into a log jam. Among them are the width of the stream, the depth of the stream, the swiftness of the current, the presence of boulders, the size of the logs, and the absence of enough lumberjacks. No one of these factors can be solely responsible for the pile-up.

Many elements entered into the legislative log jam of March, 1920. Among them were isolationism, partisanship, senatorial prerogative, confusion, apathy, personal pride, and private feuds. No one of them was solely responsible for the pile-up. *But as the pile-up finally developed, there was only one lumberjack who could break it, and that was Woodrow Wilson.* If at any time before the final vote he had told the Senate Democrats to support the treaty with the Lodge reservations, or even if he had merely told them that they were on their own, the pact would almost certainly have been approved. So "in the last analysis" the primary responsibility for the failure in March rested with Wilson.

What about Lodge? If the treaty would have passed by Wilson's surrendering, is it not equally true that it would have passed by Lodge's surrendering?

The answer is probably "Yes," but the important point is that Lodge had far less responsibility for getting the treaty through than Wilson. If Lodge had yielded, he probably would have created a schism within his ranks. His ultimate responsibility was to keep the party from breaking to pieces, and in this he succeeded. Wilson's ultimate responsibility was to get the treaty ratified, and in this he failed. With Lodge, as with any truly partisan leader, the party comes before country; with the President the country should come before party, though unhappily it often does not.

It is possible that Wilson saw all this—but not clearly enough. He might have been willing to compromise if his adversary had been any other than Lodge. But so bitter was the feeling between the two men that Wilson, rather than give way, grasped at the straw of the election of 1920.

Lodge did not like Wilson either, but he made more of a show of compromising than the President. He actually supported and drove through amendments to his original reservations which were in line with Wilson's wishes, and he probably would have gone further had the "irreconcilables" not been on his back. He fought the crippling Irish reservation, as well as others supported by the "bitter-enders." Finally, he gave the Democrats a fair chance to reconsider their vote and get on the bandwagon, but they spurned it.

If Lodge's words mean anything, and if his actions were not those of a monstrous hypocrite, he actually tried to get the treaty through with his reservations. When he found that he could not, he washed his hands of the whole business in disgust.

The charge is frequently made that, if Wilson had yielded to his adversary, Lodge would have gleefully piled on more reservations until Wilson, further humiliated, would have had to throw out the whole thing.

The strongest evidence for this view is a circumstantial story which Secretary Houston relates. During a Cabinet meeting Wilson was called to the telephone, and agreed to make certain concessions agreeable to Lodge. Before adjournment the telephone rang again, and word came that Lodge would not adhere to his original proposal.

This story is highly improbable, because Wilson attended

no Cabinet meetings between September 2, 1919, and April 13, 1920. By the latter date, all serious attempts at compromise had been dropped; by the earlier date the treaty was still before the Senate committee, and the Lodge reservations, though in an embryonic stage, were yet unborn. But, even if the story is true, it merely proves that Lodge veered about, as he frequently did under "irreconcilable" pressure.

In March, as in November, all Wilson had to do was to send over Postmaster General Burleson to the Senate a few minutes before the final vote with the quiet word that the Democrats were to vote "Yea." The treaty would then have passed with the Lodge reservations, and Lodge could hardly have dared incur for himself or his party the odium of moving to reconsider for the purpose of screwing on more reservations. Had he tried to do so, the "mild reservationists" almost certainly would have blocked him.

A few days after the disastrous final vote, Wilson's only comment to Tumulty was, "They have shamed us in the eyes of the world." If his previous words said what he really meant, he was hardly more shamed by the defeat of the treaty than by the addition of the Lodge reservations. In his eyes it all amounted to the same thing.

If the treaty had passed, would the President have been willing to go through with the exchange of ratifications? Would he not have pocketed it, as he threatened to do prior to the November vote?

Again, if Wilson's words may be taken at their face value, this is what he would have done. He had not backed down from his pre-November position. His Jackson Day message and his letter to Hitchcock made it unmistakably clear that he preferred the uncertainties of a political campaign to the certainties of ratification with the Lodge reservations. The addition of the indefensible Irish reservation provided even stronger justification for pocketing the entire pact.

It is probable that some of the loyal Democrats voted as they did partly because they were convinced that Wilson was going to pigeonhole the treaty anyhow. From their point of view it was better that the odium for defeat should seemingly rest on Lodge rather than on their President. It also seems clear that Wilson preferred, as in November, to have the blood of the treaty on the Senate doorstep rather than on his. As he wrote to Secretary Colby, on April 2, 1920, the slain pact lay heavily on the consciences of those who had stabbed it, and he was quite willing to have it lie there until those consciences were either awakened or crushed.

Yet it is one thing to say, just before Senate action, "I will pocket the treaty." It is another, after the pact is approved and sent to the White House, to assume this tremendous responsibility. The eyes of the world are upon the President; he is the only man keeping the nation out of the peace which it so urgently needs; he is the one man standing in the way of the rehabilitation which the world so desperately demands. Public pressure to ratify in such a case would be enormous—probably irresistible.

Some years later Senator Hitchcock said that in the event of senatorial approval Wilson would possibly have waited for the November election. If he had won, he would have worked for the removal of the Lodge reservations; if he had lost, then the compulsion to go through with ratification would have become overpowering. By November more than six months would have passed, and by that time Wilson might have developed a saner perspective.

But this is all speculation. Wilson gave orders that the treaty was to be killed in the Senate chamber. And there it died.

One other line of inquiry must be briefly pursued. Is it true, as some writers allege, that the thirty-odd Allied signatories of the original treaty would have rejected the Lodge reservations when officially presented? We recall that under the terms of the preamble these nations were privileged to acquiesce silently or file objections.

One will never know the answer to this question, because

Wilson denied the other signatories a chance to act. But it seems proper to point to certain probabilities.

One or more of the Latin American nations might have objected to the reservation regarding the then hated Monroe Doctrine. Yet the Monroe Doctrine would have continued to exist anyhow; it was already in the Covenant; and these neighboring republics might well have swallowed their pride in the interest of world peace.

Italy probably would have acquiesced, and the evidence is strong that France would have done likewise. The Japanese could not completely overlook the Shantung reservation, but it was generally recognized in their press as meaningless, and for this reason it might have been tolerated, though not without some loss of face. It is noteworthy that the most important Japanese newspapers regretted the Senate stalemate as an encouragement to world instability, particularly in China.

Great Britain probably would have been the chief objector. The reservation on Ireland was highly offensive but completely innocuous, for the British lion had long endured Irish-American tail-twistings in pained but dignified silence. The reservation on six-to-one was a slap at the loyal and sacrificing Dominions, but it did not mean that their vote was to be taken away. Moreover, the contingency envisaged by this proviso was unlikely to arise very often, and in the long run would doubtless have proved inconsequential.

In sum, there were only two or three reservations to which the outside powers could seriously object. If they had objected, it is probable that a satisfactory adjustment could have been threshed out through diplomatic channels. For when it became clear that only a few phrases stood between the United States and peace, the dictates of common sense and the pressure of public opinion probably would have led to an acceptable compromise. If the Senate had refused to give ground in such a case, then the onus would have been clearly on it and not on Wilson.

The World Court is a case in point. In 1926 the Senate

voted to join, but attached five reservations, four of which were accepted by the other powers. By 1935 a compromise was worked out on the fifth, but an isolationist uprising led by William Randolph Hearst and Father Coughlin turned what seemed to be a favorable vote in the Senate into a narrow defeat for the World Court. The one-third minority again triumphed, with the aging Borah and Johnson and Norris and Gore still voting their fears and prejudices.

But the World Court analogy must not be pressed too far. In 1920 Europe was in a desperate condition; the only real hope for a successful League lay in American cooperation. Unless the United States would shoulder its obligations the whole treaty system was in danger of collapse. In 1926 the powers could afford to haggle over the World Court; in 1920 there was far less temptation to haggle while Europe burned. The European nations were under strong compulsion to swallow their pride, or at the very worst not to drive too hard a bargain in seeking adjustment.

But this again is pure speculation. Wilson never gave the other powers a chance to act on the reservations, though Colonel House and others urged him to. He assumed this terrific responsibility all by himself. While thinking that he was throwing the onus on the consciences of the senators, he was in fact throwing a large share of the onus upon his own bent shoulders.

What were the reactions of our recent brothers in arms on the other side of the Atlantic?

The British viewed the Senate debacle with mixed emotions. The result had been a foregone conclusion, and there was some relief in having an end to senatorial uncertainty— at least this stage of it. Some journals were inclined to blame the two-thirds rule; others, the unbending doctrinaire in the White House. The London *Times* sorrowfully concluded that all the processes of peace would have to be suspended pending the outcome of the November election.

The French were shocked, though hardly surprised. The

Paris *Liberté* aptly referred to the state of anarchy existing between the executive and the legislative in America. Other journals, smarting under Wilson's recent blast against French militarism, blamed the autocrat in the White House. "At the most troubled moment in history," gibed the Paris *Matin,* "America has a sick President, an amateur Secretary of State, and no Treaty of Peace. A President in the clouds, a Secretary of State in the bushes, and a treaty in the cabbage patch. What a situation!"

But the French did not completely abandon hope that America might yet honor her commitments. Meanwhile they would keep their powder dry and pursue the militaristic course which widened the growing rift between Britain and France, and which proved so fatal to the peace of Europe in the 1930's. The French finally became disgusted with German excuses (which were probably encouraged by America's defection), and in April, 1920, the month after the Senate rejected the treaty, their tanks rumbled into the Ruhr and occupied several German cities as hostages for reparations payments. Bullets were fired, and some blood was shed. This was but a dress rehearsal for the catastrophic invasion of the Ruhr in 1923.

The action—or rather inaction—of the United States had other tragic consequences. It encouraged German radicals in their determination to tear up the treaty: they were finding unwitting collaborators in Senator Borah and President Wilson. It delayed by many months, as British Foreign Secretary Curzon openly charged, the treaty with Turkey, thus giving the "Sick Man of Europe" (Turkey) a chance to prove that he was the "Slick Man of Europe." It held up the economic and moral rehabilitation of the Continent, and even hampered the work of relief then going forward. It further disillusioned the liberals of Europe and others who had clung to Wilson as the major prophet of a new order. It gave new comfort to the forces of disorder everywhere. It left the

United States discredited, isolated, shorn of its prestige, and branded as a hypocrite and renegade. It marked the first unbridgeable rift in the ranks of the victorious Allies, a coalition that might have kept the peace. Instead they now went their separate ways, perhaps not as enemies, but certainly no longer as close friends. The United States was the first to break completely away.

America—and the world—paid a high price for the collapse of the treaty-making process in Washington. We are still paying it.

One final question. Who won after all these months of parliamentary jockeying?

Lodge the master parliamentarian had not won—that is, if he really wanted the treaty with his reservations. As in November, he was unable to keep the "irreconcilables" in line on the crucial vote, and he was unable to muster a two-thirds majority. He finally had to confess failure of leadership, except in so far as he prevented a schism.

The Republican party had not won. Lodge had avoided a serious split with the "bitter-enders" by knuckling under when they laid down the law. But the Republican leaders did not really want the issue in the campaign, and they had made strong efforts to keep it out. Now it was on their hands to cause them no end of embarrassment.

Wilson had not won. He has been praised for having kept the party ranks intact, and for having retained undisputed leadership of his following. But the Democrats in the Senate split 21 for the treaty to 23 against it, and that is hardly holding one's followers in line. Wilson lost irreparably because he did not get his treaty, even with reservations, and because he was doomed to lose again by insisting on a referendum where there could be no referendum.

The Democrats had not won. The treaty issue had caused a serious rift in the Senate, and Bryan, who was still a great leader, was on the rampage. Except for Wilson and some of his "yes men," there were few Democratic leaders who wanted this troublesome issue catapulted into the campaign. Yet there it was.

The United States had not won. It had won the war, to be sure; but it was now kicking the fruits of the victory back under the peace table. We had helped turn Europe into a scrap heap, and now we were scrapping the treaty. We were going to stand by the Allies—with our arms folded. We were throwing away the only hope of averting World War II.

The real victor was international anarchy.

Wilson has been savagely denounced for having made commitments at Paris which the American people were ultimately unwilling to honor.

The truth is that only the President was in a position to make such pledges for the nation, and that the assurances which Wilson gave were in line with his war addresses, which the people either had warmly applauded or had seemingly accepted. Wilson erred not so much in making commitments —for commitments of some sort had to be made—as in assuming that the same high degree of wartime idealism would continue indefinitely after the signing of the peace.

But whoever was at fault, the unwillingness or inability of the United States to carry through the promises made in its behalf was catastrophic.

(1) One result was a betrayal of the League of Nations. The newly formed organization was crippled at birth when this nation, the most powerful of its sponsors, left it an orphaned waif on the international doorstep. With the United States in a position to hamstring the boycotts of the League—the League's most potent economic weapon—the other countries had little faith in what they were doing. While preaching peace they prepared for war. They could not hope to carry through a successful disarmament program as long as the United States would have no traffic with them. Under the League ideal there were to be no neutrals: either one was for

the League, or one was against it. By not being for it, the United States was against it.

It is possible of course that the League would have proved a failure even with our participation. But that is speculation. It is a demonstrable fact that the League was weakened and demoralized at the outset by the defection of the mightiest of the nations.

(2) Another result was a betrayal of the Treaty of Versailles —or better, the Truce of Versailles. This pact became a different treaty as a result of our desertion, and a much harsher one. Wilson had counted on the Covenant—the "heart" of the treaty—to soften its punitive features and provide a forum for wronged peoples. But the treaty could not work unless the "heart" worked, and the League could not work unless we worked with it.

The two chief instruments for giving flexibility to the Treaty of Versailles were the League of Nations and the Reparations Commission. We spurned the one, while declining representation on the other. The all-important commission then fell under the domination of France, although at Paris it had been assumed that the United States would use its great influence in the direction of moderation. The result of our withdrawal was that Germany was saddled with an impossible reparations burden, which unsettled Europe (and America) economically for more than a decade, contributed to the coming of the Great Depression, and helped prepare the path for Adolf Hitler.

The same sad story must be told elsewhere. The commission for the administration of the Saar was to have been headed by a high-minded American historian, but it fell under the influence of a nationalistic Frenchman, who was made no less nationalistic by fears growing out of the retirement of the United States. This was the sort of thing that Lloyd George had in mind when he said that the great failure lay not in the Treaty of Versailles but in the failure of the powers to carry out its provisions in the manner intended. To this tragic result the United States, by mere abstention, contributed powerfully.

(3) Another result was a betrayal of the Allies. The United States, by seceding from the victorious Allied coalition, made the first major breach in an alliance which might have kept the peace. In so doing, we indirectly joined with our former enemy, Germany, against the Treaty of Versailles. If the original entente had been kept intact, Hitler today might be ranting in the beer halls of an unbombed Munich.

Our sins were sins of omission; the sins of Britain and France were sins of commission. But our failure to stand by our associates gave them justification in their own minds for blaming us for many of their ills, and provided a plausible excuse for not acting together resolutely in the face of their common dangers.

(4) Another result was a betrayal of France. Suffering from a security psychosis, the French were stunned by our renunciation of the League, of the Treaty of Versailles, and of the Security Treaty. The resulting state of "jitters" was largely responsible for harsh measures against Germany, particularly the disastrous invasion of the Ruhr in 1923, all of which further aroused German nationalism and provided combustibles for demagogues like Adolf Hitler.

(5) Another result was a betrayal of Germany. The Treaty of Versailles, as noted, became a different treaty from the one which the Germans had thought they were signing. One of the Fourteen Points was a League of Nations—presumably a potent, *world* League of Nations. It was partly on the strength of such a promise that the Germans laid down their arms in 1918. But through our defection the League was condemned to anemia, and at the outset it became essentially a European league, in large part aimed at Germany, rather than a world league with the United States as a moderating member.

(6) Another result was a betrayal of liberal opinion the world over, not only in England, France, and America, but

also in Germany. The black eye given German liberalism helped undermine faith in the Weimar Republic and smoothed the way for Adolf Hitler and other apostles of oppression.

(7) Another result was a betrayal of American boys who had died, and of American boys yet unborn. Those who had died had been assured that their lives were being expended in a war to end wars; those yet unborn had to go over and do the job—a bloodier job—all over again.

(8) Another result was a betrayal of the masses everywhere, particularly the unredeemed minorities who through Wilson had been promised a better world.

(9) Another result was a betrayal of our humanitarian, missionary, and educational interests not only in Europe, but particularly in the Near East. Our retirement from the scene delayed the Near Eastern settlement, and infused new life into the Turks, with resulting disaster to the Armenians and other peoples for whom we had something of a moral responsibility.

(10) Another result was a betrayal of the legitimate interests of American merchants, manufacturers, bankers, and investors. We adopted a policy of ostrichism: trying to play the role of a debtor nation when we were now a creditor nation; seeking to eat our cake and have it too; raising high tariff and other barriers. In so doing we contributed heavily to the economic ills of Europe in the 1920's and 1930's, which in turn prepared the foundations of the Great Depression, which in turn brought in Adolf Hitler.

(11) Another result was a betrayal of America's responsibility to assume that world leadership which had been thrust upon her. First of all, there was a kind of *Noblesse oblige*—an obligation to help the less fortunate. Secondly, there were the dictates of both selfishness and common sense—of playing an active role so as to safeguard our interests and prevent our being dragged into World War II. Instead, we cravenly retreated, while our prestige sank to a new low in Europe, the

Far East, and Latin America. Instead of trying to control events, we left ourselves at the mercy of events which inexorably drew us again into their vortex.

(12) Another result was a betrayal of the nation's plighted word and of good faith in international dealings. The world will be long in recovering completely from the shock of our desertion in 1919–1920. The cooperation of the United States had been indispensable for victory; it was no less indispensable for a victorious peace. We achieved the one gloriously; we botched the other ingloriously. Henceforth other nations, in laying their plans for a world order, must choose not what they think is desirable but what they think the political situation in America will permit the Senate to accept. All this makes for world instability, and militates against that maximum of international cooperation which might otherwise be possible.

The moral is that the ill effects of broken pledges are worse than those resulting from no pledges at all. If our government is so unworkable that we cannot carry through commitments which the President makes and a majority of the people want to honor, then we had better warn other nations in advance, so that they can count on only limited American cooperation —or no cooperation at all.

(13) Another result was a betrayal of our clear moral obligation to finish the job. If we had stayed out of the war in 1917, Europe would have worked out something different if not better—perhaps a negotiated peace. By throwing our power into the balance, we brought victory to one side and prostration to the other, all the while creating problems which we were morally bound to help solve. Vice President Marshall pointedly remarked that we were like the man who rushed into his neighbor's house to beat off a burglar, and then rushed back home, leaving the victim bleeding to death on the floor.

It ill became the United States to sit self-righteously on the side lines during the 1920's and 1930's and blame the Europeans for not solving their problems, when some of those problems would never have been created if we had stayed out altogether, or had not turned away from the plow when the furrow was only half completed.

(14) Another result was a betrayal of the American people. An overwhelming majority of our citizens clearly wanted the League—at least with some reservations. Wilson's instincts were sound when he vainly sought to find some way by which the people might express their will through their government. But our method of approving treaties is so antiquated, illogical, undemocratic, and unworkable that the American people had no mechanism through which to implement their desires. And Wilson's own inflexibility, as we have noted, tightened the deadlock.

In 1919 and in 1920, the American people were willing to forsake the ancient path of isolation, at least with reservations. By the 1930's they were in a different mood, because by that time they saw that the League (which they had helped condemn to impotence) was a failure in preventing aggression by a major power.

This long and disconcerting list of "betrayals" does not necessarily mean that our withdrawal was solely, or even primarily, responsible for all the ills that befell Europe from 1919 to 1939. But it does mean that the United States cannot escape a very considerable share of the blame for what happened.

At the conclusion of the volume *Woodrow Wilson and the Lost Peace,* certain general principles were set forth regarding peacemaking. It now seems proper to list a few maxims relating to peace-ratifying and peace-executing.

(1) Politics, in so far as possible, should be kept out of foreign affairs. Nothing should be more nonpartisan than international relations, because what is good for one party is presumably good for both parties and the entire country. This, of course, suggests the counsel of perfection: politics is a bacillus which laughs at three-mile lines. Yet we should

never wantonly throw a delicate issue on foreign affairs into the turbulence of a political campaign. The result is certain to be misleading and possibly disastrous. We must seek senators to match our mountains—men who will put the good of the country above the good of the party; who will put the advancement of humanity above the advancement of self. We should select senators and members of the House as much (if not more) for their position on foreign affairs as for their position on domestic affairs: the two, as we shall note, are inextricably intertwined.

(2) The two-thirds rule in the Senate should be eliminated. It is the refuge of the filibusterer, the obstructionist, and the devotee of minority rule, all of whom are foreign to a true democracy. This antique restriction adds immeasurably to clumsiness and deadlock in the treaty-ratifying process. In March, 1920 (though not in November, 1919), it was directly responsible for the defeat of the treaty.

(3) A postwar slump in idealism is inescapable in the cold, gray dawn that follows victory. The urge to return to a normalcy that can never be again is age-old; the growth of distrust in one's allies, once the common cause is won, is inevitable. The peacemakers should never lose sight of these things when they come to design the temple of the future, and not try to attain the unattainable.

(4) Perfectionism is impossible in this workaday world. Our statesmen and our people, whether fashioning treaties of peace or fashioning new world organizations, should seek what will work—not what seems ideally desirable. The League was not perfect. It was, said one critic, only half a League— but it was half a League onward. Even today, after more than a century and a half of experience—our Constitution is far from perfect; yet we have changed it and are changing it.

(5) Compromise may be as essential in peace-ratifying as in peacemaking. Certainly this was true in Washington during 1919–1920. A stubborn refusal to compromise when the people

demand compromise not only is undemocratic but may, as it did in 1920, lead to the defeat of the entire treaty.

(6) Sovereignty is a sacred cow tied across the path of international cooperation. It conjures up all kinds of unwarranted fears. But an impairment of sovereignty—of national freedom of action—is a characteristic of treaties entered into on a free and friendly basis. Broadly speaking, a treaty is a promise to give up, in return for something else, that which we would ordinarily do. The United States has entered into hundreds of international agreements, but our sovereignty is essentially unimpaired.

(7) Effective international cooperation demands a price. That price is the yielding of some small part of our freedom of action—our sovereignty—so that we may, through preventing international disorders, enjoy greater freedom of action. The good things of life may be free, but peace is not one of them. One of the supreme follies of the American people in the post-Versailles years was to demand rights, while shunning responsibilities. We found ourselves in the immoral and disastrous position of seeking all the immunities, privileges, and advantages of riding in the internatonal boat, while refusing to pull the laboring oar of liabilities, reponsibilities, and costs.

(8) An excess of suspicion—a Yankee horse-trading trait—is a barrier to international cooperation. Peace can be preserved only among men of good will, for it is a blessing which rests not so much on paper pacts as on attitudes of mind. Peace can no more be maintained by parchment than sobriety can be maintained by constitutional amendments.

In 1919 we were the most powerful and secluded of the great nations, yet we acted as though we were the weakest and most vulnerable. Rich though we were, we feared that we might be asked to contribute one cent more than our proper share; powerful though we were, we feared that a few thousand of our soldiers might be sent abroad to prevent ten million from following them. We confessed by our conduct that our representatives were not intelligent enough to sit down at the same table with those of other nations, even though we had the highest stack of chips and most of the high cards. If we enter a world organization for peace, eyeing our colleagues distrustfully and momentarily expecting them to try to "put something over on us," then failure is inevitable. There is usually more to be gained through an excess of confidence than through an excess of suspicion.

(9) Domestic affairs are but the obverse side of the shield of foreign affairs. In the 1920's the American people fatuously sought to crawl into a hole and pull the hole in after them. But they discovered to their sorrow—or at least some of them did—that immigration barriers, tariff walls, reparations payments, and foreign debts all stir up international reverberations. World depressions leap lightly across international boundaries; bumper wheat crops in the Argentine and Australia bring impoverishment to American farmers. The wars of Europe and Asia have an ugly and inexorable habit of becoming our wars.

(10) It is better to desert one's associates before the peace is drawn up than after. In 1919 we forced the Europeans to adopt a treaty they would not have adopted if we had stayed out. Then we left them in the lurch and loudly condemned them because they could not make our kind of peace work. If we are unwilling or unable to ratify and help execute a world peace, then we owe it to our associates to say so, in order that they may draw their plans accordingly.

(11) Isolationism as a physical fact is dead (granted that it ever existed), even though the isolationists are not. The desire to draw apart and mind one's own business is entirely natural and often commendable. But on this shriveling planet such an ideal is impracticable. With new inventions annihilating both time and distance, the Atlantic Ocean today is far smaller than the Aegean Sea was in the day of Pericles. It is now "One World," and we cannot secede from it. This whirling ball has now become so small that an international quar-

rel anywhere becomes our business. Wilson recognized all this, and it explains why he fought to the death for his ideal. Since 1689, there have been nine world wars, and the American people have been drawn into *every single one of them.* This disconcerting fact lends much force to the truism that the only sure way for us to keep out of a great world conflict is to prevent its outbreak. If we are unwilling to recognize that we are part of this planet, and if we are not utter fools, *we had better start preparing for the next world war right now.*

(12) Power creates responsibilities. The United States has become so wealthy and so powerful that, whether we do nothing or something in regard to an international organization, our influence will be felt for good or ill, positively or negatively. Aloofness merely accelerates the chaos which will inevitably engulf us. As long as this power exists, and as long as it will be felt one way or the other, elemental common sense commands us to direct it actively into channels which will be most helpful to the rest of the world and indirectly to ourselves.

(13) The United States, as the richest of the powers, has as vital an interest in world peace as any other nation. Another world war may bankrupt us. In 1919 we prided ourselves on not asking for anything at the peace table—in spurning reparations which we did not need and mandates which we did not want. But we did have an enormous material stake, *and that was in making the peace last.* Because it did not last we were forced to incur a debt of over $200,000,000,000 and mobilize a force of over 11,000,000 men. Compared with this colossal outlay, the cost of making a world order operate would be nothing.

(14) American opinion must be educated to its responsibilities in international affairs. If a new world organization is to work, we as a people must have a better appreciation of our long-run interests and our long-range responsibilities. One of the most formidable barriers to international cooperation is

the pursuit of the immediate, short-run advantage to the exclusion of the less immediate but more profitable longer-run advantage. Unless man is willing to labor for the interests of all (which are his long-run interests); unless he is prepared to avoid the selfish short-run gain which hurts his neighbor and indirectly himself; unless he can assume that most people are decent human beings striving toward a common end—then we might just as well start preparing to go back into the jungle and up into the trees. *There can be no long-range peace without a long-range view.*

A few final observations.

Should the United States have ratified the treaty and joined the League? In the face of the evidence herein presented, there can be only one answer. We had very little if anything to lose—perhaps the trivial expenses of the League; and everything to gain—possibly a preventing of so-called World War II. No nation was ever trapped in the League, as our isolationists feared: Japan got out, Germany got out, Russia was thrown out. Where the possible losses were so negligible, and the probable gains so tremendous, the United States, as Wilson repeatedly pointed out, was more than justified in taking the chance.

Would the results have been essentially different if we had joined the League?

The conclusions here must of course be more speculative. But it seems clear that some kind of "slump in idealism" would have come sooner or later, and it may legitimately be doubted whether, when the pinch came, the United States would have provided adequate support for the League of Nations. The events of the 1930's would seem to support such a view, but we must remember that the set of circumstances then encountered might not have come into being if we had joined the League in the first instance.

General Jan C. Smuts said that not Wilson but "humanity" failed at Paris. This is a striking statement that has little meaning, in part because the real failure came after Paris. If a horseman spurs his mount at a twelve-foot brick wall, who is responsible for the ensuing accident: the horse that fails to make the jump, or the rider who has attempted an impossible feat?

A horseman must know his horse and its limitations; a statesman must know his people and their limitations, as well as the limitations of foreign peoples. Otherwise he is not a statesman. He must not set for his people impossible goals, however desirable they may be in the abstract. He must train public opinion by gradations for the new tasks—not try to shoot Niagara all at once. He must educate the people in advance for the responsibility which he is asking them to shoulder. Otherwise, even though they may temporarily take on the burden, they are likely to find it too wearisome and cast it aside.

Wilson engineered a revolution in our foreign policy when he undertook to lead the American people out of the path of isolationism into that of effective world cooperation. Yet the isolationists, aided by the circumstances set forth in this book, were able to effect a counterrevolution, and take us back into the old paths. But it is possible that this counterrevolution would have come within a few years anyhow; the people were not yet fully ready for a major departure.

The great Covenanter was eternally right in recognizing that isolationism was but a mirage, and that the next war would surely drag us in, and that the new organization for peace had to be based upon justice for all. The stakes were enormous; they were worth giving one's life for. He failed in part because he seems not to have realized that his was a dual task: making a peace and changing a national—perhaps a world—psychology.

Wilson was the greatest of the neutral statesmen, the greatest mediator, the greatest war leader, the greatest peacemaker, the greatest tragedy, and the greatest disappointment. Reaching for the stars, he crashed to earth.

178   *The Supreme Infanticide*

But his was a magnificent failure, and in some ways a successful failure. Wilson once said, "Ideas live; men die." His ideas have lived. The Wilsonian tradition has been kept alive, and countless thousands of men and women have vowed that we shall not make the same mistakes again. We shall know better how to do it next time. We know better our limitations and those of other peoples, for we have before us the successes and failures of the League. We know better what machinery will work, and what will not. We know that a League without teeth is little better than a debating society.

We must never forget that there are two phases to a war: the fighting duration, and the peace duration. Partly because men did not recognize this, the Treaty of Versailles became an armistice, and the postwar era a prewar era. Only a handful of statesmen can actually draw up a treaty of peace. *But in a democracy every citizen can actively participate in its ratification and in its execution.* Upon him rests a sacred obligation not only to do so but to do so intelligently. The record is there for him to read, and he should read it—*with due regard for changed conditions.*

We do not want to have to do the ghastly job a third time.

For Further Reading

Thomas A. Bailey's *Woodrow Wilson and the Lost Peace* (1944) evaluates the role played by Wilson and the United States at the Peace Conference and complements his volume on the rejection of the treaty. Three men who accompanied Wilson to Paris have written useful acounts: Robert Lansing, *The Peace Negotiations: A Personal Narrative* (1921), Ray Stannard Baker, *Woodrow Wilson and the World Settlement* (3 vols., 1922), and Herbert Hoover, *The Ordeal of Woodrow Wilson* (1958). Excellent secondary works are Harold Nicolson, *Peacemaking, 1919* (1939), Stephen Bonsal, *Unfinished*

Business (1944), and Paul Birdsall, *Versailles Twenty Years After* (1941). Students reading John Maynard Keynes, *The Economic Consequences of the Peace* (1920), are advised to also read Etienne Mantoux, *The Carthaginian Peace, or the Economic Consequences of Mr. Keynes* (1946). On the struggle for ratification, see Denna F. Fleming, *The United States and League of Nations, 1918–1920* (1932), and W. Stull Holt, *Treaties Defeated by the Senate* (1933). Ruhl J. Bartlett's *The League to Enforce Peace* (1944) is a study of the leading groups lobbying for ratification. John A. Garraty, *Henry Cabot Lodge* (1953), does a better job of presenting the position of the majority leader than does Lodge's own account, *The Senate and the League of Nations* (1925). Bailey's judgment on Wilson may be contrasted with those of Arthur Walworth, *Woodrow Wilson World Prophet* (1958), John M. Blum, *Woodrow Wilson and the Politics of Morality* (1956), and Arthur S. Link, *Wilson the Diplomatist* (1957). Gene Smith's *When the Cheering Stopped* (1964), a controversial study of Wilson's last years, attributes his adamant attitude toward the treaty to mental deterioration.

Selig Adler, *The Isolationist Impulse: Its Twentieth Century Reaction* (1957), effectively handles a complex topic with good chapters on the liberal and hyphenate opposition to the League. But on the latter, see also Joseph P. O'Grady, ed., *The Immigrant's Influence on Wilson's Peace Policies* (1967). Marian McKenna's *Borah* (1961) is the best biography of the leader of the irreconcilables in the Senate. For the election of 1920, see Wesley M. Bagby, *The Road to Normalcy* (1962).

Manners and Morals in the 1920's

Frederick Lewis Allen

*W*arren Gamaliel Harding coined the term normalcy while campaigning for the presidency of the United States in 1920. Said the man destined to be remembered as one of the nation's worst chief executives: "America's present need is not heroics but healing; not nostrums but normalcy; not revolution but restoration ... not surgery but serenity." The dictionary did not then list the word "normalcy," but the word did express the national feeling in 1920. Harding could not compete with Woodrow Wilson as far as mastery of the English language was concerned, but he far surpassed him in gauging the public temper in the aftermath of World War I. Disillusioned by the failure of the "war to end wars" and "the war to make the world safe for democracy" to accomplish either of these purposes, tired of Wilsonian rhetoric with its appeals to

Source: Frederick Lewis Allen, *Only Yesterday: An Informal History of the Nineteen-Twenties* (New York: Harper & Row, 1931), pp. 88–122. Copyright 1931 by Frederick Lewis Allen; renewed 1959 by Agnes Rogers Allen. Reprinted by permission of Harper & Row, Publishers.

idealism and self-sacrifice, the American people wanted to be left alone to make money and enjoy themselves. In their desire to recapture normalcy, many harked back to the last decade of the previous century. We realize now that the 1890's were hardly gay, but the world certainly seemed happier and simpler then. In a sense, observed Frederick Lewis Allen (1890–1954), the 1920's became the Indian summer of the nineteenth century. In what some critics have described as the most interesting social history ever written, Allen described a decade of scandal and ballyhoo, of flappers and fanatics, of alcohol and Al Capone. Writing in 1931, he brought to his subject a sense of immediacy; he aimed his book at those who "could hardly fail to remember the entire period with which it deals." But viewing events at such close range also involves dangers of distortion. Later students of the period have accused Allen of emphasizing the outré and the sensational. Unquestionably, his portrayal of the era as a frivolous, frantic interlude between war and depression became a stereotype. Subsequent accounts had such titles as *Fantastic Interim, The Era of Wonderful Nonsense,* and *The Lawless Decade.* But in later years the decade of the twenties seemed much more serious and complex than it did to those who viewed it during the depression years. Indeed, Allen later admitted that in order to highlight the trends of the era and to enliven the book, he "illustrated some of these trends with rather extreme, though authentic, examples of odd or excited behavior." He concluded that the period was not conspicuously sillier than any other.

Much of the valid criticism of *Only Yesterday* has centered not so much on what Allen said, but on what he left unsaid. For example, he devoted little space to political history; when he did write of the political arena, he concentrated on the conservatism and complacency of the times, on the Harding scandals, and on keeping "cool with Coolidge." He emphasized the rampant bigotry and racism evident in the big Red Scare, the judicial murder of Sacco and Vanzetti, and the discriminatory immigration legislation. He dwelt on the intolerance of rural dry America—the Bible Belt—as manifested in the revival of the Ku Klux Klan, the defense of prohibition, and the attempt to deny Darwinian biology and the new biblical criticism by forbidding the teaching of evolution in the schools. This is, admittedly, a large part of the politics of the 1920's, but there is another side. For one thing, the Progressivism identified with the prewar years did not completely expire after the Armistice. To the conservatism of Harding and Coolidge, we can contrast the continuing liberalism of Robert M. LaFollette, who ran for the presidency as a Progressive in 1924, and the emergence of new leaders such as Fiorello La Guardia and Alfred E. Smith. Most of the achievements of men like Smith or La Guardia occurred at the local or state level, but Senator George Norris of Nebraska led a successful fight to prevent the sale to private interests of the government's wartime nitrate plant at Muscle Shoals, Alabama. This permitted the eventual development, through the Tennessee Valley Authority, of a vast hydroelectric and water control system enormously beneficial to the residents of the region.

Secondly, even in the election of 1928, when the old order seemed to be most resoundingly reaffirmed, it was, in fact, challenged. In his short account of the election, Allen sees Smith, a wet, a Catholic, and a product of Tammany Hall, undertaking the impossible in trying to defeat Herbert Hoover, a man who seemed to personify "the New Era" in all its success and prosperity. He duly records Hoover's sweep on the country and his breaking of the Solid South, a complete vindication of the status quo and political fundamentalism. But what Allen did not perceive—perhaps, in fairness, what he could not be expected to perceive from the perspective of only three years—was that Smith in defeat had reshaped the Democratic Party by running extremely well in the urban industrial areas of the nation. The big-city vote had gone overwhelmingly Republican in 1920; by 1928, due largely to Smith's religion and his immigrant background, it shifted to the Democrats where it formed the base for the party's success in the New Deal years and after.

Finally, Allen probably underplayed some of the technological accomplishments of the twenties and failed to realize the genuinely high level of literacy and artistic achievement. Nonetheless, *Only Yesterday* remains essentially sound in its analysis of the social upheaval following the war. In writing of the change in manners and morals in terms of a revolution, Allen is not guilty of exaggeration.

A first-class revolt against the accepted American order was certainly taking place during those early years of the Post-war Decade, but it was one with which Nikolai Lenin had nothing whatever to do. The shock troops of the rebellion were not alien agitators, but the sons and daughters of well-to-do American families, who knew little about Bolshevism and cared distinctly less, and their defiance was expressed not in obscure radical publications or in soap-box speeches, but right across the family breakfast table into the horrified ears of conservative fathers and mothers. Men and women were still shivering at the Red Menace when they awoke to the no less alarming Problem of the Younger Generation, and realized that if the Constitution were not in danger, the moral code of the country certainly was.

This code, as it currently concerned young people, might have been roughly summarized as follows: Women were the guardians of morality; they were made of finer stuff than men and were expected to act accordingly. Young girls must look forward in innocence (tempered perhaps with a modicum of physiological instruction) to a romantic love match which would lead them to the altar and to living-happily-ever-after; and until the "right man" came along they must allow no male to kiss them. It was expected that some men would succumb to the temptations of sex, but only with a special class of outlawed women; girls of respectable families were supposed to have no such temptations. Boys and girls were permitted large freedom to work and play together, with decreasing and well-nigh nominal chaperonage, but only because the code worked so well on the whole that a sort of honor system was supplanting supervision by their elders; it was taken for granted that if they had been well brought up they would never take advantage of this freedom. And although the attitude toward smoking and drinking by girls differed widely in different strata of society and different parts of the country, majority opinion held that it was morally wrong for them to smoke and could hardly imagine them showing the effects of alcohol.

The war had not long been over when cries of alarm from parents, teachers, and moral preceptors began to rend the air. For the boys and girls just growing out of adolescence were making mincemeat of this code.

The dresses that the girls—and for that matter most of the older women—were wearing seemed alarming enough. In July, 1920, a fashion-writer reported in the *New York Times* that "the American woman... has lifted her skirts far beyond any modest limitation," which was another way of saying that the hem was now all of nine inches above the ground. It was freely predicted that skirts would come down again in the winter of 1920–21, but instead they climbed a few scandalous inches farther. The flappers wore thin dresses, short-sleeved and occasionally (in the evening) sleeveless; some of the wilder young things rolled their stockings below their knees, revealing to the shocked eyes of virtue a fleeting glance of shin-bones and knee-cap; and many of them were visibly using cosmetics. "The intoxication of rouge," earnestly explained Dorothy Speare in *Dancers in the Dark*, "is an insidious vintage known to more girls than mere man can ever believe." Useless for frantic parents to insist that no lady did such things; the answer was that the daughters of ladies were doing it, and even retouching their masterpieces in public. Some of them, furthermore, were abandoning their corsets. "The men won't dance with you if you wear a corset," they were quoted as saying.

The current mode in dancing created still more consternation. Not the romantic violin but the barbaric saxophone now dominated the orchestra, and to its passionate crooning and wailing the fox-trotters moved in what the editor of the Hobart College *Herald* disgustedly called a "syncopated embrace." No longer did even an inch of space separate them; they danced as if glued together, body to body, cheek to cheek. Cried the *Catholic Telegraph* of Cincinnati in righteous indignation, "The music is sensuous, the embracing of partners—the female only half dressed—is absolutely indecent; and the motions—they are such as may not be described, with any respect for propriety, in a family newspaper. Suffice it to say that there are certain houses appropriate for such dances; but those houses have been closed by law."

Supposedly "nice" girls were smoking cigarettes—openly and defiantly, if often rather awkwardly and self-consciously. They were drinking—somewhat less openly but often all too efficaciously. There were stories of daughters of the most exemplary parents getting drunk—"blotto," as their companions cheerfully put it—on the contents of the hip-flasks of the new prohibition régime, and going out joyriding with men at four in the morning. And worst of all, even at well-regulated dances they were said to retire where the eye of the most sharp-sighted chaperon could not follow, and in darkened rooms or in parked cars to engage in the unspeakable practice of petting and necking.

It was not until F. Scott Fitzgerald, who had hardly graduated from Princeton and ought to know what his generation were doing, brought out *This Side of Paradise* in April, 1920, that fathers and mothers realized fully what was afoot and how long it had been going on. Apparently the "petting party" had been current as early as 1916, and was now widely established as an indoor sport. "None of the Victorian mothers—and most of the mothers were Victorian—had any idea how casually their daughters were accustomed to be kissed," wrote Mr. Fitzgerald. "... Amory saw girls doing things that even in his memory would have been impossible: eating three-o'clock, after-dance suppers in impossible cafés, talking of every side of life with an air half of earnestness, half of mockery, yet with a furtive excitement that Amory considered stood for a real moral let-down. But he never realized how widespread it was until he saw the cities between New York and Chicago as one vast juvenile intrigue." The book caused a shudder to run down the national spine; did not Mr. Fitzgerald represent one of his well-nurtured heroines as brazenly confessing, "I've kissed dozens of men. I suppose I'll kiss dozens more"; and another heroine as saying to a young man (*to a young man!*), "Oh, just one person in fifty has any glimmer of what sex is. I'm hipped on Freud and all that, but it's rotten that every bit of real love in the world is ninety-nine per cent passion and one little *soupçon* of jealousy"?

It was incredible. It was abominable. What did it all mean? Was every decent standard being thrown over? Mothers read the scarlet words and wondered if they themselves "had any idea how often their daughters were accustomed to be kissed."... But no, this must be an exaggerated account of the misconduct of some especially depraved group. Nice girls couldn't behave like that and talk openly about passion. But in due course other books appeared to substantiate the findings of Mr. Fitzgerald: *Dancers in the Dark, The Plastic Age, Flaming Youth*. Magazine articles and newspapers reiterated the scandal. To be sure, there were plenty of communities where nice girls did not, in actual fact, "behave like that"; and even in the more sophisticated urban centers there were plenty of girls who did not. Nevertheless, there was enough fire beneath the smoke of these sensational revelations to make the Problem of the Younger Generation a topic of anxious discussion from coast to coast.

The forces of morality rallied to the attack. Dr. Francis E. Clark, the founder and president of the Christian Endeavor

Society, declared that the modern "indecent dance" was "an offense against womanly purity, the very fountainhead of our family and civil life." The new style of dancing was denounced in religious journals as "impure, polluting, corrupting, debasing, destroying spirituality, increasing carnality," and the mothers and sisters and church members of the land were called upon to admonish and instruct and raise the spiritual tone of these dreadful young people. President Murphree of the University of Florida cried out with true Southern warmth, "The low-cut gowns, the rolled hose and short skirts are born of the Devil and his angels, and are carrying the present and future generations to chaos and destruction." A group of Episcopal church-women in New York, speaking with the authority of wealth and social position (for they included Mrs. J. Pierpont Morgan, Mrs. Borden Harriman, Mrs. Henry Phipps, Mrs. James Roosevelt, and Mrs. E. H. Harriman), proposed an organization to discourage fashions involving an "excess of nudity" and "improper ways of dancing." The Y. W. C. A. conducted a national campaign against immodest dress among high-school girls, supplying newspapers with printed matter carrying headlines such as "Working Girls Responsive to Modesty Appeal" and "High Heels Losing Ground Even in France." In Philadelphia a Dress Reform Committee of prominent citizens sent a questionnaire to over a thousand clergymen to ask them what would be their idea of a proper dress, and although the gentlemen of the cloth showed a distressing variety of opinion, the committee proceeded to design a "moral gown" which was endorsed by ministers of fifteen denominations. The distinguishing characteristics of this moral gown were that it was very loose-fitting, that the sleeves reached just below the elbows, and that the hem came within seven and a half inches of the floor.

Not content with example and reproof, legislators in several states introduced bills to reform feminine dress once and for all. The *New York American* reported in 1921 that a bill was pending in Utah providing fine and imprisonment for those who wore on the streets "skirts higher than three inches above the ankle." A bill was laid before the Virginia legislature which would forbid any woman from wearing shirtwaists or evening gowns which displayed "more than three inches of her throat." In Ohio the proposed limit of decolletage was two inches; the bill introduced in the Ohio legislature aimed also to prevent the sale of any "garment which unduly displays or accentuates the lines of the female figure," and to prohibit any "female over fourteen years of age" from wearing "a skirt which does not reach to that part of the foot known as the instep."

Meanwhile innumerable families were torn with dissension over cigarettes and gin and all-night automobile rides. Fathers and mothers lay awake asking themselves whether their children were not utterly lost; sons and daughters evaded questions, lied miserably and unhappily, or flared up to reply rudely that at least they were not dirty-minded hypocrites, that they saw no harm in what they were doing and proposed to go right on doing it. From those liberal clergymen and teachers who prided themselves on keeping step with all that was new, came a chorus of reassurance: these young people were at least franker and more honest than their elders had been; having experimented for themselves, would they not soon find out which standards were outworn and which represented the accumulated moral wisdom of the race? Hearing such hopeful words, many good people took heart again. Perhaps this flare-up of youthful passion was a flash in the pan, after all. Perhaps in another year or two the boys and girls would come to their senses and everything would be all right again.

They were wrong, however. For the revolt of the younger generation was only the beginning of a revolution in manners and morals that was already beginning to affect men and women of every age in every part of the country.

A number of forces were working together and interacting upon one another to make this revolution inevitable.

First of all was the state of mind brought about by the war and its conclusion. A whole generation had been infected by the eat-drink-and-be-merry-for-tomorrow-we-die spirit which accompanied the departure of the soldiers to the training camps and the fighting front. There had been an epidemic not only of abrupt war marriages, but of less conventional liaisons. In France, two million men had found themselves very close to filth and annihilation and very far from the American moral code and its defenders; prostitution had followed the flag and willing mademoiselles from Armentières had been plentiful; American girls sent over as nurses and war workers had come under the influence of continental manners and standards without being subject to the rigid protections thrown about their continental sisters of the respectable classes; and there had been a very widespread and very natural breakdown of traditional restraints and reticences and taboos. It was impossible for this generation to return unchanged when the ordeal was over. Some of them had acquired under the pressure of war-time conditions a new code which seemed to them quite defensible; millions of them had been provided with an emotional stimulant from which it was not easy to taper off. Their torn nerves craved the anodynes of speed, excitement, and passion. They found themselves expected to settle down into the humdrum routine of American life as if nothing had happened, to accept the moral dicta of elders who seemed to them still to be living in a Pollyanna land of rosy ideals which the war had killed for them. They couldn't do it, and they very disrespectfully said so.

"The older generation had certainly pretty well ruined this world before passing it on to us," wrote one of them (John F. Carter in the *Atlantic Monthly,* September, 1920), expressing accurately the sentiments of innumerable contemporaries. "They give us this thing, knocked to pieces, leaky, red-hot, threatening to blow up; and then they are surprised that we don't accept it with the same attitude of pretty, decorous enthusiasm with which they received it, way back in the 'eighties."

The middle generation was not so immediately affected by

the war neurosis. They had had time enough, before 1917, to build up habits of conformity not easily broken down. But they, too, as the let-down of 1919 followed the war, found themselves restless and discontented, in a mood to question everything that had once seemed to them true and worthy and of good report. They too had spent themselves and wanted a good time. They saw their juniors exploring the approaches to the forbidden land of sex, and presently they began to play with the idea of doing a little experimenting of their own. The same disillusion which had defeated Woodrow Wilson and had caused strikes and riots and the Big Red Scare furnished a culture in which the germs of the new freedom could grow and multiply.

The revolution was accelerated also by the growing independence of the American woman. She won the suffrage in 1920. She seemed, it is true, to be very little interested in it once she had it; she voted, but mostly as the unregenerate men about her did, despite the efforts of women's clubs and the League of Women Voters to awaken her to womanhood's civic opportunity; feminine candidates for office were few, and some of them—such as Governor Ma Ferguson of Texas —scarcely seemed to represent the starry-eyed spiritual influence which, it had been promised, would presently ennoble public life. Few of the younger women could rouse themselves to even a passing interest in politics: to them it was a sordid and futile business, without flavor and without hope. Nevertheless, the winning of the suffrage had its effect. It consolidated woman's position as man's equal.

Even more marked was the effect of woman's growing independence of the drudgeries of housekeeping. Smaller houses were being built, and they were easier to look after. Families were moving into apartments, and these made even less claim upon the housekeeper's time and energy. Women were learning how to make lighter work of the preparation of meals. Sales of canned foods were growing, the number of delicatessen stores had increased three times as fast as the population during the decade 1910–20, the ouput of bakeries increased by 60 per cent during the decade 1914–24. Much of what had once been housework was now either moving out of the home entirely or being simplified by machinery. The use of commercial laundries, for instance, increased by 57 per cent between 1914 and 1924. Electric washing-machines and electric irons were coming to the aid of those who still did their washing at home; the manager of the local electric power company at "Middletown," a typical small American city, estimated in 1924 that nearly 90 per cent of the homes in the city already had electric irons. The housewife was learning to telephone her shopping orders, to get her clothes ready-made and spare herself the rigors of dress-making, to buy a vacuum cleaner and emulate the lovely carefree girls in the magazine advertisements who banished dust with such delicate fingers. Women were slowly becoming emancipated from routine to "live their own lives."

And what were these "own lives" of theirs to be like? Well, for one thing, they could take jobs. Up to this time girls of the middle classes who had wanted to "do something" had been largely restricted to school-teaching, social-service work, nursing, stenography, and clerical work in business houses. But now they poured out of the schools and colleges into all manner of new occupations. They besieged the offices of publishers and advertisers; they went into tearoom management until there threatened to be more purveyors than consumers of chicken patties and cinnamon toast; they sold antiques, sold real estate, opened smart little shops, and finally invaded the department stores. In 1920 the department store was in the mind of the average college girl a rather bourgeois institution which employed "poor shop girls"; by the end of the decade college girls were standing in line for openings in the misses' sports-wear department and even selling behind the counter in the hope that some day fortune might smile upon them and make them buyers or stylists. Small-town girls who once would have been contented to stay in Sauk Center all their days were now borrowing from father to go to New York or Chicago to seek their fortunes—in Best's or Macy's or Marshall Field's. Married women who were encumbered with children and could not seek jobs consoled themselves with the thought that home-making and child-rearing were really "professions," after all. No topic was so furiously discussed at luncheon tables from one end of the country to the other as the question whether the married woman should take a job, and whether the mother had a right to. And as for the unmarried woman, she no longer had to explain why she worked in a shop or an office; it was idleness, nowadays, that had to be defended.

With the job—or at least the sense that the job was a possibility—came a feeling of comparative economic independence. With the feeling of economic independence came a slackening of husbandly and parental authority. Maiden aunts and unmarried daughters were leaving the shelter of the family roof to install themselves in kitchenette apartments of their own. For city-dwellers the home was steadily becoming less of a shrine, more of a dormitory—a place of casual shelter where one stopped overnight on the way from the restaurant and the movie theater to the office. Yet even the job did not provide the American woman with that complete satisfaction which the management of a mechanized home no longer furnished. She still had energies and emotions to burn; she was ready for the revolution.

Like all revolutions, this one was stimulated by foreign propaganda. It came, however, not from Moscow, but from Vienna. Sigmund Freud had published his first book on psychoanalysis at the end of the nineteenth century, and he and Jung had lectured to American psychologists as early as 1909, but it was not until after the war that the Freudian gospel began to circulate to a marked extent among the American lay public. The one great intellectual force which had not suffered disrepute as a result of the war was science; the more-or-less educated public was now absorbing a quantity of popularized information about biology and anthropology which gave a general impression that men and women were merely animals of a rather intricate variety, and that moral codes had no universal validity and were often based on curious superstitions. A fertile ground was ready for the seeds of Freudianism, and presently one began to hear even from the lips of flappers that "science taught" new and disturbing things about sex. Sex, it appeared, was the central and pervasive force which moved mankind. Almost every human motive was attributable to it: if you were patriotic or liked the violin, you were in the grip of sex—in a sublimated form. The first requirement of mental health was to have an uninhibited sex life. If you would be well and happy, you must obey your libido. Such was the Freudian gospel as it imbedded itself in the American mind after being filtered through the successive minds of interpreters and popularizers and guileless readers and people who had heard guileless readers talk about it. New words and phrases began to be bandied about the cocktail-tray and the Mah Jong table—inferiority complex, sadism, masochism, Œdipus complex. Intellectual ladies went to Europe to be analyzed; analysts plied their new trade in American cities, conscientiously transferring the affections of their fair patients to themselves; and clergymen who preached about the virtue of self-control were reminded by outspoken critics that self-control was out-of-date and really dangerous.

The principal remaining forces which accelerated the revolution in manners and morals were all 100 per cent American. They were prohibition, the automobile, the confession and sex magazines, and the movies.

When the Eighteenth Amendment was ratified, prohibition seemed, as we have already noted, to have an almost united country behind it. Evasion of the law began immediately, however, and strenuous and sincere opposition to it—especially in the large cities of the North and East—quickly gathered force. The results were the bootlegger, the speakeasy, and a spirit of deliberate revolt which in many communities made drinking "the thing to do." From these facts in turn flowed further results: the increased popularity of distilled as against fermented liquors, the use of the hip-flask, the cocktail party, and the general transformation of drinking from a masculine prerogative to one shared by both sexes together. The old-time saloon had been overwhelmingly masculine; the speakeasy usually catered to both men and women. As Elmer Davis put it, "The old days when father spent his evenings at Cassidy's bar with the rest of the boys are gone, and probably gone forever; Cassidy may still be in business at the old stand and father may still go down there of evenings, but since prohibition mother goes down with him." Under the new régime not only the drinks were mixed, but the company as well.

Meanwhile a new sort of freedom was being made possible by the enormous increase in the use of the automobile, and particularly of the closed car. (In 1919 hardly more than 10 per cent of the cars produced in the United States were closed; by 1924, the percentage had jumped to 43, by 1927 it had reached 82.8.) The automobile offered an almost universally available means of escaping temporarily from the supervision of parents and chaperons, or from the influence of neighborhood opinion. Boys and girls now thought nothing, as the Lynds pointed out in *Middletown,* of jumping into a car and driving off at a moment's notice—without asking anybody's permission—to a dance in another town twenty miles away, where they were strangers and enjoyed a freedom impossible among their neighbors. The closed car, moreover, was in effect a room protected from the weather which could be occupied at any time of the day or night and could be moved at will into a darkened byway or a country lane. The Lynds quoted the judge of the juvenile court in "Middletown" as declaring that the automobile had become a "house of prostitution on wheels," and cited the fact that of thirty girls brought before his court in a year on charges of sex crimes, for whom the place where the offense had occurred was recorded, nineteen were listed as having committed it in an automobile.

Finally, as the revolution began, its influence fertilized a bumper crop of sex magazines, confession magazines, and lurid motion pictures, and these in turn had their effect on a class of readers and movie-goers who had never heard and never would hear of Freud and the libido. The publishers of the sex adventure magazines, offering stories with such titles as "What I Told My Daughter the Night Before Her Marriage," "Indolent Kisses," and "Watch Your Step-Ins," learned to a nicety the gentle art of arousing the reader without arousing the censor. The publishers of the confession magazines, while always instructing their authors to provide a moral ending and to utter pious sentiments, concentrated on the description of what they euphemistically called "missteps." Most of their fiction was faked to order by hack writers who could write one day "The Confessions of a Chorus Girl" and the next day recount, again in the first person, the temptations which made it easy for the taxi-driver to go wrong. Both classes of magazines became astonishingly numerous and successful. Bernarr McFadden's *True-Story*, launched as late as 1919, had over 300,000 readers by 1923; 848,000 by 1924; over a million and a half by 1925; and almost two million by 1926—a record of rapid growth probably unparalleled in magazine publishing.

Crowding the news stands along with the sex and confession magazines were motion-picture magazines which depicted "seven movie kisses" with such captions as "Do you recognize your little friend, Mae Busch? She's had lots of kisses, but she never seems to grow *blasé*. At least you'll agree that she's giving a good imitation of a person enjoying this one." The movies themselves, drawing millions to their doors every day and every night, played incessantly upon the same lucrative theme. The producers of one picture advertised "brilliant men, beautiful jazz babies, champagne baths, midnight revels, petting parties in the purple dawn, all ending in one terrific smashing climax that makes you gasp"; the venders of another promised "neckers, petters, white kisses, red kisses, pleasure-mad daughters, sensation-craving mothers, . . . the truth—bold, naked, sensational." Seldom did the films offer as much as these advertisements promised, but there was enough in some of them to cause a sixteen-year-old girl (quoted by Alice Miller Mitchell) to testify, "Those pictures with hot love-making in them, they make girls and boys sitting together want to get up and walk out, go off somewhere, you know. Once I walked out with a boy before the picture was even over. We took a ride. But my friend, she all the time had to get up and go out with her boy friend."

A storm of criticism from church organizations led the motion-picture producers, early in the decade, to install Will H. Hays, President Harding's Postmaster-General, as their arbiter of morals and of taste, and Mr. Hays promised that all would be well. "This industry must have," said he before the Los Angeles Chamber of Commerce, "toward that sacred thing, the mind of a child, toward that clean virgin thing, that unmarked slate, the same responsibility, the same care about the impressions made upon it, that the best clergyman or the most inspired teacher of youth would have." The result of Mr. Hays's labors in behalf of the unmarked slate was to make the moral ending as obligatory as in the confession magazines, to smear over sexy pictures with pious platitudes, and to blacklist for motion-picture production many a fine novel and play which, because of its very honesty, might be construed as seriously or intelligently questioning the traditional sex ethics of the small town. Mr. Hays, being something of a genius, managed to keep the churchmen at bay. Whenever the threats of censorship began to become ominous he would promulgate a new series of moral commandments for the producers to follow. Yet of the practical effects of his supervision it is perhaps enough to say that the quotations given above all date from the period of his distatorship. Giving lip-service to the old code, the movies diligently and with consummate vulgarity publicized the new.

Each of these diverse influences—the post-war disillusion, the new status of women, the Freudian gospel, the automobile, prohibition, the sex and confession magazines, and the movies—had its part in bringing about the revolution. Each of them, as an influence, was played upon by all the others; none of them could alone have changed to any great degree the folkways of America; together their force was irresistible.

The most conspicuous sign of what was taking place was the immense change in women's dress and appearance.

In Professor Paul H. Nystrom's *Economics of Fashion,* the trend of skirt-length during the Post-war Decade is ingeniously shown by the sort of graph with which business analysts delight to compute the ebb and flow of car-loadings or of stock averages. The basis of this graph is a series of measurements of fashion-plates in the *Delineator;* the statistician painstakingly measured the relation, from month to month, of the height of the skirt hem above the ground to the total height of the figure, and plotted his curve accordingly. This very unusual graph shows that in 1919 the average distance of the hem above the ground was about 10 per cent of the woman's height—or to put it in another way, about six or seven inches. In 1920 it curved upward from 10 to about 20 per cent. During the next three years it gradually dipped to 10 per cent again, reaching its low point in 1923. In 1924, however, it rose once more to between 15 and 20 per cent, in 1925 to more than 20 per cent; and the curve continued steadily upward until by 1927 it had passed the 25 per cent mark—in other words, until the skirt had reached the knee. There it remained until late in 1929.

This graph, as Professor Nystrom explains, does not accurately indicate what really happened, for it represents for any given year or month, not the average length of skirts actually worn, but the length of the skirt which the arbiters of fashion, not uninfluenced by the manufacturers of dress goods, expected and wanted women to wear. In actual fact, the dip between 1921 and 1924 was very slight. Paris dressmakers predicted the return of longer skirts, the American stylists and manufacturers followed their lead, the stores bought the longer skirts and tried to sell them, but women kept on buying the shortest skirts they could find. During the fall of 1923 and the spring of 1924, manufacturers were deluged with complaints from retailers that skirts would have to be shorter. Shorter they finally were, and still shorter. The knee-length dress proved to be exactly what women wanted. The unlucky manufacturers made valiant efforts to change the fashion. Despite all they could do, however, the knee-length skirt remained standard until the decade was approaching its end.

With the short skirt went an extraordinary change in the weight and material and amount of women's clothing. The boyishly slender figure became the aim of every woman's ambition, and the corset was so far abandoned that even in so short a period as the three years from 1924 to 1927 the combined sales of corsets and brassières in the department stores of the Cleveland Federal Reserve District fell off 11 per cent. Silk or rayon stockings and underwear supplanted cotton, to the distress of cotton manufacturers and the delight of rayon manufacturers; the production of rayon in American plants, which in 1920 had been only eight million pounds, had by 1925 reached fifty-three million pounds. The flesh-colored stocking became as standard as the short skirt. Petticoats almost vanished from the American scene; in fact, the tendency of women to drop off one layer of clothing after another became so pronounced that in 1928 the *Journal of Commerce* estimated that in 15 years the amount of material required for a woman's complete costume (exclusive of her stockings) had declined from 19¼ yards to 7 yards. All she could now be induced to wear, it seemed, was an overblouse (2 yards), a skirt (2¼ yards), vest or shirt (¾), knickers (2), and stockings—and all of them were made of silk or rayon!

This latter statement, it is true, was a slight exaggeration; but a survey published in 1926 by the National Retail Dry Goods Association, on the basis of data from department stores all over the country, showed that only 33 per cent of the women's underwear sold was made of cotton, whereas 36 per cent was made of rayon, and 31 per cent of silk. No longer were silk stockings the mark of the rich; as the wife of a workingman with a total family income of $1,638 a year told the authors of *Middletown,* "No girl can wear cotton stockings to high school. Even in winter my children wear silk stockings with lisle or imitations underneath."

Not content with the freedom of short and skimpy clothes, women sought, too, the freedom of short hair. During the early years of the decade the bobbed head—which in 1918, as you may recall, had been regarded by the proprietor of the Palm Garden in New York as a sign of radicalism—became increasingly frequent among young girls, chiefly on the ground of convenience. In May, 1922, the *American Hairdresser* predicted that the bob, which persisted in being popular, "will probably last through the summer, anyway." It not only did this, it so increased in popularity that by 1924 the same journal was forced to feature bobbed styles and give its subscribers instructions in the new art, and was reporting the progress of a lively battle between the professional hairdressers and the barbers for the cream of this booming business. The ladies' hairdressers very naturally objected to women going to barbers' shops; the barbers, on the other hand, were trying to force legislation in various states which would forbid the "hairdressing profession" to cut hair unless they were licensed as barbers. Said the *Hairdresser,* putting the matter on the loftiest basis, "The effort to bring women to barber shops for hair-cutting is against the best interests of the public, the free and easy atmosphere often prevailing in barber shops being unsuitable to the high standard of American womanhood." But all that American womanhood appeared to insist upon was the best possible shingle. In the latter years of the decade bobbed hair became almost universal among girls in their twenties, very common among women in their thirties and forties, and by no means rare among women of sixty; and for a brief period the hair was not only bobbed, but in most cases cropped close to the head like a man's. Women universally adopted the small cloche hat which fitted tightly on the bobbed head, and the manufacturer of milliner's materials joined the hair-net manufacturer, the hairpin manufacturer, and the cotton goods and woolen goods and corset manufacturers, among the ranks of depressed industries.

For another industry, however, the decade brought new and enormous profits. The manufacturers of cosmetics and the proprietors of beauty shops had less than nothing to complain of. The vogue of rouge and lipstick, which in 1920 had so alarmed the parents of the younger generation, spread swiftly to the remotest village. Women who in 1920 would have thought the use of paint immoral were soon applying it regularly as a matter of course and making no effort to disguise the fact; beauty shops had sprung up on every street to give "facials," to apply pomade and astringents, to make war against the wrinkles and sagging chins of age, to pluck and trim and color the eyebrows, and otherwise to enhance and restore the bloom of youth; and a strange new form of surgery, "face-lifting," took its place among the applied sciences of the day. Back in 1917, according to Frances Fisher Dubuc, only two persons in the beauty culture business had paid an income tax; by 1927 there were 18,000 firms and individuals in this field listed as income-tax payers. The "beautician" had arrived.

As for the total amount of money spent by American women on cosmetics and beauty culture by the end of the decade, we may probably accept as conservative the prodigious figure of three-quarters of a billion dollars set by Professor Paul H. Nystrom in 1930; other estimates, indeed, ran as high as two billion. Mrs. Christine Frederick tabulated in 1929 some other equally staggering figures: for every adult woman in the country there were being sold annually over a pound of face powder and no less than eight rouge compacts; there were 2,500 brands of perfume on the market and 1,500 face creams; and if all the lipsticks sold in a year in the United States were placed end to end, they would reach from New York to Reno—which to some would seem an altogether logical destination.

Perhaps the readiest way of measuring the change in the public attitude toward cosmetics is to compare the advertisements in a conservative periodical at the beginning of the decade with those at its end. Although the June, 1919, issue of the *Ladies' Home Journal* contained four advertisements which listed rouge among other products, only one of them commented on its inclusion, and this referred to its rouge as one that was "imperceptible if properly applied." In those days the woman who used rouge—at least in the circles in which the *Journal* was read—wished to disguise the fact. (Advertisements of talc, in 1919, commonly displayed a mother leaning affectionately over a bouncing baby.) In the June, 1929, issue, exactly ten years later, the *Journal* permitted a lipstick to be advertised with the comment, "It's comforting to know that the alluring note of scarlet will stay with you for hours." (Incidentally, the examination of those two magazines offers another contrast: in 1919 the Listerine advertisement said simply, "The prompt application of Listerine may prevent a minor accident from becoming a major infection," whereas in 1929 it began a tragic rhapsody with the words, "Spring! for everyone but her . . .")

These changes in fashion—the short skirt, the boyish form, the straight, long-waisted dresses, the frank use of paint—were signs of a real change in the American feminine ideal (as well, perhaps, as in men's idea of what was the feminine ideal). Women were bent on freedom—freedom to work and to play without the trammels that had bound them heretofore to lives of comparative inactivity. But what they sought was not the freedom from man and his desires which had put the suffragists of an earlier day into hard straw hats and mannish suits and low-heeled shoes. The woman of the nineteen-twenties wanted to be able to allure man even on the golf links and in the office; the little flapper who shingled her hair and wore a manageable little hat and put on knickerbockers for the week-ends would not be parted from her silk stockings and her high-heeled shoes. Nor was the postwar feminine ideal one of fruitful maturity or ripened wisdom or practiced grace. On the contrary: the quest of slenderness, the flattening of the breasts, the vogue of short skirts (even when short skirts still suggested the appearance of a little girl), the juvenile effect of the long waist,—all were signs that, consciously or unconsciously, the women of this decade worshiped not merely youth, but unripened youth: they wanted to be—or thought men wanted them to be—men's casual and light-hearted companions; not broad-hipped mothers of the race, but irresponsible playmates. Youth was their pattern, but not youthful innocence: the adolescent whom they imitated was a hard-boiled adolescent, who thought not in terms of romantic love, but in turns of sex, and who made herself desirable not by that sly art which conceals art, but frankly and openly. In effect, the woman of the Post-war Decade said to man, "You are tired and disillusioned, you do not want the cares of a family or the companionship of mature wisdom, you want exciting play, you want the thrills of sex without their fruition, and I will give them to you." And to herself she added, "But I will be free."

One indication of the revolution in manners which her headlong pursuit of freedom brought about was her rapid acceptance of the cigarette. Within a very few years millions of American women of all ages followed the lead of the flappers of 1920 and took up smoking. Custom still generally frowned upon their doing it on the street or in the office, and in the evangelical hinterlands the old taboo died hard; but in restaurants, at dinner parties and dances, in theater lobbies, and in a hundred other places they made the air blue. Here again the trend in advertising measured the trend in public opinion. At the beginning of the decade advertisers realized that it would have been suicidal to portray a woman smoking; within a few years, however, they ventured pictures of pretty girls imploring men to blow some of the smoke their way; and by the end of the decade billboards boldly displayed a smart-looking woman cigarette in hand, and in some of the magazines, despite floods of protests from rural readers, tobacco manufacturers were announcing that "now women may enjoy a companionable smoke with their husbands and brothers." In the ten years between 1918 and 1928 the total production of cigarettes in the United States *more than doubled*. Part of this increase was doubtless due to the death of the one-time masculine prejudice against the cigarette as unmanly, for it was accompanied by somewhat of a decrease in the production of cigars and smoking tobacco, as well as—mercifully—of chewing tobacco. Part of it was attributable to the fact that the convenience of the cigarette made the masculine smoker consume more tobacco than in the days when he preferred a cigar or a pipe. But the increase could never have been so large had it not been for the women who now strewed the dinner table with their ashes, snatched a puff between the acts, invaded the masculine sanctity of the club car, and forced department stores to place ornamental ash-trays between the chairs in their women's shoe departments. A formidable barrier between the sexes had broken down. The custom of separating them after formal dinners, for example, still lingered, but as an empty rite. Hosts who laid in a stock of cigars for their male guests often found them untouched; the men in the dining-room were smoking the very same brands of cigarettes that the ladies consumed in the living-room.

Of far greater social significance, however, was the fact that men and women were drinking together. Among well-to-do people the serving of cocktails before dinner became almost socially obligatory. Mixed parties swarmed up to the curtained grills of speakeasies and uttered the mystic password, and girls along with men stood at the speakeasy bar with one foot on the old brass rail. The late afternoon cocktail party became a new American institution. When dances were held in hotels, the curious and rather unsavory custom grew up of hiring hotel rooms where reliable drinks could be served in suitable privacy; guests of both sexes lounged on the beds and tossed off mixtures of high potency. As houses and apartments became smaller, the country club became the social center of the small city, the suburb, and the summer resort; and to its pretentious clubhouse, every Saturday night, drove men and women (after a round of cocktails at somebody's house) for the weekly dinner dance. Bottles of White Rock and of ginger ale decked the tables, out of capacious masculine hip pockets came flasks of gin (once the despised and rejected of bartenders, now the most popular of all liquors), and women who a few years before would have gasped at the thought that they would ever be "under the influence of alcohol" found themselves matching the men drink for drink and enjoying the uproarious release. The next day gossip would report that the reason Mrs. So-and-so disappeared from the party at eleven was because she had had too many cocktails and had been led to the dressing-room to be sick, or that somebody would have to meet the club's levy for breakage, or that Mrs. Such-and-such really oughtn't to drink so much because three cocktails made her throw bread about the table. A passing scandal would be created by a dance at which substantial married men amused themselves by tripping up waiters, or young people bent on petting parties drove right out on the golf-links and made wheel-tracks on the eighteenth green.

Such incidents were of course exceptional and in many communities they never occurred. It was altogether probable, though the professional wets denied it, that prohibition succeeded in reducing the total amount of drinking in the country as a whole and of reducing it decidedly among the workingmen of the industrial districts. The majority of experienced college administrators agreed—rather to the annoyance of some of their undergraduates—that there was less drinking among men students than there had been before prohibition and that drinking among girl students, at least while they were in residence, hardly offered a formidable problem. Yet the fact remained that among the prosperous classes which set the standards of national social behavior, alcohol flowed more freely than ever before and lubricated an unprecedented informality—to say the least—of manners.

It lubricated, too, a new outspokenness between men and women. Thanks to the spread of scientific skepticism and especially to Sigmund Freud, the dogmas of the conservative moralists were losing force and the dogma that salvation lay in facing the facts of sex was gaining. An upheaval in values was taking place. Modesty, reticence, and chivalry were going out of style; women no longer wanted to be "ladylike" or could appeal to their daughters to be "wholesome"; it was too widely suspected that the old-fashioned lady had been a sham and that the "wholesome" girl was merely inhibiting a nasty mind and would come to no good end. "Victorian" and "Puritan" were becoming terms of opprobrium: up-to-date people thought of Victorians as old ladies with bustles and inhibitions, and of Puritans as blue-nosed, ranting spoilsports. It was better to be modern,—everybody wanted to be modern, —and sophisticated, and smart, to smash the conventions and to be devastatingly frank. And with a cocktail glass in one's hand it was easy at least to be frank.

"Listen with a detached ear to a modern conversation," wrote Mary Agnes Hamilton in 1927, "and you will be struck, first, by the restriction of the vocabulary, and second, by the high proportion in that vocabulary of words such as, in the older jargon, 'no lady could use.'" With the taste for strong liquors went a taste for strong language. To one's lovely dinner partner, the inevitable antithesis for "grand" and "swell" had become "lousy." An unexpected "damn" or "hell" uttered on the New York stage was no longer a signal for the sudden sharp laughter of shocked surprise; such words were becoming the commonplace of everyday talk. The barroom anecdote of the decade before now went the rounds of aristocratic bridge tables. Every one wanted to be unshockable; it was delightful to be considered a little shocking; and so the competition in boldness of talk went on until for a time, as Mrs. Hamilton put it, a conversation in polite circles was like a room decorated entirely in scarlet—the result was overemphasis, stridency, and eventual boredom.

Along with the new frankness in conversation went a new frankness in books and the theater. Consider, for example, the themes of a handful of the best plays produced in New York during the decade: *What Price Glory,* which represented the amorous marines interlarding their talk with epithets new to the stage; *The Road to Rome,* the prime comic touch of which was the desire of a Roman matron to be despoiled by the Carthaginians; *Strange Interlude,* in which a wife who found there was insanity in her husband's family but wanted to give him a child decided to have the child by an attractive young doctor, instead of by her husband, and forthwith fell in love with the doctor; *Strictly Dishonorable,* in which a charming young girl walked blithely and open-eyed into an affair of a night with an opera-singer; and *The Captive,* which revealed to thousands of innocents the fact that the world contained such a phenomenon as homosexuality. None of these plays could have been tolerated even in New York before the Post-war Decade; all of them in the nineteen-twenties were not merely popular, but genuinely admired by intelligent audiences. The effect of some of them upon these audiences is suggested by the story of the sedate old lady who, after two acts of *What Price Glory,* reprimanded her grandson with a "God damn it, Johnny, sit down!"

The same thing was true of the novels of the decade; one after another, from *Jurgen* and *Dark Laughter* through the tales of Michael Arlen to *An American Tragedy* and *The Sun Also Rises* and *The Well of Loneliness* and *Point Counter Point*, they dealt with sex with an openness or a cynicism or an unmoral objectivity new to the English-speaking world. Bitterly the defenders of the Puritan code tried to stem the tide, but it was too strong for them. They banned *Jurgen*—and made a best seller of it and a public reputation for its author. They dragged Mary Ware Dennett into court for distributing a pamphlet for children which explained some of the mysteries of sex—only to have her upheld by a liberal judge and endorsed by intelligent public opinion. In Boston, where they were backed by an alliance between stubborn Puritanism and Roman Catholicism, they banned books wholesale, forebade the stage presentation of *Strange Interlude*, and secured the conviction of a bookseller for selling *Lady Chatterley's Lover*—only to find that the intellectuals of the whole country were laughing at them and that ultimately they were forced to allow the publication of books which they would have moved to ban ten years before. Despite all that they could do, the taste of the country demanded a new sort of reading matter.

Early in the decade a distinguished essayist wrote an article in which she contended that the physical processes of childbirth were humiliating to many women. She showed it to the editor of one of the best magazines, and he and she agreed that it should not be printed: too many readers would be repelled by the subject matter and horrified by the thesis. Only a few years later, in 1927, the editor recalled this manuscript and asked if he might see it again. He saw it—and wondered why it had ever been disqualified. Already such frankness seemed quite natural and permissible. The article was duly published, and caused only the mildest of sensations.

If in 1918 the editors of a reputable magazine had accepted a story in which one gangster said to another, "For Christ's sake, Joe, give her the gas. Some lousy bastard has killed Eddie," they would have whipped out the blue pencil and changed the passage to something like "For the love of Mike, Joe, give her the gas. Some dirty skunk has killed Eddie." In 1929 that sentence appeared in a story accepted by a magazine of the most unblemished standing, and was printed without alteration. A few readers objected, but not many. Times had changed. Even in the great popular periodicals with huge circulations and a considerable following in the strongholds of rural Methodism the change in standards was apparent. Said a short-story writer in the late nineteen-twenties, "I used to write for magazines like the *Saturday Evening Post* and the *Pictorial Review* when I had a nice innocuous tale to tell and wanted the money, and for magazines like *Harper's* and *Scribner's* when I wanted to write something searching and honest. Now I find I can sell the honest story to the big popular magazines too."

With the change in manners went an inevitable change in morals. Boys and girls were becoming sophisticated about sex at an earlier age; it was symptomatic that when the authors of *Middletown* asked 241 boys and 315 girls of high-school age to mark as true or false, according to their opinion, the extreme statement, "Nine out of every ten boys and girls of high-school age have petting parties," almost precisely half of them marked it as true. How much actual intercourse there was among such young people it is of course impossible to say; but the lurid stories told by Judge Lindsey—of girls who carried contraceptives in their vanity cases, and of "Caroline," who told the judge that fifty-eight girls of her acquaintance had had one or more sex experiences without a single pregnancy resulting—were matched by the gossip current in many a town. Whether prostitution increased or decreased during the decade is likewise uncertain; but certain it is that the prostitute was faced for the first time with an amateur competition of formidable proportions.

As for the amount of outright infidelity among married couples, one is again without reliable data, the private relations of men and women being happily beyond the reach of the statistician. The divorce rate, however, continued its steady increase; for every 100 marriages there were 8.8 divorces in 1910, 13.4 divorces in 1920, and 16.5 divorces in 1928—almost one divorce for every six marriages. There was a corresponding decline in the amount of disgrace accompanying divorce. In the urban communities men and women who had been divorced were now socially accepted without question; indeed, there was often about the divorced person just enough of an air of unconventionality, just enough of a touch of scarlet, to be considered rather dashing and desirable. Many young women probably felt as did the New York girl who said, toward the end of the decade, that she was thinking of marrying Henry, although she didn't care very much for him, because even if they didn't get along she could get a divorce and "it would be much more exciting to be a divorcée than to be an old maid."

The petting party, which in the first years of the decade had been limited to youngsters in their teens and twenties, soon made its appearance among older men and women: when the gin-flask was passed about the hotel bedroom during a dance, or the musicians stilled their saxophones during the Saturday-night party at the country club, men of affairs and women with half-grown children had their little taste of raw sex. One began to hear of young girls, intelligent and well born, who had spent week-ends with men before marriage and had told their prospective husbands everything and had been not merely forgiven, but told that there was nothing to forgive; a little "experience," these men felt, was all to the good for any girl. Millions of people were moving toward acceptance of what a *bon-vivant* of earlier days had said was his idea of the proper state of morality—"A single standard, and that a low one."

It would be easy, of course, to match every one of these cases with contrasting cases of men and women who still thought and behaved at the end of the decade exactly as the president of the Epworth League would have wished. Two women who conducted newspaper columns of advice in affairs of the heart testified that the sort of problem which was worrying young America, to judge from their bulging correspondence, was not whether to tell the boy friend about the illegitimate child, but whether it was proper to invite the boy friend up on the porch if he hadn't yet come across with an invitation to the movies, or whether the cake at a pie social should be cut with a knife. In the hinterlands there was still plenty of old-fashioned sentimental thinking about sex, of the sort which expressed itself in the slogan of a federated women's club: "Men are God's trees, women are His flowers." There were frantic efforts to stay the tide of moral change by law, the most picturesque of these efforts being the ordinance actually passed in Norphelt, Arkansas, in 1925, which contained the following provisions:

"Section 1. Hereafter it shall be unlawful for any man and woman, male or female, to be guilty of committing the act of sexual intercourse between themselves at any place within the corporate limits of said town.

"Section 3. Section One of this ordinance shall not apply to married persons as between themselves, and their husband and wife, unless of a grossly improper and lascivious nature."

Nevertheless, there was an unmistakable and rapid trend away from the old American code toward a philosophy of sex relations and of marriage wholly new to the country: toward a feeling that the virtues of chastity and fidelity had been rated too highly, that there was something to be said for what Mrs. Bertrand Russell defined as "the right, equally shared by men and women, to free participation in sex experience," that it was not necessary for girls to deny themselves this right before marriage or even for husbands and wives to do so after marriage. It was in acknowledgment of the spread of this feeling that Judge Lindsey proposed, in 1927, to establish "companionate marriage" on a legal basis. He wanted to legalize birth control (which, although still outlawed, was by this time generally practiced or believed in by married couples in all but the most ignorant classes) and to permit legal marriage to be terminated at any time in divorce by mutual consent, provided there were no children. His suggestion created great consternation and was widely and vigorously denounced; but the mere fact that it was seriously debated showed how the code of an earlier day had been shaken. The revolution in morals was in full swing.

A time of revolution, however, is an uneasy time to live in. It is easier to tear down a code than to put a new one in its place, and meanwhile there is bound to be more or less wear and tear and general unpleasantness. People who have been brought up to think that it is sinful for women to smoke or drink, and scandalous for sex to be discussed across the luncheon table, and unthinkable for a young girl to countenance strictly dishonorable attentions from a man, cannot all at once forget the admonitions of their childhood. It takes longer to hard-boil a man or a woman than an egg. Some of the apostles of the new freedom appeared to imagine that habits of thought could be changed overnight, and that if you only dragged the secrets of sex out into the daylight and let every one do just as he pleased at the moment, society would at once enter upon a state of barbaric innocence like that of the remotest South Sea Islanders. But it couldn't be done. When you drag the secrets of sex out into the daylight, the first thing that the sons and daughters of Mr. and Mrs. Grundy do is to fall all over themselves in the effort to have a good look, and for a time they can think of nothing else. If you let every one do just as he pleases, he is as likely as not to begin by making a nuisance of himself. He may even shortly discover that making a nuisance of himself is not, after all, the recipe for lasting happiness. So it happened when the old codes were broken down in the Post-war Decade.

One of the most striking results of the revolution was a widely pervasive obsession with sex. To listen to the conversation of some of the sons and daughters of Mr. and Mrs. Grundy was to be reminded of the girl whose father said that she would talk about anything; in fact, she hardly ever talked about anything else. The public attitude toward any number of problems of the day revealed this obsession: to give a single example, the fashionable argument against women's colleges at this period had nothing to do with the curriculum or with the intellectual future of the woman graduate, but pointed out that living with girls for four years was likely to distort a woman's sex life. The public taste in reading matter revealed it: to say nothing of the sex magazines and the tabloids and the acres of newspaper space devoted to juicy scandals like that of Daddy Browning and his Peaches, it was significant that almost every one of the novelists who were ranked most highly by the post-war intellectuals was at outs with the censors, and that the Pulitzer Prize juries had a hard time meeting the requirements that the prize-winning novel should "present the wholesome atmosphere of American life and the highest standard of American manners and manhood," and finally had to alter the terms of the award, substituting "whole" for "wholesome" and omitting reference to "highest standards." There were few distinguished novels being written which one could identify with a "wholesome atmosphere" without making what the Senate would call interpretive reservations. Readers who considered themselves "modern-minded" did not want them: they wanted the philosophical promiscuity of Aldous Huxley's men and women, the perfumed indiscretions of Michael Arlen's degenerates, Ernest Hemingway's unflinching account of the fleeting amours of the drunken Brett Ashley, Anita Loo's comedy of two kept women and their gentlemen friends, Radclyffe Hall's study of homosexuality. Young men and women who a few years before would have been championing radical economic or political doctrines were championing the new morality and talking about it everywhere and thinking of it incessantly. Sex was in the limelight, and the Grundy children could not turn their eyes away.

Another result of the revolution was that manners became

no merely different, but—for a few years—unmannerly. It was no mere coincidence that during this decade hostesses—even at small parties—found that their guests couldn't be bothered to speak to them on arrival or departure; that "gate-crashing" at dances became an accepted practice; that thousands of men and women made a point of not getting to dinners within half an hour of the appointed time lest they seem insufficiently *blasé*; that house parties of flappers and their wide-trousered swains left burning cigarettes on the mahogany tables, scattered ashes light-heartedly on the rugs, took the porch cushions out in the boats and left them there to be rained on, without apology; or that men and women who had had—as the old phrase went—"advantages" and considered themselves highly civilized, absorbed a few cocktails and straightway turned a dinner party into a boisterous rout, forgetting that a general roughhouse was not precisely the sign of a return to the Greek idea of the good life. The old bars were down, no new ones had been built, and meanwhile the pigs were in the pasture. Some day, perhaps, the ten years which followed the war may aptly be known as the Decade of Bad Manners.

Nor was it easy to throw overboard the moral code and substitute another without confusion and distress. It was one thing to proclaim that married couples should be free to find sex adventure wherever they pleased and that marriage was something independent of such casual sport; it was quite another thing for a man or woman in whom the ideal of romantic marriage had been ingrained since early childhood to tolerate infidelities when they actually took place. Judge Lindsey told the story of a woman who had made up her mind that her husband might love whom he pleased; she would be modern and think none the less of him for it. But whenever she laid eyes on her rival she was physically sick. Her mind, she discovered, was hard-boiled only on the surface. That woman had many a counterpart during the revolution in morals; behind the grim statistics of divorce there was many a case of husband and wife experimenting with the new freedom and suddenly finding that there was dynamite in it which wrecked that mutual confidence and esteem without which marriage—even for the sake of their children—could not be endured.

The new code had been born in disillusionment, and beneath all the bravado of its exponents and the talk about entering upon a new era the disillusionment persisted. If the decade was ill-mannered, it was also unhappy. With the old order of things had gone a set of values which had given richness and meaning to life, and substitute values were not easily found. If morality was dethroned, what was to take its place? Honor, said some of the prophets of the new day: "It doesn't matter much what you do so long as you're honest about it." A brave ideal—yet it did not wholly satisfy; it was too vague, too austere, too difficult to apply. If romantic love was dethroned, what was to take its place? Sex? But as Joseph Wood Krutch explained, "If love has come to be less often a sin, it has also come to be less often a supreme privilege." And as Walter Lippmann, in *A Preface to Morals,* added after quoting Mr. Krutch, "If you start with the belief that love is the pleasure of a moment, is it really surprising that it yields only a momentary pleasure?" The end of the pursuit of sex alone was emptiness and futility—the emptiness and futility to which Lady Brett Ashley and her friends in *The Sun Also Rises* were so tragically doomed.

There were not, to be sure, many Brett Ashleys in the United States during the Post-war Decade. Yet there were millions to whom in some degree came for a time the same disillusionment and with it the same unhappiness. They could not endure a life without values, and the only values they had been trained to understand were being undermined. Everything seemed meaningless and unimportant. Well, at least one could toss off a few drinks and get a kick out of physical passion and forget that the world was crumbling. . . . And so the saxophones wailed and the gin-flask went its rounds and the dancers made their treadmill circuit with half-closed eyes, and the outside world, so merciless and so insane, was shut away for a restless night. . . .

It takes time to build up a new code. Not until the decade was approaching its end did there appear signs that the revolutionists were once more learning to be at home in their world, to rid themselves of their obsession with sex, to adjust themselves emotionally to the change in conventions and standards, to live the freer and franker life of this new era gracefully, and to discover among the ruins of the old dispensation a new set of enduring satisfactions.

For Further Reading

In *Since Yesterday* (1939), Allen carries his informal history through 1939. Two other early efforts to assess the twenties deserve mention: James C. Malin, *The United States After the World War* (1930), and Preston W. Slosson, *The Great Crusade and After, 1914–1928* (1930). Social histories patterned on *Only Yesterday* include Henry Morton Robinson, *Fantastic Interim* (1943), and Laurence Greene, *The Era of Wonderful Nonsense* (1939). A contemporary assessment of the revolution in morals is Freda Kirchway, ed., *Our Changing Morality: A Symposium* (1924). See also Walter Lippmann, *A Preface to Morals* (1929). William E. Leuchtenburg, *The Perils of Prosperity: 1914–32* (1958), covers a somewhat broader period but is admirable on the 1920's. Also recommended is Paul Carter, *The Twenties in America* (1968), which is really a long, interpretative and perceptive essay, and John D. Hicks, *Republican Ascendancy, 1921–1933* (1960).

On political history Arthur Schlesinger, Jr., *The Crisis of the Old Order, 1918–1933* (1957), offers a critical but convincing indictment of the old politics. Even less restrained is Karl Shriftgiesser, *This War Normalcy* (1948). On the Harding administration, the traditional account by Samuel Hopkins Adams, *Incredible Era, the Life and Times of Warren Gamaliel Harding* (1939), has been amplified and revised to a certain extent by Andrew Sinclair, *The Available Man* (1965), and Francis Russell, *The Shadow of Blooming Grove* (1968), both biographies of Harding.

William Allen White, *A Puritan in Babylon: The Story of Calvin Coolidge* (1938), enables us to understand its subject better than does Claude Feuss, *Calvin Coolidge* (1940). Good, full-length studies are needed for both the 1928 candidates. On Smith, Oscar Handlin's *Al Smith and His America* (1958) is an excellent short biography. For Hoover, see Ray L. Wilbur and Arthur Hyde, *The Hoover Policies* (1937).

Monographic studies of various aspects of the 1920's are plentiful. Robert K. Murray, *Red Scare* (1955), is competent and well written. The literature on Sacco-Vanzetti is enormous, but of particular value are G. Louis Joughin and Edmund M. Morgan, *The Legacy of Sacco and Vanzetti* (1948), and Francis Russell, *Tragedy in Dedham* (1962), which offers an intriguing new explanation.

The rise and fall of prohibition is described in Andrew Sinclair, *The Era of Excess* (1962). Claude Merz's *The Dry Decade* (1931) was written while the "noble experiment" was still going on. Arnold S. Rice's *The Ku Klux Klan in America* (1962) is well researched and thoughtful. On the evolution controversy, consult Ray Ginger, *Six Days or Forever?* (1958), and Norman F. Furniss, *The Fundamentalist Controversy, 1918–1931* (1954).

The Great Crash: Cause and Consequence

John Kenneth Galbraith

According to the calendar, the 1920's ended on December 31, 1929, but the Prosperity Decade had symbolically expired two months earlier on October 24. On this day, Black Thursday, the great stock market crash began. In a frenzy of excitement thousands of speculators who had ridden a roaring bull market for years rushed to get out while the getting was good. More than 12,890,000 shares changed hands amid a scene of panic and confusion. At an emergency meeting leading New York bankers agreed to shore up the market by a fresh infusion of money, but this succeeded in stabilizing the situation for only a few days. By the end of October it was quite evident that, as the theater publication *Variety* expressed it, Wall Street had laid an egg. Stockholders had suffered paper losses of more than $15 billion in less than a week; by the end of the year the total would reach $40 billion. But even this decline proved to be only the beginning of the end.

Source: John Kenneth Galbraith, *The Great Crash, 1929* (Boston: Houghton Mifflin Company, 1955), pp. 173–199. Copyright 1955 by John Kenneth Galbraith. Reprinted by permission of the publisher.

Between September 1929 and January 1930, the value of thirty industrial stocks on the Dow-Jones index declined from $364.90 to $62.60. Other securities tumbled at an even more incredible rate: U.S. Steel dropped from 262 in September 1929 to 150 in November and to 22 in the summer of 1932; during the same period Montgomery Ward declined from 138 to 49 to 4.

Immediately after the stock market debacle efforts were made to assure the nation that the basic prosperity of the country had not been imperiled. The *Wall Street Journal* scoffed at suggestions that the "wiping out of paper profits will reduce the country's real purchasing power" and bankers and government officials competed with each other in issuing optimistic prognostications on business recovery. But the cycle of economic disaster did not stop. More than three thousand banks failed in the three years following the crash, bankruptcies became everyday occurrences throughout the country, and the gross national product for 1933 fell to its lowest level since 1907. Unemployment was staggering, reaching at least thirteen million by 1933. New York City had more than one million unemployed but in some industrial cities the ratio was much higher. According to William E. Leuchtenburg, in Cleveland 50 per cent were jobless, in Akron, 60 per cent, in Toledo, 80 per cent. In Donora, Pennsylvania, only 277 of 13,900 workers held regular jobs. In the three years after the crash, an average of one hundred thousand workers were fired every week.

One can hardly exaggerate the effect of the crisis on President Herbert Hoover. When he assumed office in March 1929, every indicator pointed to a successful administration by the leading technician of "the New Era." Hoover embodied the American ideal of the self-made man. Born on an Iowa farm, he had successively made a fortune as a mining engineer, directed the relief of starving Belgians, and served magnificently as Food Administrator in World War I. As Secretary of Commerce under Harding and Coolidge, he came to be regarded as the outstanding Republican statesman in the country, not excluding the Presidents he had served. During the 1928 presidential campaign, he spoke often of the glorious future that lay ahead for a nation about to celebrate its final triumph over poverty; others had more prosaically promised two chickens in every pot and two cars in every garage. Few doubted Hoover's predictions; if anything his popularity increased after his inauguration. Then with abrupt suddenness came the crash, followed by the depression. By 1933, the President had become an object of bitter scorn. Shantytowns that arose on the edges of cities became known as Hoovervilles, and newspapers used to cover the unemployed who were sleeping on park benches were Hoover blankets. Bewildered by the failure of the economy to correct itself, Hoover handled the crisis ineptly. Because he did not really understand either the causes or the consequences of the crash, he tended to minimize the crisis and to assure the nation that prosperity was just around the corner. In his *Memoirs,* he explained the large number of men selling apples on the street corners as part of a conspiracy by the apple growers associations and made the astonishing assertion: "Many persons left their jobs for the more profitable one of selling apples." When the Democrats charged that Hoover and the Republicans caused the depression and kept it going by their policies, Hoover countered that the U.S. economy suffered because of the worldwide depression, and later claimed that full recovery had been prevented only by the Democratic victory in 1932.

In the following selection, John Kenneth Galbraith (b. 1908), perhaps the best-known American economist of the post-World War II era, disregards these simplistic partisan explanations and shows just how weak the economy had become by 1929. Of itself, the panic could not have caused the great depression. The day after Black Thursday, Hoover expressed the common belief of the financial community and that of most of the nation's economists when he stated: "The fundamental business of the country—that is, the production and distribution of goods and services—is on a sound and prosperous basis." Even such an eminent authority as the British economist John Maynard Keynes argued that commodity prices would improve since the money previously absorbed by the swollen market would now be available for the use of industry. But Hoover and Keynes were wrong; they had not gauged the situation correctly. Galbraith, who served as Ambassador to India from 1961 to 1963 and is a foremost proponent of plans to devote more of the nation's wealth to public services and less to private consumption, focuses on the factors that made the economy fundamentally unsound.

*A*fter the Great Crash came the Great Depression which lasted, with varying severity, for ten years. In 1933, Gross National Product (total production of the economy) was nearly a third less than in 1929. Not until 1937 did the physical volume of production recover to the levels of 1929, and then it promptly slipped back again. Until 1941 the dollar value of production remained below 1929. Between 1930 and 1940 only once, in 1937, did the average number unemployed during the year drop below eight million. In 1933 nearly thirteen million were out of work, or about one in every four in the labor force. In 1938 one person in five was still out of work.

It was during this dreary time that 1929 became a year of myth. People hoped that the country might get back to twenty-nine; in some industries or towns when business was phenomenally good it was almost as good as in twenty-nine; men of outstanding vision, on occasions of exceptional solemnity, were heard to say that 1929 "was no better than Americans deserve."

On the whole, the great stock market crash can be much more readily explained than the depression that followed it. And among the problems involved in assessing the causes of depression none is more intractable than the responsibility to be assigned to the stock market crash. Economics still does not allow final answers on these matters. But, as usual, something can be said.

As already so often emphasized, the collapse in the stock market in the autumn of 1929 was implicit in the speculation that went before. The only question concerning that speculation was how long it would last. Sometime, sooner or later, confidence in the short-run reality of increasing common stock values would weaken. When this happened, some people would sell, and this would destroy the reality of increasing values. Holding for an increase would now become meaningless; the new reality would be falling prices. There would be a rush, pellmell, to unload. This was the way past speculative orgies had ended. It was the way the end came in 1929. It is the way speculation will end in the future.

We do not know why a great speculative orgy occurred in 1928 and 1929. The long accepted explanation that credit was easy and so people were impelled to borrow money to buy common stocks on margin is obviously nonsense. On numerous occasions before and since credit has been easy, and there has been no speculation whatever. Furthermore, much of the 1928 and 1929 speculation occurred on money borrowed at interest rates which for years before, and in any period since, would have been considered exceptionally astringent. Money, by the ordinary tests, was tight in the late twenties.

Far more important than rate of interest and the supply of credit is the mood. Speculation on a large scale requires a pervasive sense of confidence and optimism and conviction that ordinary people were meant to be rich. People must also have faith in the good intentions and even in the benevolence of others, for it is by the agency of others that they will get rich. In 1929 Professor Dice observed: "The common folks believe in their leaders. We no longer look upon the captains of industry as magnified crooks. Have we not heard their voices over the radio? Are we not familiar with their thoughts, ambitions, and ideals as they have expressed them to us almost as a man talks to his friend?" Such a feeling of trust is essential for a boom. When people are cautious, questioning, misanthropic, suspicious, or mean, they are immune to speculative enthusiasms.

Savings must also be plentiful. Speculation, however it may rely on borrowed funds, must be nourished in part by those who participate. If savings are growing rapidly, people will place a lower marginal value on their accumulation; they will be willing to risk some of it against the prospect of a greatly enhanced return. Speculation, accordingly, is most likely to break out after a substantial period of prosperity, rather than in the early phases of recovery from a depression. Macaulay noted that between the Restoration and the Glorious Revolution, Englishmen were at loss to know what to do with their savings and that the "natural effect of this state of things was that a crowd of projectors, ingenious and absurd, honest and knavish, employed themselves in devising new schemes for the employment of redundant capital." Bagehot and others have attributed the South Sea Bubble to roughly the same causes. In 1720 England had enjoyed a long period of prosperity, enhanced in part by war expenditures, and during this time private savings are believed to have grown at an unprecedented rate. Investment outlets were also few and returns low. Accordingly, Englishmen were anxious to place their savings at the disposal of the new enterprises and were quick to believe that the prospects were not fantastic. So it was in 1928 and 1929.

Finally, a speculative outbreak has a greater or less immunizing effect. The ensuing collapse automatically destroys the very mood speculation requires. It follows that an outbreak of speculation provides a reasonable assurance that another outbreak will not immediately occur. With time and the dimming of memory, the immunity wears off. A recurrence becomes possible. Nothing would have induced Americans to launch a speculative adventure in the stock market in 1935. By 1955 the chances are very much better.

As noted, it is easier to account for the boom and crash in the market than to explain their bearing on the depression which followed. The causes of the Great Depression are still far from certain. A lack of certainty, it may also be observed, is not evident in the contemporary writing on the subject. Much of it tells what went wrong and why with marked firmness. However, this paradoxically can itself be an indication of uncertainty. When people are least sure they are often most dogmatic. We do not know what the Russians intend, so we state with great assurance what they will do. We compensate for our inability to foretell the consequences of, say, rearming Germany by asserting positively just what the consequences will be. So it is in economics. Yet, in explaining what happened in 1929 and after, one can distinguish between explanations that might be right and those that are clearly wrong.

A great many people have always felt that a depression was inevitable in the thirties. There had been (at least) seven good years; now by an occult or biblical law of compensation there would have to be seven bad ones. Perhaps, consciously or unconsciously, an argument that was valid for the stock market was brought to bear on the economy in general. Because the market took leave of reality in 1928 and 1929, it had at some time to make a return to reality. The disenchantment was bound to be as painful as the illusions were beguiling. Similarly, the New Era prosperity would some day evaporate; in its wake would come the compensating hardship.

There is also the slightly more subtle conviction that economic life is governed by an inevitable rhythm. After a certain time prosperity destroys itself and depression corrects itself. In 1929 prosperity, in accordance with the dictates of the business cycle, had run its course. This was the faith confessed by the members of the Harvard Economic Society in the spring of 1929 when they concluded that a recession was somehow overdue.

Neither of these beliefs can be seriously supported. The twenties by being comparatively prosperous established no imperative that the thirties be depressed. In the past, good times have given way to less good times and less good or bad to good. But change is normal in a capitalist economy. The degree of regularity in such movements is not great, though often thought to be. No inevitable rhythm required the collapse and stagnation of 1930–40.

Nor was the economy of the United States in 1929 subject to such physical pressure or strain as the result of its past level of performance that a depression was bound to come. The notion that the economy requires occasional rest and resuscitation has a measure of plausibility and also a marked viability. During the summer of 1954 a professional economist on President Eisenhower's personal staff explained the then current recession by saying that the economy was enjoying a brief (and presumably well-merited) rest after the exceptional exertions of preceding years. In 1929 the labor force was not tired; it could have continued to produce indefinitely at the best 1929 rate. The capital plant of the country was not depleted. In the preceding years of prosperity, plant had been renewed and improved. In fact, depletion of the capital plant occurred during the ensuing years of idleness when new investment was sharply curtailed. Raw materials in 1929 were ample for the current rate of production. Entrepreneurs were never more eupeptic. Obviously if men, materials, plant, and management were all capable of continued and even enlarged exertions a refreshing pause was not necessary.

Finally, the high production of the twenties did not, as some have suggested, outrun the wants of the people. During these years people were indeed being supplied with an increasing volume of goods. But there is no evidence that their desire for automobiles, clothing, travel, recreation, or even food was sated. On the contrary, all subsequent evidence showed (given the income to spend) a capacity for a large further increase in consumption. A depression was not needed so that people's wants could catch up with their capacity to produce.

What, then, are the plausible causes of the depression? The task of answering can be simplified somewhat by dividing the problem into two parts. First there is the question of why economic activity turned down in 1929. Second there is the vastly more important question of why, having started down, on this unhappy occasion it went down and down and down and remained low for a full decade.

As noted, the Federal Reserve indexes of industrial activity and of factory production, the most comprehensive monthly measures of economic activity then available, reached a peak in June. They then turned down and continued to decline throughout the rest of the year. The turning point in other indicators—factory payrolls, freight-car loadings, and department store sales—came later, and it was October or after before the trend in all of them was clearly down. Still, as economists have generally insisted, and the matter has the high authority of the National Bureau of Economic Research, the economy had weakened in the early summer well before the crash.

This weakening can be variously explained. Production of industrial products, for the moment, had outrun consumer and investment demand for them. The most likely reason is that business concerns, in the characteristic enthusiasm of good times, misjudged the prospective increase in demand and acquired larger inventories than they later found they needed. As a result they curtailed their buying, and this led to a cutback in production. In short, the summer of 1929 marked the beginning of the familiar inventory recession. The proof is not conclusive from the (by present standards) limited figures available. Department store inventories, for which figures are available, seem not to have been out of line early in the year. But a mild slump in department store sales in April could have been a signal for curtailment.

Also there is a chance—one that students of the period have generally favored—that more deep-seated factors were at work and made themselves seriously evident for the first time during that summer. Throughout the twenties production and productivity per worker grew steadily: between 1919 and 1929, output per worker in manufacturing industries increased by about 43 per cent. Wages, salaries, and prices all remained comparatively stable, or in any case underwent no comparable increase. Accordingly, costs fell and with prices the same, profits increased. These profits sustained the spending of the well-to-do, and they also nourished at least some of the expectations behind the stock marked boom. Most of all they encouraged a very high level of capital investment. During the twenties, the production of capital goods increased at an average annual rate of 6.4 per cent a year; non-durable consumers' goods, a category which includes such objects of mass consumption as food and clothing, increased at a rate of only 2.8 per cent. (The rate of increase for durable consumers' goods such as cars, dwellings, home furnishings, and the like, much of it representing expenditures of the well-off to well-to-do, was 5.9 per cent.) A large and increasing investment in capital goods was, in other words, a principal device by which the profits were being spent. It follows that anything that interrupted the investment outlays—anything, indeed, which kept them from showing the necessary rate of increase—could cause trouble. When this occurred, compensation through an increase in consumer spending could not automatically be expected. The effect therefore, of insufficient investment—investment that failed to keep pace with the steady increase in profits—could be falling total demand reflected in turn in falling orders and output. Again there is no final proof of this point, for unfortunately we do not know how rapidly investment had to grow to keep abreast of the current increase in profits. However, the explanation is broadly consistent with the facts.

There are other possible explanations of the downturn.

Back of the insufficient advance in investment may have been the high interest rates. Perhaps, although less probably, trouble was transmitted to the economy as a whole from some weak sector like agriculture. Further explanations could be offered. But one thing about this experience is clear. Until well along in the autumn of 1929 the downturn was limited. The recession in business activity was modest and underemployment relatively slight. Up to November it was possible to argue that not much of anything had happened. On other occasions, as noted—in 1924 and 1927 and of late in 1949— the economy has undergone similar recession. But, unlike these other occasions, in 1929 the recession continued and continued and got violently worse. This is the unique feature of the 1929 experience. This is what we need really to understand.

There seems little question that in 1929, modifying a famous cliché, the economy was fundamentally unsound. This is a circumstance of first-rate importance. Many things were wrong, but five weaknesses seem to have had an especially intimate bearing on the ensuing disaster. They are:

1) The bad distribution of income. In 1929 the rich were indubitably rich. The figures are not entirely satisfactory, but it seems certain that the 5 per cent of the population with the highest incomes in that year received approximately one third of all personal income. The proportion of personal income received in the form of interest, dividends, and rent—the income, broadly speaking, of the well-to-do—was about twice as great as in the years following the Second World War.

This highly unequal income distribution meant that the economy was dependent on a high level of investment or a high level of luxury consumer spending or both. The rich cannot buy great quantities of bread. If they are to dispose of what they receive it must be on luxuries or by way of investment in new plants and new projects. Both investment and luxury spending are subject, inevitably, to more erratic influences and to wider fluctuations than the bread and rent outlays of the $25-a-week workman. This high-bracket spending and investment was especially susceptible, one may assume, to the crushing news from the stock market in October of 1929.

2) *The bad corporate structure.* In November 1929, a few weeks after the crash, the Harvard Economic Society gave as a principal reason why a depression need not be feared its reasoned judgment that "business in most lines has been conducted with prudence and conservatism." The fact was that American enterprise in the twenties had opened its hospitable arms to an exceptional number of promoters, grafters, swindlers, impostors, and frauds. This, in the long history of such activities, was a kind of flood tide of corporate larceny.

The most important corporate weakness was inherent in the vast new structure of holding companies and investment trusts. The holding companies controlled large segments of the utility, railroad, and entertainment business. Here, as with the investment trusts, was the constant danger of devastation by reverse leverage. In particular, dividends from the operating companies paid the interest on the bonds of upstream holding companies. The interruption of the dividends meant default on the bonds, bankruptcy, and the collapse of the structure. Under these circumstances, the temptation to curtail investment in operating plant in order to continue dividends was obviously strong. This added to deflationary pressures. The latter, in turn, curtailed earnings and helped bring down the corporate pyramids. When this happened, even more retrenchment was inevitable. Income was earmarked for debt repayment. Borrowing for new investment became impossible. It would be hard to imagine a corporate system better designed to continue and accentuate a deflationary spiral.

3) *The bad banking structure.* Since the early thirties, a generation of Americans has been told, sometimes with amusement, sometimes with indignation, often with outrage, of the banking practices of the late twenties. In fact, many

of these practices were made ludicrous only by the depression. Loans which would have been perfectly good were made perfectly foolish by the collapse of the borrower's prices or the markets for his goods or the value of the collateral he had posted. The most responsible bankers—those who saw that their debtors were victims of circumstances far beyond their control and sought to help—were often made to look the worst. The bankers yielded, as did others, to the blithe, optimistic, and immoral mood of times but probably not more so. A depression such as that of 1929–32, were it to begin as this is written, would also be damaging to many currently impeccable banking reputations.

However, although the bankers were not unusually foolish in 1929, the banking structure was inherently weak. The weakness was implicit in the large numbers of independent units. When one bank failed, the assets of others were frozen while depositors elsewhere had a pregnant warning to go and ask for their money. Thus one failure led to other failures, and these spread with a domino effect. Even in the best of times local misfortune or isolated mismanagement could start such a chain reaction. (In the first six months of 1929, 346 banks failed in various parts of the country with aggregate deposits of nearly $115 million.) When income, employment, and values fell as the result of a depression bank failures could quickly become epidemic. This happened after 1929. Again it would be hard to imagine a better arrangement for magnifying the effects of fear. The weak destroyed not only the other weak, but weakened the strong. People everywhere, rich and poor, were made aware of the disaster by the persuasive intelligence that their savings had been destroyed.

Needless to say, such a banking system, once in the convulsions of failure, had a uniquely repressive effect on the spending of its depositors and the investment of its clients.

4) The dubious state of the foreign balance. This is a familiar story. During the First World War, the United States became a creditor on international account. In the decade

following, the surplus of exports over imports which once had paid the interest and principal on loans from Europe continued. The high tariffs, which restricted imports and helped to create this surplus of exports remained. However, history and traditional trading habits also accounted for the persistence of the favorable balance, so called.

Before, payments on interest and principal had in effect been deducted from the trade balance. Now that the United States was a creditor, they were added to this balance. The latter, it should be said, was not huge. In only one year (1928) did the excess of exports over imports come to as much as a billion dollars; in 1923 and 1926 it was only about $375,000,000. However, large or small, this difference had to be covered. Other countries which were buying more than they sold, and had debt payments to make in addition, had somehow to find the means for making up the deficit in their transactions with the United States.

During most of the twenties the difference was covered by cash—i.e., gold payments to the United States—and by new private loans by the United States to other countries. Most of the loans were to governments—national, state, or municipal bodies—and a large proportion were to Germany and Central and South America. The underwriters' margins in handling these loans were generous; the public took them up with enthusiasm; competition for the business was keen. If unfortunately corruption and bribery were required as competitive instruments, these were used. In late 1927 Juan Leguia, the son of the President of Peru, was paid $450,000 by J. and W. Seligman and Company and the National City Company (the security affiliate of the National City Bank) for his services in connection with a $50,000,000 loan which these houses marketed for Peru. Juan's services, according to later testimony, were of a rather negative sort. He was paid for not blocking the deal. The Chase extended President Machado of Cuba, a dictator with a marked predisposition toward murder, a generous personal line of credit which at one time reached $200,000. Machado's son-in-law was employed by the Chase. The bank did a large business in Cuban bonds. In contemplating these loans, there was a tendency to pass quickly over anything that might appear to the disadvantage of the creditor. Mr. Victor Schoepperle, a vice-president of the National City Company with the responsibility for Latin American loans, made the following appraisal of Peru as a credit prospect:

> Peru: Bad debt record, adverse moral and political risk, bad internal debt situation, trade situation about as satisfactory as that of Chile in the past three years. Natural resources more varied. On economic showing Peru should go ahead rapidly in the next 10 years.

On such showing the National City Company floated a $15,000,000 loan for Peru, followed a few months later by a $50,000,000 loan, and some ten months thereafter by a $25,000,000 issue. (Peru did prove a highly adverse political risk. President Leguia, who negotiated the loans, was thrown violently out of office, and the loans went into default.)

In all respects these operations were as much a part of the New Era as Shenandoah and Blue Ridge. They were also just as fragile, and once the illusions of the New Era were dissipated they came as abruptly to an end. This, in turn, forced a fundamental revision in the foreign economic position of the United States. Countries could not cover their adverse trade balance with the United States with increased payments of gold, at least not for long. This meant that they had either to increase their exports to the United States or reduce their imports or default on their past loans. President Hoover and the Congress moved promptly to eliminate the first possibility—that the accounts would be balanced by larger imports—by sharply increasing the tariff. Accordingly, debts, including war debts, went into default and there was a precipitate fall in American exports. The reduction was not vast in relation to total output of the American economy, but it contributed to the general distress and was especially hard on farmers.

5) The poor state of economic intelligence. To regard the people of any time as particularly obtuse seems vaguely improper, and it also establishes a precedent which members of this generation might regret. Yet it seems certain that the economists and those who offered economic counsel in the late twenties and early thirties were almost uniquely perverse. In the months and years following the stock market crash, the burden of reputable economic advice was invariably on the side of measures that would make things worse. In November of 1929, Mr. Hoover announced a cut in taxes; in the great no-business conferences that followed he asked business firms to keep up their capital investment and to maintain wages. Both of these measures were on the side of increasing spendable income, though unfortunately they were largely without effect. The tax reductions were negligible except in the higher income brackets; businessmen who promised to maintain investment and wages, in accordance with a well-understood convention, considered the promise binding only for the period within which it was not financially disadvantageous to do so. As a result investment outlays and wages were not reduced until circumstances would in any case have brought their reduction.

Still, the effort was in the right direction. Thereafter policy was almost entirely on the side of making things worse. Asked how the government could best advance recovery, the sound and responsible adviser urged that the budget be balanced. Both parties agreed on this. For Republicans the balanced budget was, as ever, high doctrine. But the Democratic Party platform of 1932, with an explicitness which politicians rarely advise, also called for a "federal budget annually balanced on the basis of accurate executive estimates within revenues..."

A commitment to a balanced budget is always comprehensive. It then meant there could be no increase in government outlays to expand purchasing power and relieve distress. It meant there could be no further tax reduction. But taken literally it meant much more. From 1930 on the budget was far out of balance, and balance, therefore, meant an increase in taxes, a reduction in spending, or both. The Democratic platform in 1932 called for an "immediate and drastic reduction of governmental expenditures" to accomplish at least a 25 per cent decrease in the cost of government.

The balanced budget was not a subject of thought. Nor was it, as often asserted, precisely a matter of faith. Rather it was a formula. For centuries avoidance of borrowing had protected people from slovenly or reckless public housekeeping. Slovenly or reckless keepers of the public purse had often composed complicated arguments to show why balance of income and outlay was not a mark of virtue. Experience had shown that however convenient this belief might seem in the short run, discomfort or disaster followed in the long run. Those simple precepts of a simple world did not hold amid the growing complexities of the early thirties. Mass unemployment in particular had altered the rules. Events had played a very bad trick on people, but almost no one tried to think out the problem anew.

The balanced budget was not the only strait jacket on policy. There was also the bogey of "going off" the gold standard and, most surprisingly, of risking inflation. Until 1932 the United States added formidably to its gold reserves, and instead of inflation the country was experiencing the most violent deflation in the nation's history. Yet every sober adviser saw dangers here, including the danger of runaway price increases. Americans, though in years now well in the past, had shown a penchant for tinkering with the money supply and enjoying the brief but heady joys of a boom in prices. In 1931 or 1932, the danger or even the feasibility of such a boom was nil. The advisers and counselors were not, however, analyzing the danger or even the possibility. They were serving only as the custodians of bad memories.

The fear of inflation reinforced the demand for the balanced budget. It also limited efforts to make interest rates low, credit plentiful (or at least redundant) and borrowing as easy as possible under the circumstances. Devaluation of the dollar was, of course, flatly ruled out. This directly violated the gold standard rules. At best, in such depression times, monetary policy is a feeble reed on which to lean. The current economic clichés did not allow even the use of that frail weapon. And again, these attitudes were above party. Though himself singularly open-minded, Roosevelt was careful not to offend or disturb his followers. In a speech in Brooklyn toward the close of the 1932 campaign, he said:

> The Democratic platform specifically declares, "We advocate a sound currency to be preserved at all hazards." That is plain English. In discussing this platform on July 30, I said, "Sound money is an international necessity, not a domestic consideration for one nation alone." Far up in the Northwest, at Butte, I repeated the pledge . . . In Seattle I reaffirmed my attitude . . .

The following February, Mr. Hoover set forth his view, as often before, in a famous letter to the President-elect:

> It would steady the country greatly if there could be prompt assurance that there will be no tampering or inflation of the currency; that the budget will be unquestionably balanced even if further taxation is necessary; that the Government credit will be maintained by refusal to exhaust it in the issue of securities.

The rejection of both fiscal (tax and expenditure) and monetary policy amounted precisely to a rejection of all affirmative government economic policy. The economic advisers of the day had both the unanimity and the authority to force the leaders of both parties to disavow all the available steps to check deflation and depression. In its own way this was a marked achievement—a triumph of dogma over thought. The consequences were profound.

It is in light of the above weaknesses of the economy that the role of the stock market crash in the great tragedy of the thirties must be seen. The years of self-depreciation by Wall Street to the contrary, the role is one of respectable importance. The collapse in securities values affected in the first instance the wealthy and the well-to-do. But we see that in the world of 1929 this was a vital group. The members disposed of a large proportion of the consumer income; they were the source of a lion's share of personal saving and investment. Anything that struck at the spending or investment by this group would of necessity have broad effects on expenditure and income in the economy at large. Precisely such a blow was struck by the stock market crash. In addition, the crash promptly removed from the economy the support that it had been deriving from the spending of stock market gains.

The stock market crash was also an exceptionally effective way of exploiting the weaknesses of the corporate structure. Operating companies at the end of the holding-company chain were forced by the crash to retrench. The subsequent collapse of these systems and also of the investment trusts effectively destroyed both the ability to borrow and the willingness to lend for investment. What have long looked like purely fiduciary effects were, in fact, quickly translated into declining orders and increasing unemployment.

The crash was also effective in bringing to an end the foreign lending by which the international accounts had been balanced. Now the accounts had, in the main, to be balanced by reduced exports. This put prompt and heavy pressure on export markets for wheat, cotton, and tobacco. Perhaps the foreign loans had only delayed an adjustment in the balance which had one day to come. The stock market crash served nonetheless to precipitate the adjustment with great suddenness at a most unpropitious time. The instinct of farmers who traced their troubles to the stock market was not totally misguided.

Finally, when the misfortune had struck, the attitudes of

the time kept anything from being done about it. This, perhaps, was the most disconcerting feature of all. Some people were hungry in 1930 and 1931 and 1932. Others were tortured by the fear that they might go hungry. Yet others suffered the agony of the descent from the honor and respectability that goes with income into poverty. And still others feared that they would be next. Meanwhile everyone suffered from a sense of utter hopelessness. Nothing, it seemed, could be done. And given the ideas which controlled policy, nothing could be done.

Had the economy been fundamentally sound in 1929 the effect of the great stock market crash might have been small. Alternatively, the shock to confidence and the loss of spending by those who were caught in the market might soon have worn off. But business in 1929 was not sound; on the contrary it was exceedingly fragile. It was vulnerable to the kind of blow it received from Wall Street. Those who have emphasized this vulnerability are obviously on strong ground. Yet when a greenhouse succumbs to a hailstorm something more than a purely passive role is normally attributed to the storm. One must accord similar significance to the typhoon which blew out of lower Manhattan in October 1929.

The military historian when he has finished his chronicle is excused. He is not required to consider the chance for a renewal of war with the Indians, the Mexicans, or the Confederacy. Nor will anyone press him to say how such acrimony can be prevented. But economics is taken more seriously. The economic historian, as a result, is invariably asked whether the misfortunes he describes will afflict us again and how they may be prevented.

The task of this book, as suggested on an early page, is only to tell what happened in 1929. It is not to tell whether or when the misfortunes of 1929 will recur. One of the pregnant lessons of that year will by now be plain: it is that very specific and personal misfortune awaits those who presume to believe that the future is revealed to them. Yet, without undue risk, it may be possible to gain from our view of this useful year some insights into the future. We can distinguish, in particular, between misfortunes that could happen again and others which events, many of them in the aftermath of 1929, have at least made improbable. And we can perhaps see a little of the form and magnitude of the remaining peril.

At first glance the least probable of the misadventures of the late twenties would seem to be another wild boom in the stock market with its inevitable collapse. The memory of that autumn, although now much dimmed, is not yet gone. As those days of disenchantment drew to a close, tens of thousands of Americans shook their heads and muttered, "Never again." In every considerable community there are yet a few survivors, aged but still chastened, who are still muttering and still shaking their heads. The New Era had no such guardians of sound pessimism.

Also, there are the new government measures and controls. The powers of the Federal Reserve Board—now styled the Board of Governors, the Federal Reserve System—have been strengthened both in relation to the individual Reserve banks and the member banks. Mitchell's defiance of March 1929 is now unthinkable. What was then an act of arrogant but not abnormal individualism would now be regarded as idiotic. The New York Federal Reserve Bank retains a measure of moral authority and autonomy, but not enough to resist a strong Washington policy. Now also there is power to set margin requirements. If necessary, the speculator can be made to post the full price of the stock he buys. While this may not completely discourage him, it does mean that when the market falls there can be no outsurge of margin calls to force further sales and insure that the liquidation will go through continuing spasms. Finally, the Securities and Exchange Commission is a bar, one hopes effective, to large-scale market manipulation, and it also keeps rein on the devices and the salesmanship by which new speculators are recruited.

Yet, in some respects, the chances for a recurrence of a

speculative orgy are rather good. No one can doubt that the American people remain susceptible to the speculative mood—to the conviction that enterprise can be attended by unlimited rewards in which they, individually, were meant to share. A rising market can still bring the reality of riches. This, in turn, can draw more and more people to participate. The government preventatives and controls are ready. In the hands of a determined government their efficacy cannot be doubted. There are, however, a hundred reasons why a government will determine not to use them. In our democracy an election is in the offing even on the day after an election. The avoidance of depression and the prevention of unemployment have become for the politician the most critical of all questions of public policy. Action to break up a boom must always be weighed against the chance that it will cause unemployment at a politically inopportune moment. Booms, it must be noted, are not stopped until after they have started. And after they have started the action will always look, as it did to the frightened men in the Federal Reserve Board in February 1929, like a decision in favor of immediate as against ultimate death. As we have seen, the immediate death not only has the disadvantage of being immediate but of identifying the executioner.

The market will not go on a speculative rampage without some rationalization. But during the next boom some newly rediscovered virtuosity of the free enterprise system will be cited. It will be pointed out that people are justified in paying the present prices—indeed, almost any price—to have an equity position in the system. Among the first to accept these rationalizations will be some of those responsible for invoking the controls. They will say firmly that controls are not needed. The newspapers, some of them, will agree and speak harshly of those who think action might be in order. They will be called men of little faith.

A new adventure in stock market speculation sometime in the future followed by another collapse would not have the same effect on the economy as in 1929. Whether it would show the economy to be fundamentally sound or unsound is something, unfortunately, that will not be wholly evident until after the event. There can be no question, however, that many of the points of extreme weakness exposed in 1929 or soon thereafter have since been substantially strengthened. The distribution of income is no longer quite so lopsided. Between 1929 and 1948 the share of total personal income going to the 5 per cent of the population with the highest income dropped from nearly a third to less than a fifth of the total. Between 1929 and 1950 the share of all family income which was received as wages, salaries, pensions, and unemployment compensation increased from approximately 61 per cent to approximately 71 per cent. This is the income of everyday people. Although dividends, interest, and rent, the income characteristically of the well-to-do, increased in total amount, the share dropped from just over 22 to just over 12 per cent of total family personal income.

Similarly, in the years since 1929, the great investment trust promotions have been folded up and put away, or they have become cautious and respectable. The SEC, aided by the bankruptcy laws, has flattened out the great utility holding company pyramids. There has been a new age of mergers, but it does not seem yet to have produced any such Napoleonic bandits as Kreuger or so far to have encouraged illusions of destiny in stock jobbers like Hopson or Insull. Federal insurance of bank deposits, even to this day, has not been given full credit for the revolution that it has worked in the nation's banking structure. With this one piece of legislation the fear which operated so efficiently to transmit weakness was dissolved. As a result the grievous defect of the old system, by which failure begot failure, was cured. Rarely has so much been accomplished by a single law.

The problem of the foreign balance is much changed from what it was twenty-five years ago. Now the United States finds itself with a propensity to buy or spend as much and more than it sells and receives. And now any disequilibrium is filled or more than filled by military aid, Export-Import and International Bank loans and economic aid. In contrast with the loans to Latin American republics and the German municipalities, these payments are relatively invulnerable to shock. A crash in the stock market would affect them but little if at all.

Finally, there has been a modest accretion of economic knowledge. A developing depression would not now be met with a fixed determination to make it worse. Without question, no-business conferences would be assembled at the White House. We would see an explosion of reassurance and incantation. Many would urge waiting and hoping as the best policy. Not again, however, would people suppose that the best policy would be—as Secretary Mellon so infelicitously phrased it—to "liquidate labor, liquidate stocks, liquidate the farmers, liquidate real estate." Our determination to deal firmly and adequately with a serious depression is still to be tested. But there is still a considerable difference between a failure to do enough that is right and a determination to do much that is wrong.

Other weaknesses in the economy have been corrected. The much maligned farm program provides a measure of security for farm income and therewith for spending by farmers. Unemployment compensation accomplishes the same result, if still inadequately, for labor. The remainder of the social security system—pensions and public assistance—helps protect the income and consequently the expenditures of yet other segments of the population. The tax system is a far better servant of stability than it was in 1929. An angry god may have endowed capitalism with inherent contradictions. But at least as an afterthought he was kind enough to make social reform surprisingly consistent with improved operation of the system.

Yet all this reinforcement notwithstanding, it would probably be unwise to expose the economy to the shock of another major speculative collapse. Some of the new reinforcements might buckle. Instead of the investment trusts we have the mutual funds and the contraction here would be sharp. Fissures might open at other new and perhaps unexpected places. Even the quick withdrawal from the economy of the spending that comes from stock market gains might be damaging. Any collapse, even though the further consequences were small, would not be good for the public reputation of Wall Street.

Wall Street, in recent times, has become, as a learned phrase has it, very "public relations conscious." Since a speculative collapse can only follow a speculative boom, one might expect that Wall Street would lay a heavy hand on any resurgence of speculation. The Federal Reserve would be asked by bankers and brokers to lift margins to the limit; it would be warned to enforce the requirement sternly against those who might try to borrow on their own stocks and bonds in order to buy more of them. The public would be warned sharply and often of the risks inherent in buying stocks for the rise. Those who persisted, nonetheless, would have no one to blame but themselves. The position of the Stock Exchange, its members, the banks, and the financial community in general would be perfectly clear and as well protected in the event of a further collapse as sound public relations allow.

As noted, all this might logically be expected. It will not come to pass. This is not because the instinct for self-preservation in Wall Street is poorly developed. On the contrary, it is probably normal and may be above. But now, as throughout history, financial capacity and political perspicacity are inversely correlated. Long-run salvation by men of business has never been highly regarded if it means disturbance of orderly life and convenience in the present. So inaction will be advocated in the present even though it means deep trouble in the future. Here, at least equally with communism, lies the threat to capitalism. It is what causes men who know that things are going quite wrong to say that things are fundamentally sound.

For Further Reading

Other accounts of the 1929 debacle include Francis W. Hirst, *Wall Street and Lombard Street* (1931), and Irving Fisher, *The Stock Market Crash—and After* (1930). The latter work is by one of the most optimistic supporters of the bull market who was taken by surprise at its collapse. For a lively, informal survey of the crash, see Joe Alex Morris, *What a Year* (1956).

George Soule's *Prosperity Decade: From War to Depression 1917–1929* (1947) is excellent economic history, comprehensive and eminently readable. On the distribution or maldistribution of income, see the original study, Simon S. Kuznets, *National Income and Its Composition, 1919–1938* (1941). James Prothro, *The Dollar Decade* (1959), irreverently surveys the business thought of the decade. There are several works of the muckraking genre: Stuart Chase, *Prosperity: Fact or Myth* (1929), John T. Flynn, *Investment Trusts Gone Wrong* (1931), and Thurman W. Arnold, *The Folklore of Capitalism* (1937). The best sources for studying overseas business expansion are Herbert Feis, *The Diplomacy of the Dollar, First Era 1919–1932* (1950), and Cleona Lewis, *America's Stake in International Investments* (1938), which details the consequence of transformation of the United States into the world's leading creditor nation. Harris G. Waylord, *Herbert Hoover and the Great Depression* (1959), is an excellent account of the administrative attitude toward the crisis. The desperate state of the farmers receives attention in D. Black, *Agricultural Discontent in the Middle West, 1900–1939* (1951). For the problems encountered by labor during the "prosperity years," see Irving Bernstein, *The Lean Years: A History of the American Worker, 1920–1933* (1960).

On the depression, Lionel Robbins' *The Great Depression* (1934) and Broadus Mitchell's *Depression Decade* (1947) are good economic histories, while Mauritz Hallgren, *Seeds of Revolt* (1933), and Gilbert Seldes, *Years of the Locust* (1933), emphasize the social aspects of the period. Roger W. Babson, *Cheer Up! Better Times Ahead* (1932) should be read in conjunction with Edward Angly, ed., *Oh Yeah?* (1931), for maximum effect. David Shannon, ed., *The Great Depression* (1960), and Bernard Sternsher, ed., *The New Deal: Doctrines and Democracy* (1966), are two excellent collections, the first dealing with source materials, the second with the various proposals advanced to stabilize the economy.